T0016494

USA TODAY

LAZY DAY
LOGIC
200 PUZZLES

Can't get enough of USA TODAY puzzles?

Play more at puzzles.usatoday.com or by downloading our FREE apps!

(Get them on Google Play or iTunes or just scan the QR Codes below with your smartphone camera.)

USA TODAY

LAZY DAY LOGIC
200 PUZZLES

Andrews McMeel
PUBLISHING®

USA TODAY Lazy Day Logic copyright © 2022 by USA TODAY.
All rights reserved. Printed in the United States of America. No part of this book
may be used or reproduced in any manner whatsoever without written permission
except in the case of reprints in the context of reviews.

Andrews McMeel Publishing
a division of Andrews McMeel Universal
1130 Walnut Street, Kansas City, Missouri 64106

www.andrewsmcmeel.com

Logic puzzles copyright of Puzzler Media Ltd. All puzzles supplied under license
from Puzzler Media Ltd.—www.puzzler.com

USA TODAY®, its logo, and associated graphics are federally registered trademarks.
All rights are reserved. All USA TODAY text, graphics, and photographs are used pursuant
to a license and may not be reproduced, distributed, or otherwise used without the
express written consent of Gannett Co., Inc.

22 23 24 25 26 PAH 10 9 8 7 6 5 4 3 2 1

ISBN: 978-1-5248-6994-6

Editor: Patty Rice
Art Director/Designer: Holly Swayne
Production Editor: David Shaw
Production Manager: Julie Skalla

ATTENTION: SCHOOLS AND BUSINESSES
Andrews McMeel books are available at quantity discounts with bulk purchase
for educational, business, or sales promotional use. For information,
please e-mail the Andrews McMeel Publishing Special Sales Department:
specialsales@amuniversal.com.

Solving Tips

The next few pages have all the instructions you'll need to tackle all the puzzles in this book. They may look a little complicated but you'll soon get the hang of things.

Logic Problems

With each standard problem we provide a chart that takes into account every possibility to be considered in the solution. First, you carefully read the statement of the problem in the introduction, and then consider the clues. Next, you enter in the chart all the information immediately apparent from the clues, using an **X** to show a definite **no** and a ✓ to show a definite **yes**. You'll find that this narrows down the possibilities and might even reveal some new definite information. So now you re-read the clues with these new facts in mind to discover further positive/negative relationships. Be sure to enter information in all the relevant places in the chart, and to transfer newly discovered information from one part of the chart to all the other relevant parts. The smaller grid at the end of each problem is simply a quick-reference chart for all your findings.

Now try your hand at working through the example below—you'll soon get the hang of it.

EXAMPLE

Three children live on the same street. From the two clues given below, can you discover each child's full name and age?

Clues

1. Miss Brown is three years older than Mary.
2. The child whose surname is White is 9 years old.

Solution

Miss Brown (clue 1) cannot be Brian, so you can place an **X** in the Brian/Brown box. Clue 1 tells us that she is not Mary either, so you can put an **X** in the Mary/Brown box. Miss Brown is therefore Anne, the only possibility remaining. Now place a ✓ in that box in the chart, with corresponding **X**'s against the other possible surnames for Anne.

If Anne Brown is three years older than Mary (clue 1), she must be 10 and Mary, 7. So place ✓'s in the Anne/10, Brown/10 and Mary/7 boxes, and **X**'s in all the empty boxes in each row and column containing these ✓'s. The chart now reveals Brian's age as 9, so you can place a ✓ in the Brian/9 box. Clue 2 tells us that White is 9 years old too, so he must be Brian. Place a ✓ in the White/9 box and X's in the remaining empty boxes in that row and column, then place a ✓ in the Brian/White box and X's in all the remaining empty boxes in that row and column. You can see now that the remaining unfilled boxes in the chart must contain ✓'s, since their rows and columns contain only X's, so they reveal Green as the surname of 7-year-old Mary.

Anne Brown, 10.
Brian White, 9.
Mary Green, 7.

The solving system for the puzzles that don't have grids is very similar. Read through the clues and insert any positive information onto the diagram. Then read through the clues again and use a process of elimination to start positioning the

	Brown	Green	White	7	9	10
Anne	✓	X	X	X	X	✓
Brian	X			X		X
Mary	X			✓	X	X
7	X					
9	X					
10	✓	X	X			

	Brown	Green	White	7	9	10
Anne	✓	X	X	X	X	✓
Brian	X	X	✓	X	✓	X
Mary	X		X	✓	X	X
7	X		X			
9	X	X	✓			
10	✓	X	X			

remaining elements of the puzzle. You may find it easier to make a few notes about which elements of the puzzle you know are linked but that cannot yet be entered on the diagram. These can be positioned once the other examples of those elements are positioned. If you find it difficult to know where to begin, use the starting tip printed upside down at the foot of the page.

Battleships

Before you look at the numbers around the grid, there are a number of squares you can fill in from the starter pieces given. If an end piece of a ship is given, then the square next to it, in the direction indicated by the end, must also be part of a ship. If a middle piece is given, then the pieces on either side must also be ship parts; in this instance, you need some more information before you can decide which way the ship runs. Also, any square that is adjacent to an end piece (apart from those squares in the direction of the rest of the ship), any square touching the corners of a middle piece, and all squares around destroyers (one-square ships) must be sea.

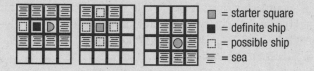

= starter square
■ = definite ship
□ = possible ship
☰ = sea

Now, look at the numbers around the grid and eliminate rows and columns in which the large aircraft carrier might be. Either from this or by looking at the next consequences of the remaining possibilities, you should be able to position this ship. Now fill in the sea squares around the carrier and move on to the smaller ships.

Domino Search

Starting this puzzle is just a matter of finding one domino (number pair) that is unique in the grid. It is often easiest to look for the double numbers first (0 0; 6 6). When you have discovered one or more of these unique possibilities, you will find that their position in the grid forces you to place one or more dominoes in order to fill in the shape of the grid left. Cross off all these dominoes in the check-grid for future reference. Now, look at the dominoes you have managed to fill in and check around the grid, especially near the edge of the grid or next to dominoes already positioned, where the possibilities are reduced, to find other examples of those number pairs. Since you have already positioned that domino, you know that the second example you have found is not a pair and the domino must run in one of the other possible directions. Carry on in this vein, finding dominoes and then eliminating possibilities elsewhere in the grid until the puzzle is cracked.

Logi-5

Start by looking at the intersection of columns and rows that contain at least two starter letters, preferably more, and then use the "shapes" to further eliminate possible letters from that intersection square. You may well find that you can now position at least one letter exactly. There is one more "trick" to help: If, in your eliminating, you find two squares in a row or column, each of which must contain one of the same pair, then the other squares in the row or column cannot contain those letters and can be eliminated.

Sign In

When solving Sign In puzzles, the clues that aren't there are just as important as the ones that are. In the second row of our example puzzle, the 5 can only be positioned in column two, since placing it elsewhere in that row would mean that a 6 would have to be entered according to the signs. Following the 5, a 4 can now be written in below it. Now here's where the clues that aren't there come into play. If the 2 was placed in either of the shaded squares, either a 1 or 3 must be next to it. And there is no + or—sign linking these two squares. Therefore the 2 must be placed at the top.

Sudoku

The basic Sudoku puzzle is a 9 × 9 square grid, split into 9 square blocks, each containing 9 cells. Each puzzle starts off with roughly 20 to 35 of the cells filled in with any of the numbers 1 to 9. There is just one rule: The rest of the cells must be filled in with the missing numbers from 1 to 9 so that no number appears twice in any row, column, or 3 × 3 block. Use the numbers provided to eliminate places where the same number can't appear. For example, if there is already 1 in a cell, then 1 cannot appear again in that same row, column, or 3 × 3 block. By scanning all the cells that the various 1 values rule out, often you can find where the remaining 1s must go.

Killer Sudoku

This puzzle uses the solving skills of Sudoku, but in addition, the digits within each dotted-line shape imposed on top of the Sudoku grid must add up to the number in the top left corner of each shape. No digit may be repeated within a dotted-line shape. Look for the unique digit answers in the dotted-line shapes. For example, two squares totaling 17 must contain a 9 and an 8. Two squares totaling 4 must contain a 1 and a 3, as two 2s would not be allowed. Don't get so involved in the totals that you forget to use normal Sudoku solving methods as well.

Battleships

Do you remember the old game of battleships? These puzzles are based on that idea. Your task is to find the vessels in the diagram. Some parts of boats or sea squares have already been filled in, and a number next to a row or column refers to the number of occupied squares in that row or column. The boats may be positioned horizontally or vertically, but no two boats or parts of boats are in adjacent squares—horizontally, vertically, or diagonally.

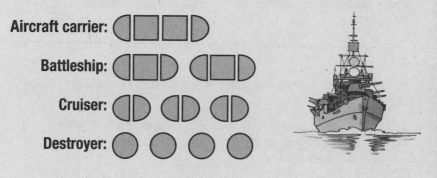

Aircraft carrier:

Battleship:

Cruiser:

Destroyer:

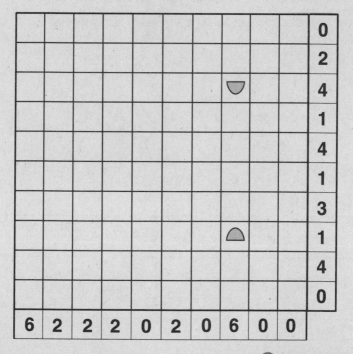

When in Rome

In the 2nd century AD, a ship is about to sail from the Roman-British port of Dubris carrying five male passengers on their way to Rome on business, official or private. Each of the five is accompanied by one other person. Can you work out the name and occupation of each man, in which Roman town he lives or is stationed, and the identity of his companion?

Clues

1. Junius Marinus, from Camulodunum, isn't a soldier, and is not accompanied by his daughter.

2. The officer from the legionary fortress at Segedunum is a widower, traveling with his son.

3. Flavius Emilius is not the junior centurion commanding a maniple of the 10th Legion.

4. Neither Decimus Arbanus nor Flavius Emilius is traveling with a female companion; Servius Valusius' companion is a local gladiator who he is hoping will become famous in Rome.

5. Decimus Arbanus, who is a wine merchant, does not live in Mamucium.

6. The administrator from Glevum has a female traveling companion.

Name	Description

 ● USA TODAY

	Administrator	Junior centurion	Senior centurion	Servant dealer	Wine merchant	Camulodunum	Glevum	Londinium	Mamucium	Segedunum	Brother	Daughter	Gladiator	Mother	Son
Decimus Arbanus															
Flavius Emilius															
Junius Marinus															
Publius Scaevolus															
Servius Valusius															
Brother															
Daughter															
Gladiator															
Mother															
Son															
Camulodunum															
Glevum															
Londinium															
Mamucium															
Segedunum															

i-i; i-vee; vee-i; vee-i-i-i,
who do we identify?

Colosseum cheerleaders

Town	Companion

Unwanted Job

The McKay's Department Store has been experiencing problems employing someone to manage their Customer Services for their Home Textiles Department. The department has recently developed a bad reputation for shoddy goods after a cost-cutting exercise, and most of the day for the manager would be taken up fielding calls from irate customers. So the store offered each new member of staff to whom they offered the role, a different incentive, but in the end they still left the job after just a few weeks. Can you work out what incentive was offered to each employee, how many weeks they stayed and the name of the customer who pushed them a bit too far, causing them to resign from the job?

Clues

1. Bev's offer of a new job was sweetened with the promise of McKay's very own shopping vouchers; she wasn't the employee who persisted in the job for just three weeks and who left after being rudely spoken to by Mrs. Kay.

2. The last straw for Fay was Miss Harringay complaining that her curtains were too short, too thin and far too yellow.

3. Dan decided the role of Home Textiles manager wasn't for him at the end of five weeks; during that time he never had the pleasure of dealing with either Mr. Stevens or Mr. Wilkes.

4. The bonus pay incentive for high sales wasn't enough to keep one employee, who wasn't Hal or Joy, beyond two weeks; Joy stayed for longer in the Home Textiles department than Hal did.

5. Although one employee was offered extra holidays to take the Home Textile role, it wasn't enough of a draw to stop that person handing back the key to the executive washroom after a particularly angry encounter with Mr. Miles.

6. The employee who managed the Home Textiles team for four weeks wasn't enticed with the promise of gym membership or medical insurance, the latter of which wasn't offered to the employee who stayed for a full six weeks before going back to their old job, who didn't encounter the wrath of Mr. Wilkes.

Employee	Incentive

USA TODAY

	Bonus pay	Extra holidays	Gym membership	Medical insurance	Shopping vouchers	2 weeks	3 weeks	4 weeks	5 weeks	6 weeks	Miss Harringay	Mrs. Kay	Mr. Miles	Mr. Stevens	Mr. Wilkes
Bev															
Dan															
Fay															
Hal															
Joy															
Miss Harringay															
Mrs. Kay															
Mr. Miles															
Mr. Stevens															
Mr. Wilkes															
2 weeks															
3 weeks															
4 weeks															
5 weeks															
6 weeks															

Weeks	Customer

The Specialists

Harmony House Medical Clinic currently has five full-time partners and, coincidentally, none were born in the US. Each also has a speciality—a medical one, that is. Dr. Jackson's mastery of BBQ is neither here nor there. Can you work out the name of each doctor, where they were born, their medical speciality, and how long ago they joined Harmony House?

Clues

1. The doctor with the pediatric speciality, who was born in Seoul, South Korea, is not Dr. Lee, and has been at Harmony House twice as long as Dr. Taverner.

2. Dr. Jackson, who has a wide knowledge of sports medicine, came to Harmony House a year after Dr. Taverner.

3. The doctor born in Singapore has been at Harmony House longer than the one born in Port Antonio, in Jamaica.

4. The doctor who comes from Madrid has been based at Harmony House for two years; he or she is not the alternative medicine specialist, who wasn't born in Singapore.

5. It's Dr. Winston Drake who was born in Jamaica.

6. The doctor who has special training in dealing with cases of diabetes has been at Harmony House longer than the one whose speciality is geriatrics.

Doctor	Hometown

USA TODAY

	Madrid	Omagh	Port Antonio	Seoul	Singapore	Alternative medicine	Diabetes	Geriatrics	Pediatrics	Sports medicine	1 year	2 years	3 years	4 years	5 years
Dr. Drake															
Dr. Jackson															
Dr. Lee															
Dr. Park															
Dr. Taverner															
1 year															
2 years															
3 years															
4 years															
5 years															
Alternative medicine															
Diabetes															
Geriatrics															
Pediatrics															
Sports medicine															

Homeopathic Medicines

Absolutely no side effects - guaranteed

Speciality	Time

Room Service

The GalaxyCorp is a remarkably successful space trading organization born from the GloboCorp company of the 21st century, and during the 24th century branched out into passenger liners. The interplanetary liners of GalaxyCorp Spaceways, as the new division was named, carry all kinds of passengers, some of whom have very unusual requirements and can't make use of the normal accommodation, so cabins 1 to 5 on each of GalaxyCorp's vessels are fitted up for quick and easy adaptation. The details below relate to one flight of the liner from Terra to Carremon, a world in orbit around the star Merseia Dexter. Can you work out the name of the passenger in each of the special cabins, their planetary origin, and their particular requirement?

Clues

1. The cabin that has been provided with a methane atmosphere has a higher number than the one assigned to the Pimtrian passenger, and is numbered immediately below the cabin in which Bodi-Nadi will be traveling.

2. The Gunitrian's cabin has to be totally dark, because even the lowest light-levels would cause him/her (Gunitrians switch genders cyclically) unbearable pain.

3. Sinuwei has been assigned the cabin numbered immediately above the one adapted to provide its occupant with the sub-zero temperature it requires.

4. The cabin adapted to provide low gravity is not Y'Alidan's, which isn't cabin 1.

5. Cabin 3's atmosphere is being filtered to remove all water vapor, which could poison the passenger who is to travel in it.

6. The Dravian traveler's cabin is numbered lower than the Jirrizic's but higher than the Ordolase's.

7. Lurimeg will be accommodated in cabin 5.

Cabin	Passenger

	Bodi-Nadi	Hravpak	Lurimeg	Sinuwei	Y'Alidan	Dravian	Gunitrian	Jirrizic	Ordolase	Pimtrian	Low gravity	Methane atmos.	No water vapor	Sub-zero temp.	Total darkness
1															
2															
3															
4															
5															
Low gravity															
Methane atmos.															
No water vapor															
Sub-zero temp.															
Total darkness															
Dravian															
Gunitrian															
Jirrizic															
Ordolase															
Pimtrian															

Planet	Requirement

Playing for Courage

Five Knock-Kneed Knights of the Round Table had recently read and discussed an article suggesting that listening to music was an effective way of calming fears. As a result, each applied to the Minstrel Agency in Camelot and engaged the services of a different minstrel for one evening each week. While this did not result in any noticeable increase in their courage factor, it did at least provide some enjoyment during the long winter evenings in their castles. Can you work out which knight hired which minstrel on which evening and match the minstrels with their instruments?

Clues

1. Blodwen played her dulcimer on a later evening in the week than Sir Poltroon's music night.

2. Aled was not the Friday performer, and the lute was not played on Thursday evenings.

3. The viol was the instrument played by the Saturday songster.

4. Tuesday was music night in the castle of Sir Spyneless de Feete.

5. Idris was hired by Sir Sorely à Frayde.

6. Madoc performed regularly the night before the harp was played in the Great Hall of Sir Coward's castle.

Knight	Minstrel

	Aled	Blodwen	Idris	Madoc	Myfanwy	Monday	Tuesday	Thursday	Friday	Saturday	Dulcimer	Harp	Lute	Lyre	Viol
Sir Coward de Custarde															
Sir Poltroon à Ghaste															
Sir Sorely à Frayde															
Sir Spyneless de Feete															
Sir Timid de Shayke															
Dulcimer															
Harp															
Lute															
Lyre															
Viol															
Monday															
Tuesday															
Thursday															
Friday															
Saturday															

Evening	Instrument

Barbies and Kens

With the weathermen forecasting a BBQ Summer, it's time for the residents of Charcoal Lane to get ready for the balmy evenings ahead, and the five we meet below (coincidentally, all called Ken) have been down to the local Homestore warehouse to choose one of the latest models to ensure plenty of well-cooked ribs and steaks. Can you work out at which house in the street (traditionally numbered with odd and even numbers on opposite sides) each Ken lives, as well as the brand he has chosen with its particular unique selling point?

Clues

1. Ken de la Bras lives on the opposite side of the road from the man who bought the new model from Dundee's and in the next higher-numbered house from his neighbor who went for the model with the Acu-Timer setting.

2. The model with the convenient Auto-Turn facility was the choice of Ken Singh-Tungor.

3. The resident of 8 Charcoal Lane decided on the BBQ made by Foster's; the Ken who chose the revolutionary high-powered Solar Flare model lives at an odd number.

4. Swagman's new machine was the choice of Ken Tuckey.

5. Everage's well-reviewed Deep Char model was bought by a Ken living at an even-numbered house.

6. Ken Airey doesn't live at 2 Charcoal Lane, whose resident settled on the model with the time-saving Self-Basting button.

Resident	House number

	No.2	No.4	No.5	No.7	No.8	Dundee's	Everage's	Foster's	Kelly's	Swagman's	Acu-Timer	Auto-Turn	Deep Char	Self-Basting	Solar Flare
Ken Airey															
Ken Aloney															
Ken de la Bras															
Ken Singh-Tungor															
Ken Tuckey															
Acu-Timer															
Auto-Turn															
Deep Char															
Self-Basting															
Solar Flare															
Dundee's															
Everage's															
Foster's															
Kelly's															
Swagman's															

WHAT'S A NICE GRILL LIKE YOU DOING IN A PLACE LIKE THIS?

Barbecue pick-up lines

Make	Feature

Logi-5

Each line, across and down, is to have each of the letters A, B, C, D, and E, appearing once. Also, every shape—shown by the thick lines—must also have each of the letters in it. Can you fill in the grid?

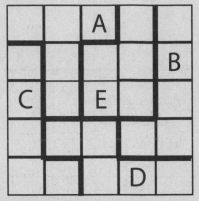

Killer Sudoku

The normal rules of Sudoku apply. In addition, the digits in each inner shape (marked by dots) must add up to the number in the top corner of that box.

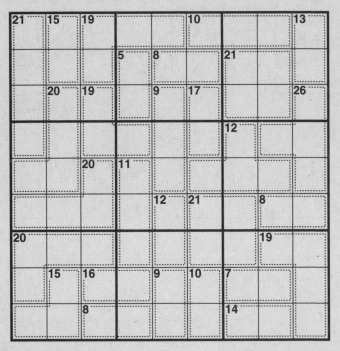

Battleships

Do you remember the old game of battleships? These puzzles are based on that idea. Your task is to find the vessels in the diagram. Some parts of boats or sea squares have already been filled in, and a number next to a row or column refers to the number of occupied squares in that row or column. The boats may be positioned horizontally or vertically, but no two boats or parts of boats are in adjacent squares— horizontally, vertically, or diagonally.

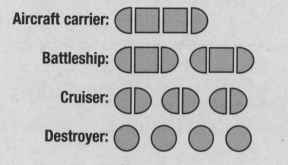

Aircraft carrier:

Battleship:

Cruiser:

Destroyer:

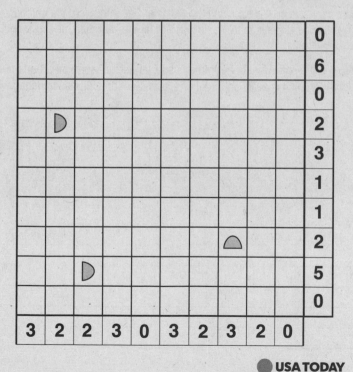

Forum Fashion

While Ancient Rome's Emperor Domitian is in top-level talks with Cardatianus, a millionaire spice-mogul from the provinces, he has arranged for his guest's celebrity womenfolk to be entertained by the senatorial bosses of five servants. They have taken the opportunity for a bit of top-level retail therapy in the Empire's capital and are currently out and about among the designer stalls of the Forum, with the hapless handful traipsing along in their tow weighed down beneath their bags. Can you work out which celebrity lady each servant is following around, what their main purchase has been, and how much it has cost?

Clues

1. The model trailing Cluelus in her wake spent the least amount, only parting with a mere 100 sesterces.

2. Cailia, followed meekly around the Forum by Gormlus, was not the visitor who spent 250 sesterces on a dress from top designers the Versatii.

3. The glamorous lady whose purchases Branelus was trying hard not to drop as she swept all before her was not Cortnia, who didn't spend exactly 200 sesterces; Branelus' eager shopper didn't spend the most.

4. Some very stylish new sandals from Dulce et Decorum were the purchase of the lady who had Hopelus in tow; this wasn't Cimmia, who had the top spend of 300 sesterces.

5. Cloia spent a small part of her father's substantial net worth on a Guttii belt; the celebrity leading Euselus around didn't splash out on a Pradae handbag.

Servant	Celebrity lady

USA TODAY

	Cailia	Cennia	Cimmia	Cloia	Cortnia	Belt	Dress	Fur jacket	Handbag	Sandals	100 sesterces	150 sesterces	200 sesterces	250 sesterces	300 sesterces
Branelus															
Cluelus															
Euselus															
Gormlus															
Hopelus															
100 sesterces															
150 sesterces															
200 sesterces															
250 sesterces															
300 sesterces															
Belt															
Dress															
Fur jacket															
Handbag															
Sandals															

Purchase	Cost

Animal Magnetism

Country vet Jane Merriott has had a busy week. Aside from her work with pets at her veterinary clinic, on successive days she was called out to different farms to attend to a variety of sick farm animals. Can you say which farm she visited on each day, name its owner, and say which animal she treated on each occasion?

Clues

1. Jane's week started with a call out to Crabtree Farm.

2. Farmer Olroyd's carthorse, which does not live at Willoughby Farm, was treated later in the week than the cow.

3. Farmer Carrick was visited the day before Farmer Burtenshaw.

4. The ailing sheepdog was treated the day after Jane's visit to Angleton Farm, but earlier in the week than her meeting with Farmer Mirfield.

5. The pig fell ill at Rockerby Farm, but not on Tuesday.

6. The sick sheep was Jane's Wednesday patient.

Day	Farm

USA TODAY

	Angleton Farm	Crabtree Farm	Melrose Farm	Rockerby Farm	Willoughby Farm	Burtenshaw	Carrick	Hirst	Mirfield	Olroyd	Carthorse	Cow	Pig	Sheep	Sheepdog
Monday															
Tuesday															
Wednesday															
Thursday															
Friday															
Carthorse															
Cow															
Pig															
Sheep															
Sheepdog															
Burtenshaw															
Carrick															
Hirst															
Mirfield															
Olroyd															

Old MacDonald had an eye test...

Farmer	Animal

Friends of Friends

Five friends visited the Georgetown Charity Fundraiser. Each bought something from a fund-raising stall and each won a small prize in the raffle. From the clues, can you work out which stall each visited, what they bought, and what they won?

Clues

1. Liam, who did not buy anything from the Friends of Willow Park, won a voucher for a free haircut in the raffle, which was unfortunate as he was completely bald. He was not the friend who bought a book from the Friends of St. Bernard's Home for Lost Dogs.

2. Norma patronized the Friends of Kirkdale Market stall. She was not the sweet-toothed person who bought the jam and won the chocolates, nor did she buy the painting, which was not the purchase from the Friends of St. Barnabas Church.

3. Mandy bought a lovely potted plant but she did not visit the Friends of Willow Park stall, which did not sell the mug. She didn't win a teddy bear in the raffle.

4. Oliver didn't patronize either of the "saintly" stalls and neither of the two who did won a bottle of wine in the raffle.

Name	Friends of . . .

● USA TODAY

	Fernwick Forest	Kirkdale Market	St. Barnabas	St. Bernard's	Willow Park	Book	Jam	Mug	Painting	Plant	Chocolates	Haircut	Perfume	Teddy	Wine
Liam															
Mandy															
Norma															
Oliver															
Paul															
Chocolates															
Haircut															
Perfume															
Teddy															
Wine															
Book															
Jam															
Mug															
Painting															
Plant															

Purchase	Prize

Extra Time

The Central Casting Department at Ivywood Studios has detailed five extras—the people who fill in the background behind film stars—to get costumed for scenes in different movies in production. Can you work out what costume each has to put on, which sound stage they need to report to, and which film is being shot there?

Clues

1. Linda Jones will be wearing motorcycling leathers and a crash-helmet for her role.

2. Peter Smith will be seen in the background of a scene from *Judgment*—so long as his few frames don't end up on the cutting room floor, that is.

3. *Close Friends* is being shot on Stage 5.

4. John Green is on his way, via the Wardrobe Department, to Stage 1, which isn't where they're filming *Like a King*; the extra who is going to be in *Like a King* won't be wearing overalls.

5. *I Confess* is not the Regency costume drama, which is not being made on Stage 2.

6. *Sparks*, for which one man will be donning medieval doublet and hose, is being filmed on a sound stage numbered two higher than that on which Susan West will be strutting her stuff.

Extra	Costume

	Beach clothes	Doublet and hose	Motorcycle leathers	Overalls	Regency costume	Stage 1	Stage 2	Stage 3	Stage 4	Stage 5	Close Friends	I Confess	Judgment	Like a King	Sparks
Alan Brown															
John Green															
Linda Jones															
Peter Smith															
Susan West															
Close Friends															
I Confess															
Judgment															
Like a King															
Sparks															
Stage 1															
Stage 2															
Stage 3															
Stage 4															
Stage 5															

Sound stage	Film

Early Profits

Money-market guru Gordon Gerbil likes to get things going at the start of the week by buying a few inexpensive (for him) shares before his morning coffee. Scanning the movements of the stock market last Monday, he bought five blocks of shares in up-and-coming companies which he knew would make him a good profit by lunchtime. Can you work out at what time during the first hour's work each purchase was made, the name of the company, the price paid per share, and the number bought?

Clues

1. At 9:30 Gordon logged on to MakeApacket.com—his favored website—to buy shares in Euro-Amalgamated; he paid less per share than for those he acquired in Imperial Holdings, and bought 100 more of the former than the latter.

2. The AD&G shares weren't Gordon's first purchase, but were on offer at $12.60 a share; he bought an even number of hundreds of them—the math is easier.

3. The 600 shares he bought just as his tablet computer chimed 10 am did not cost $4 each.

4. There were 10 minutes between Gordon's acquisition of blocks of shares in Albion Group and BBF, in that order.

5. The shares bought at 9:50 were priced at $11.

6. He bought 400 shares in one company at $7.30 per share.

Time	Company

USA TODAY

	AD&G	Albion Group	BBF	Euro-Amalgamated	Imperial Holdings	$4	$7.30	$11	$12.60	$14.20	200 shares	300 shares	400 shares	500 shares	600 shares
9:00 a.m.															
9:20 a.m.															
9:30 a.m.															
9:50 a.m.															
10:00 a.m.															
200 shares															
300 shares															
400 shares															
500 shares															
600 shares															
$4															
$7.30															
$11															
$12.60															
$14.20															

PLANNING FOR THE FUTURE?

YES, I'M SAVING FOR A HEDGE

HEDGE FUND

Price	Number

Flower Rearrangement

Rose Budd's Florists can usually be relied upon to fulfill customers' wishes beautifully and accurately. But with the proprietor herself taking a short vacation, her stand-in staff have got themselves into a complete muddle over today's orders. Not only have the flowers requested by the five clients below been sent out to the wrong recipients, the greeting card attached also bears no relation to the blooms dispatched. Can you match each sender with the person they intended to surprise, discover what mistaken type of floral offering was actually sent out, and what unfortunate wording was on the card accompanying this?

Clues

1. Chris Anthemum had ordered a floral gift for his girlfriend; fortunately she wasn't the person who received a large cheese-plant with a misplaced message reading "Made me think of you."

2. Someone's boss was surprised to receive an offering with a card which read "Love from Flopsy Bunny"; this didn't accompany the gift sent by busy project manager Lizzie Potts.

3. It wasn't someone's fellow worker whose delivery came with a card, apparently from Rhoda Dendran, congratulating them on a successful road test. Even more awkwardly, the wording "You passed it!" had also got muddled, with "You" turning into "You're."

4. A rather embarrassed relative had a lot of explaining to do when their elderly maiden aunt received a large memorial wreath; the accompanying message at least wasn't "You're passed it" or "Deepest sympathy"; William Sweet doesn't have an aunt.

5. Daisy Cheyne was mortified when her intended recipient received a single romantic red rose.

6. The wedding bouquet was not sent to someone's brother.

Sender	Recipient

	Aunt	Boss	Brother	Girlfriend	Fellow worker	Bonsai tree	Cheese-plant	Memorial wreath	Single rose	Wedding bouquet	Deepest sympathy	Love from Flopsy	Made me think of you	Saying it with flowers	You're passed it
Chris Anthemum															
Daisy Cheyne															
Lizzie Potts															
Rhoda Dendran															
William Sweet															
Deepest sympathy															
Love from Flopsy															
Made me think of you															
Saying it with flowers															
You're passed it															
Bonsai tree															
Cheese-plant															
Memorial wreath															
Single rose															
Wedding bouquet															

Flowers	Message

Getting Lost

Five passengers are in line at the Lost & Found office at Madison's central station, having inadvertently left items on trains earlier that morning on their way to work. Can you discover the item each has mislaid, the train each had traveled on, and where each train had begun its journey?

Clues

1. The umbrella was left on the Ceefield train, while the suitcase belonged to Miss Knighton.

2. The pair of gloves wasn't the item left on the 8:05 from Beaford that morning.

3. The passenger on the 8:42 forgot to pick up their parcel.

4. Mr. Cox traveled on the 8:23 train, but not from Deeleigh; the Deeleigh train left earlier than Mr. Farrell's train.

5. Mrs. Hughes traveled in from Aywood on a train that left earlier than the one on which the shopping bag was left.

6. Mr. Nichols didn't come into town on the 8:40 train.

Passenger	Lost item

 USA TODAY

	Gloves	Parcel	Shopping bag	Suitcase	Umbrella	8:05	8:23	8:40	8:42	8:51	Aywood	Beaford	Ceefield	Deeleigh	Eamouth
Mr. Cox															
Mr. Farrell															
Mrs. Hughes															
Miss Knighton															
Mr. Nichols															
Aywood															
Beaford															
Ceefield															
Deeleigh															
Eamouth															
8:05					
8:23					
8:40					
8:42					
8:51					

I'VE LOST AN UMBRELLA

LOST PROPERTY

CAN YOU DESCRIBE IT?

IT WAS ATTACHED TO MY WIFE

Train	From

Bastille Day

The French nation celebrates the Fall of the Bastille and the subsequent French Revolution on July 14 every year. The French version of the date, QUATORZE JUILLET is spelt out in the 15 squares in our diagram, each of which contains a different letter of the phrase. Your task is to place them correctly.

Clues

1. The Q in square C2 does not have a U in any adjoining square, horizontally, vertically or diagonally.

2. None of the four repeated letters appears twice in the same row or column, one such pair being in B3 and D2, and one of another pair being in E1.

3. The word JET reads diagonally downwards somewhere in the layout; you must decide in which direction; squares A1 and C3 both contain a consonant; one U is diagonally above and to the right of the Z.

4. The letter in B2 is from the second half of the alphabet; an I appears immediately above a U in one vertical column, which is not column E; one T is directly below the O.

Letters to be placed:
A; E; E; I; J; L; L; O; Q; R; T; T; U; U; Z

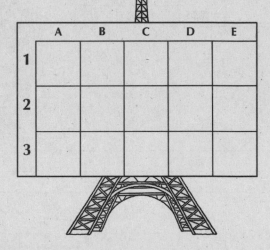

	A	B	C	D	E
1					
2					
3					

Starting tip: Start by placing the U below an I.

Battleships

Do you remember the old game of battleships? These puzzles are based on that idea. Your task is to find the vessels in the diagram. Some parts of boats or sea squares have already been filled in, and a number next to a row or column refers to the number of occupied squares in that row or column. The boats may be positioned horizontally or vertically, but no two boats or parts of boats are in adjacent squares—horizontally, vertically, or diagonally.

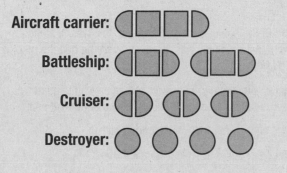

Aircraft carrier:

Battleship:

Cruiser:

Destroyer:

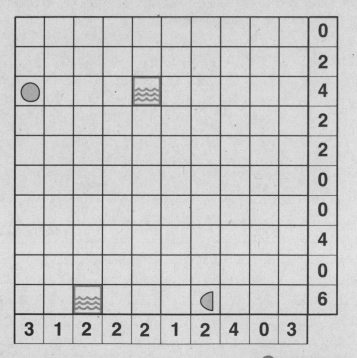

Easy Electro-rider

Although he's really pleased with his new electric bicycle, Dennis Fonder is determined to put it properly through its paces and check out the performance of each of the different power levels. So each day this week he concentrated on one of the settings, choosing an appropriate venue in the town to get the most out of his ride and confirm that he's made the right choice. Can you work out in which street he tried out each power level on each day and by what name the manufacturers have (in some cases, rather bizarrely) designated each level?

Clues

1. On Tuesday, Dennis put the Green power setting to the test; this wasn't as he rode up Cheyne Rise, which unsurprisingly was the road where he had the bike on its highest level setting of 4.

2. Dennis tried out the Distance setting along Spowke Lane; this wasn't Thursday's trip, where he used human pedal power only for the purposes of comparison.

3. Gere Avenue was the venue chosen for Friday's experimental run.

4. Confusingly perhaps, the power setting at level 2 is called Boost.

5. Dennis tried out the level 1 setting the day before he tested Travel power, but the day after he rode along Peddle Street.

Day	Power level

	Off	1	2	3	4	Cheyne Rise	Gere Avenue	Peddle Street	Saddell Road	Spowke Lane	Boost	Cruise	Distance	Green	Travel
Monday															
Tuesday															
Wednesday															
Thursday															
Friday															
Boost															
Cruise															
Distance															
Green															
Travel															
Cheyne Rise															
Gere Avenue															
Peddle Street															
Saddell Road															
Spowke Lane															

Venue	Name

Going Dutch

In her heyday, around the turn of the 20th century, Miss Raffles—the more successful criminal sister of the famous amateur safecracker—had contacts throughout Europe, although most of them never knew her true identity. For instance, there were five men in the Netherlands of whose services she regularly made use. Can you work out each man's name, profession, the city or town in which he lived, and the name Miss Raffles used when contacting him?

Clues

1. The diamond cutter from Haarlem had a shorter surname than the man who came from Nijmegan.

2. Frans Drees had a legal job in the diamond trade, although it was his not-so-legal business on the side that made him rich; he wasn't the man who knew Miss Raffles as Marie LaBonne, who was not based in Amsterdam.

3. Jan Hertzog from Hilversum was not the engineer who designed specialist equipment for the woman he knew as Rosa Van Dyck.

4. Miss Raffles did not pose as Irish-born adventurer Kitty O'Riley when negotiating with the diamond dealer.

5. Dirk Cort thought that Miss Raffles was Else De Geer, of the Transeurope Syndicate—an organization that had no existence outside her fertile imagination.

6. Miss Raffles used the name Lili Kruger—and a German accent and a large wig—when visiting her contact in Rotterdam.

7. Willem Wolf was one of Holland's top burglars, and was often used by Miss Raffles to augment her gang or create a diversion—though he never realized who he was working for.

Name	Profession

	Burglar	Diamond cutter	Diamond dealer	Engineer	Forger	Amsterdam	Haarlem	Hilversum	Nijmegen	Rotterdam	Else de Geer	Kitty O'Riley	Lili Kruger	Marie LaBonne	Rosa Van Dyck
Dirk Cort															
Frans Drees															
Jan Hertzog															
Pieter Swart															
Willem Wolf															
Else de Geer															
Kitty O'Riley															
Lili Kruger															
Marie LaBonne															
Rosa Van Dyck															
Amsterdam															
Haarlem															
Hilversum															
Nijmegen															
Rotterdam															

Home town	Name knew

Dog Days

St. Bernard's Home for Lost Dogs has produced a charity calendar featuring dogs wearing some sort of garment. Can you find out which breed of dog features in each month and what they are wearing? (They're not all St. Bernards, of course, we've just drawn it like that so as not to give the game away. Lefts and rights are from our point of view.)

Clues

1. January's dog is, of course, a St. Bernard and December's is wearing a Santa hat. The red setter in a sweater, and the pooch in a fleece are in the other two corners of the layout shown here.

2. The boxer, the dog in the panama hat, and the one in a high-vis jacket are all in months beginning with J. One is shown directly beneath the dog in a sailor hat. The Jack Russell and the mutt in a swimsuit, one of which is shown directly above the borzoi, are in months beginning with A. The collie, shown directly below a dog in a hat, is later than both the Jack Russell and the dog in the swimsuit while the Yorkshire terrier is earlier than both.

3. The Dalmatian can be spotted next right of the Labrador, next left of the pooch in a tutu, and directly below the dog in boots.

4. The chihuahua appears earlier than the dog in a hoodie, three months later than the one in a tank top and three months before the Pekinese.

Dogs: Alsatian; borzoi; boxer; chihuahua; collie; Dalmatian; Jack Russell; Labrador; Pekinese; red setter; St. Bernard; Yorkshire terrier

Garments: bow tie; fleece; high-vis jacket; hoodie; panama hat; sailor hat; Santa hat; sweater; swimsuit; tank top; tutu; boots

USA TODAY

January

_____
_____

February

_____
_____

March

_____
_____

April

_____
_____

May

_____
_____

June

_____
_____

July

_____
_____

August

_____
_____

September

_____
_____

October

_____
_____

November

_____
_____

December

_____
_____

Starting tip: Spot the dog in the sailor hat.

Spending Spree

Five office workers went out on a minor errand only to have their attention drawn to fabulous items in the winter sales. Can you work out what each worker set out to buy and what two items they returned to the office with? (Lefts and rights are from our point of view.)

Clues

1. The woman who popped out for a newspaper and came back with a picnic hamper is shown directly right of Rowan and immediately left of the shopper who fell for an irresistible pair of shoes.

2. Charlotte had only wanted a sandwich and woman D had just popped out for a phone top-up. Woman B was Alison, who wasn't the worker who arrived back at the office with a pair of velvet pants and a set of gold dinner plates. Woman C acquired a gorgeous bedspread at an absolute bargain price.

3. The shopper who had gone out for a coffee is shown more than two places left of the woman who had intended to buy a chocolate bar but had returned clutching a top-quality handbag but not a set of crystal wine glasses. The chocolate buyer was not Tina, who did not splurge on the pants or the ravishing evening dress.

Names: Alison; Charlotte; Margaret; Rowan; Tina
Popped out for: chocolate bar; coffee; newspaper; phone top-up; sandwich
First items: dress; handbag; jacket; shoes; pants
Second items: bedspread; curtains; picnic hamper; plates; wine glasses

A　B　C　D　E

_____　_____　_____　_____　_____
_____　_____　_____　_____　_____
_____　_____　_____　_____　_____
_____　_____　_____　_____　_____

Starting tip: Place the person who purchased the newspaper and picnic basket.

Curses

When the girls at Backsaddles School for Students of Witchcraft misbehave, they are not given detention. Instead they are cursed with an unpleasant affliction for ten minutes and then sent off to do a disagreeable task. From the clues, can you find out each pupil's offense, the affliction they were cursed with, and the chore they were ordered to do?

Clues

1. The girl caught cursing a classmate was cursed herself with a hefty dose of boils for ten minutes.

2. Hazel was caught drawing on her desk. Her teacher did not afflict her with a headache or stomach ache or order her to clean out the familiars' cages.

3. The girl punished for running in the corridor, who wasn't Cassandra, was tasked with putting down food for the school mascot as it rampaged around the cellar roaring and rattling its chains.

4. Circe was made to mix a potion from the smelliest ingredients available and the girl afflicted with a headache was ordered to test the potion by inhaling its vapors.

5. Cassandra was cursed with a cramp but Hecate was not given a headache. Zelda was not punished for fighting, but only because the teacher did not catch her—this time.

Witch	Infraction

	Answering back	Cursing	Drawing	Fighting	Running	Boils	Cramp	Headache	Itching	Stomachache	Clean cages	Collect toadstools	Feed mascot	Mix potion	Test potion
Cassandra															
Circe															
Hazel															
Hecate															
Zelda															
Clean cages															
Collect toadstools															
Feed mascot															
Mix potion															
Test potion															
Boils															
Cramp															
Headache															
Itching															
Stomachache															

Curse	Chore

The Meal Deal

Sam Goodyear is a local restaurant critic in the small town of Woodruff City, on the borders of Utah and Wyoming in the USA and last week—like most weeks—he dined at a different establishment, offering different cuisine, every night looking for a suitable candidate to receive his treasured Goodyear star (or it would be treasured if he had ever awarded one). Can you identify what he ate each night, where, and the address of the restaurant?

Clues

1. On Monday, Sam ate sole at a restaurant which specialized in fish—which wasn't the Tower and wasn't located on Union Street.

2. Sam had dinner at the Imperial on Tuesday; he had chicken two nights after dining in the restaurant on 24th Street.

3. The restaurant where Sam dined on Thursday was on 6th Street and had more than one word in its name.

4. Goldberg's, where Sam ate salt beef, is on a street with a number.

5. Chez Maurice wasn't where Sam had the pork chops.

6. Sam had lamb in the restaurant on 10th Street.

Day	Dish

USA TODAY

	Beef	Chicken	Lamb	Pork	Sole	Chez Maurice	Goldberg's	Imperial	Ma Tante Adele	Tower	6th Street	Temple Street	10th Street	24th Street	Union Street
Monday															
Tuesday															
Wednesday															
Thursday															
Friday															
6th Street															
Temple Street															
10th Street															
24th Street															
Union Street															
Chez Maurice															
Goldberg's															
Imperial															
Ma Tante Adele															
Tower															

Restaurant	Address

Soap Opera

Five medical students live in rented accommodation together. Friday evenings are usually mayhem, as they each try to use their one small shower before going out for the evening with their separate friends. Last Friday, as each one showered, they realized that they had run out or were about to run out of an essential item. Can you work out the order each student took their shower, who was first to discover they had run out of something, and where they planned on going for the evening?

Clues

1. Callum was the third one to hit the shower.

2. Kelvin wanted to smarten himself up as he and his girlfriend were to try out the new posh wine bar; he wasn't the person who discovered that the only towel available was the damp one from the previous user.

3. Lucy realized just as she got into the shower that there wasn't any shower gel left, so she made do with the nearby bar of soap.

4. The person who used the shower first hadn't left the water heater on for long enough and so the water ran cold halfway through. Fortunately the water had heated again by the time the next person, who wasn't Jenny or Nathan, stepped into the shower; Nathan wasn't going to the movie theater or the pub.

5. The person who had tickets to see a show at the theater, who wasn't Nathan, found an empty bottle of shampoo left in the shower, so used the shower gel for their hair instead.

6. The person who was fourth to use the shower was getting ready to go to the Italian restaurant.

7. The person who was fifth to use the shower wasn't getting ready to go to the movie theater.

Order	Name

USA TODAY

	Callum	Jenny	Kelvin	Lucy	Nathan	Clean, dry towel	Hair conditioner	Hot water	Shampoo	Shower gel	Italian restaurant	Movie theater	Pub	Theater	Wine bar
First															
Second															
Third															
Fourth															
Fifth															
Italian restaurant															
Movie theater															
Pub															
Theater															
Wine bar															
Clean, dry towel															
Hair conditioner															
Hot water															
Shampoo															
Shower gel															

Item	Destination

Bard Chart

This year The Netherlipp Amateur Players are staging the little-known Shakespeare play, *Much Taming of the Gentlemen of Windsor's Dream . . . and Juliet*. From the following verse, can you discover which actors have taken the five principal male roles, in which of the five scenes of Act 1 each makes his first entrance, and how many lines each speaks during that scene?

Verses

Forsooth, 'tis John who makes Duke Pedro's part,
While Craig hath twenty-five more lines than he.
Orlando in Scene One doth make his start
With twice the lines of Craig in memory.

Orlando's role is not for Ralph to take;
While he that ent'reth in Scene Two hath more
To say than Ben, who in Scene Three doth make
his entrance. Scene Two doth not see Godwin's fore.

Nor in Scene Four will Godwin's role arise.
But he that doth hath fifty lines to play.
Lorenzo hath more lines within his guise
Than he that feigns as Edmund has to say.

So now divine which role each man portrayed,
Its length and in which scene his entrance made.

Actor	Role

	Roles					Scene 1	Scene 2	Scene 3	Scene 4	Scene 5	25 lines	50 lines	75 lines	100 lines	125 lines
	Duke Pedro	Edmund	Godwin	Lorenzo	Orlando										
Ben															
Craig															
John															
Peter															
Ralph															
25 lines															
50 lines															
75 lines															
100 lines															
125 lines															
Scene 1															
Scene 2															
Scene 3															
Scene 4															
Scene 5															

Actors

Owing to an unfortunate typing error, the Netherlipp Players present Rodeo and Juliet.

Entrance	Lines

Wild Wilde Life

As usual, the five Wilde brothers have booked a range of adventure vacations this year. Can you discover for what part of the world each is bound, what they will be doing there, and for how many weeks? (For clarity, Austria and the Pyrenees are in Europe.)

Clues

1. The five brothers' names are in alphabetical order in reverse order of their births, and neither the youngest, Alexander, nor the climber is off to Europe, but both will be away for fewer weeks than the brother vacationing in the Pyrenees.

2. The brother bound for the Pyrenees was born immediately after the one flying to Brazil.

3. Ranulph is going pony-trekking, and is older than his brother who is spending two weeks in Austria.

4. The hiker's vacation will be longer than the one spent in Mexico.

5. One of the brothers will spend five weeks cycling, while Hector will be away for just one week.

6. One of the brothers is going diving in the Seychelles.

Brother	Country

	Austria	Brazil	Mexico	Pyrenees	Seychelles	Climbing	Cycling	Diving	Hiking	Pony-trekking	1 week	2 weeks	3 weeks	4 weeks	5 weeks
Alexander															
Ferdinand															
Hector															
Ranulph															
Sebastian															
1 week															
2 weeks															
3 weeks															
4 weeks															
5 weeks															
Climbing															
Cycling															
Diving															
Hiking															
Pony-trekking															

Activity	Weeks

Head to the Hills

Six members of the Dayton Hiking Club—three women Win, Sue, and Una and three men Rob, Tom, and Vic—have gathered to set off for a week of "back to nature" in the surrounding hills. Unfortunately each member has forgotten two of the items listed. Can you work out which two items should be in each of the named knapsacks but are not?

Clues

1. Each of the items listed have been forgotten by two hikers and no two people have forgotten the same two things; each of the six missing items is missing once from each row of knapsacks.

2. The gloves are missing from opposite ends of different rows of knapsacks; one man has forgotten both his spare socks and his airbed but Rob has remembered his socks.

3. No woman has forgotten her airbed; no man has forgotten his woolly hat.

4. Win has brought both her sleeping bag and her toothbrush; Tom has remembered to pack his toothbrush.

Missing items: airbed; gloves; sleeping bag; spare socks; toothbrush; woolly hat

Tom   Win   Sue

Rob   Una   Vic

Starting tip: Work out what Win has forgotten.

Sign In

Each row and column is to contain the digits 1-6. The given signs tell you if a digit in a cell is plus 1 (+) or minus 1 (-) the digit next to it. Signs between consecutive digits always work from left to right or top to bottom. Examples: 3 + 4 or 2 over 1 ALL occurrences of consecutive digits have been marked by a sign.

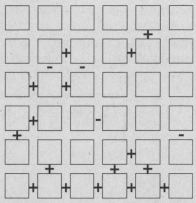

Sudoku

Complete this grid so that each column, each row, and each marked 3 X 3 square contains each of the numbers 1 to 9.

			4					
	5			8				6
4	8				3			9
	9	4			8			5
	1			4			6	
7			3			8	2	
9			1				7	2
6				3			5	
					2			

Domino Search

A standard set of dominoes has been laid out, using numbers instead of dots for clarity. Using a sharp pencil and a keen brain, can you draw in the lines to show where each domino has been placed? You may find the check grid useful—crossing off each domino as you find it.

0	3	4	4	2	4	6	4
1	6	5	6	3	1	3	0
1	6	2	4	5	1	0	6
0	3	6	0	0	2	4	6
6	3	2	5	1	5	3	5
1	2	0	5	5	3	2	2
1	4	2	1	3	4	5	0

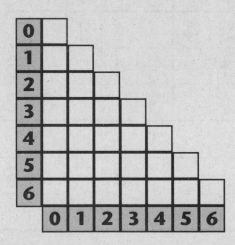

USA TODAY

Barbershop Bassmen

The Barbershop Bassmen group is a part-time quartet of double bass players who sing and play in a combination of rockabilly and barbershop harmony. Although they're making a bit of a name for themselves in their local bars and clubs, they still have their day jobs—for the moment anyway. Name each bassman, say what barbershop part he takes and work out what he does as a job. (Lefts and rights are from our point of view.)

Clues

1. Jed is somewhere left of the baritone singer and somewhere right of the bassman who spends his days in silence as a librarian but who doesn't sing the tenor part.

2. Mac sings the lead part; the bass-singing bassman is somewhere to the right of the bassman who slicks down his magnificent quiff during the day for his job in a bank.

3. Leo, who spends his days as a house painter, is immediately right of the bassman who is a nurse, who is separated from Kit by at least one other bassman.

Names: Jed; Kit; Leo; Mac
Voice: baritone; bass; lead; tenor
Job: banker; house painter; librarian; nurse

Starting tip: Work out bassman D's day job.

Soames and Wearson

The great Victorian detective Mr. Hemlock Soames has had a busy week, with five new cases being brought to his rooms at 122A Candlestickmaker Street. Can you detect the day he learned of each case, the person who visited him and his companion Doctor Wearson in their consulting room, the nature of the crime, and the district of London where each took place?

Clues

1. A robbery was described to Soames and Wearson on Monday, but the case was not brought to him by Silas Hodgson and it had not taken place in Paddington.

2. Sir Caleb Dewar called at Candlestickmaker Street on Tuesday, while an appeal for help in solving a crime in Kentish Town was brought to him on Thursday by one of the two female visitors.

3. Soames was told of the kidnapping case two days after he heard of the crime in Peckham.

4. The mysterious disappearance described by Edward Nicholson had not taken place in either Camberwell or Paddington.

5. Lady Grant did not come to Soames and Wearson for their help in a blackmail case.

6. The murder had taken place in Stepney.

Day	Visitor

	Miss Campbell	Sir Caleb Dewar	Lady Grant	Silas Hodgson	Edward Nicholson	Blackmail	Disappearance	Kidnapping	Murder	Robbery	Camberwell	Kentish Town	Paddington	Peckham	Stepney
Monday															
Tuesday															
Wednesday															
Thursday															
Friday															
Camberwell															
Kentish Town															
Paddington															
Peckham															
Stepney															
Blackmail															
Disappearance															
Kidnapping															
Murder															
Robbery															

Case	Area

Click and Collect

Nine customers have used Selfham's new click-and-collect service to order goods online. The staff at the Selfham's store have selected the goods from their shelves and placed them in boxes on shelves at the Customer Services desk. Can you work out who ordered each package on the shelf and what it contains? (Lisa, Mary, Polly, and Susan are women, the others are men.)

Clues

1. Polly looked in horror at her big square box (numbered 1, 5, or 6), which did not contain a coat. "I'll never get it home," she said. It was immediately above Mark's purchase and directly right of the splendid oriental bedspread.

2. Bernard has ordered a toy truck for his little daughter.

3. Consignment no.2 has been purchased by Mary but is not the DVDs, which are in a box of the same size and shape. The buyers of nos.4 and 5 share a first name initial.

4. The saucepan, selected by a man, has a number twice that of Mike's purchase, and the perfume is numbered three times Susan's consignment.

5. The shoes were directly left of the dress, on a higher shelf than Lisa's purchase but not in vertical alignment with it.

Customers: Bernard; Bryan; Lisa; Malcolm; Mark; Mary; Mike; Polly; Susan
Purchases: bedspread; coat; dress; DVDs; jacket; perfume; saucepan; shoes; toy

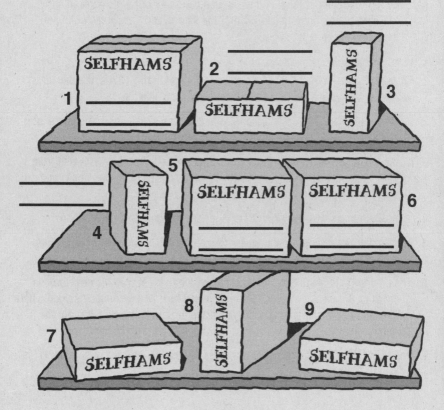

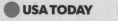

Behind Bars

The Arizona Historical Association has recently discovered and published the diaries of Phineas McGillivray, a saloon keeper who ran various drinking establishments across Arizona in the great days of the Wild West, during which time he encountered a number of famous figures. Can you work out which saloon, in which town, McGillivray was operating in each of the listed years, and which famous characters came in for a drink?

Clues

1. Phineas didn't run the North Star Saloon in Tucson in the 1870s, the decade in which he served a drink to Jesse James, who was killed in 1882.

2. William F. "Buffalo Bill" Cody drank at one of Phineas' saloons some years after Phineas had played host to another famous American in Yuma.

3. It was while he was running a saloon in Phoenix that Phineas had a visit from Martha "Calamity Jane" Canary—who, from his description, was foul-mouthed, scary, and nothing like Doris Day.

4. In 1883, Phineas was owner and manager of the Rancher's Rest Saloon.

5. The Golden Horseshoe Saloon, where Phineas once played host to Wyatt Earp, wasn't in Flagstaff.

6. The Liberty Bell Saloon was Phineas' saloon when he served his next famous guest after Samuel Langhorne Clemens, alias Mark Twain; the next saloon where he encountered a celebrity after meeting one at the Liberty Bell was not the Queen of Spades.

7. It was in 1886 that Phineas served a glass of whiskey to a famous visitor in his saloon in Tombstone.

Year	Saloon

	Golden Horseshoe	Liberty Bell	North Star	Queen of Spades	Rancher's Rest	Flagstaff	Phoenix	Tombstone	Tucson	Yuma	Buffalo Bill	Calamity Jane	Jesse James	Mark Twain	Wyatt Earp
1869															
1872															
1876															
1883															
1886															
Buffalo Bill															
Calamity Jane															
Jesse James															
Mark Twain															
Wyatt Earp															
Flagstaff															
Phoenix															
Tombstone															
Tucson															
Yuma															

Town	Drinker

Original Features

Crumbleigh Cottage was a cozy family home from 1849 to 1949, but for the past 70 years it has been boarded up and derelict. In 2019, developer Archie Tecked bought it for a knock-down price and set about restoring it to an ultramodern standard while conserving some of its period features to retain its charm and character. An article on the property pages of the *Georgetown Messenger* gives the details of five rooms, illustrated with photographs. Can you name the room in each photograph and work out which new and original features it contains?

Clues

1. The kitchen retains its original cast-iron range which keeps it comfortably warm, so neither it nor the room with the Art Nouveau fireplace has now been fitted with state-of-the-art ionic heating.

2. The original oak Paneling in one room conceals a cunning cupboard in which an array of domestic robots is stored.

3. The bathroom has been refurbished with an ultrasonic shower. It is shown in the picture numbered one higher than the room that harbors a house battery to store the energy from the solar roof and garden wind turbine to power all the gadgets and one lower than the one with the original fireplace, which is not the nursery.

4. Photograph 1 shows the living room, which does not feature the floor with patterned tiles, which is shown in a picture numbered two lower than that of the room with ionic heating. The room in photograph 5 retains its original stained-glass window.

Photograph	Room

	Bathroom	Bedroom	Kitchen	Living room	Nursery	Fireplace	Paneling	Patterned tiles	Range	Stained-glass window	Holographic TV	House battery	Ionic heating	Robots	Ultrasonic shower
Photograph 1															
Photograph 2															
Photograph 3															
Photograph 4															
Photograph 5															
Holographic TV															
House battery															
Ionic heating															
Robots															
Ultrasonic shower															
Fireplace															
Paneling															
Patterned tiles															
Range															
Stained-glass window															

NEWTON'S DEMOLITION CO.

Old feature	New feature

Regal Regalia

The historic Crown Jewels of the small country of Rigalia are famed throughout Europe and some details are given below. Can you discover the name carried by each item, the century in which each was crafted, and the principal jewels decorating each?

Clues

1. The sceptre was made in the 17th century, while the jeweled cross is known as the Cross of Alpenburg.

2. The ring contains a single huge ruby, and is not as old as the orb, which is not named after King Humbert.

3. The oldest of the five pieces is adorned with sapphires but does not bear the name of a King of Rigalia.

4. The piece dedicated to King Julius is neither adorned with emeralds nor the 16th-century item.

5. The diamond-encrusted treasure is 200 years older than that carrying St. Ludwig's name.

6. The most recent piece carries the name of St. Sylvester.

Item	Name

	of Alpenburg	of King Humbert	of King Julius	of St. Ludwig	of St. Sylvester	15th century	16th century	17th century	18th century	19th century	Diamonds	Emeralds	Pearls	Ruby	Sapphires
Cross															
Crown															
Orb															
Ring															
Sceptre															
Diamonds															
Emeralds															
Pearls															
Ruby															
Sapphires															
15th century															
16th century															
17th century															
18th century															
19th century															

Century	Jewels

I Scream

Mandy Dwyer always says that she makes a good living out of dying—though not, of course, literally. Mandy is a movie actress, appearing exclusively in horror movies. Known as one of the best screamers in the business, she specializes in horrible deaths at the hands or claws of whichever monster the screenwriter has dreamed up. Last year, she perished five times in movies which the public flocked to see. Can you work out in which month each movie was released, what it was called, Mandy's role, and what killed her?

Clues

1. The movie in which Mandy played a prying journalist was released some time after the one in which she met her end at the hands of a ferocious gorilla.

2. It was a vampire that did Mandy in in *Claw of the Demon*, although he was only the secondary villain—the main one was, of course, a demon with a claw.

3. Mandy played an entomology student in the movie in which she was bumped off by a giant spider; she was slain by a slimy alien in the movie that came out immediately before the one in which she played a tough city policewoman, which wasn't premiered in June.

4. In the August release, Mandy played a maid.

5. *Fires of Hell* came out in November.

6. The October release, in which Mandy was killed by zombies, was not *The Curse*.

7. Mandy appeared as a dedicated nurse in *Night of Terror*.

Month	Movie

	Claw of the Demon	Devil's Dawn	Fires of Hell	Night of Terror	The Curse	Journalist	Maid	Nurse	Policewoman	Student	Alien	Giant spider	Gorilla	Vampire	Zombies
March															
June															
August															
October															
November															
Alien															
Giant spider															
Gorilla															
Vampire															
Zombies															
Journalist															
Maid															
Nurse															
Policewoman															
Student															

Role	Killer

Hand-me-down Sports

One of the advantages of being the youngest of six siblings for Harvey, 11, is that his five elder brothers and sisters pass down sporting equipment they have grown out of or got bored with, so Harvey was able to easily try all of these sports. Can you work out the age of each of Harvey's siblings, the activity each tried, and how many months they stuck at it before moving on? (Lewis and Alfie are Harvey's brothers, the other three are sisters.)

Clues

1. Lewis is 13; he has never been interested in fencing or horse riding and, being 13, currently isn't interested in anything but sleeping and eating.

2. Hayley, who is older than Jessica, stuck at her activity for ten months.

3. Vicky had a go at baseball until she realized that it was likely to take up too much of weekends, when there are much better things to do.

4. Harvey inherited a pair of roller skates from his 15-year-old sister.

5. Harvey fancied having a go at kendo after watching his sibling sporting the outfit, but had to wait 9 months before the mask, armor, and shinai were passed down to him.

6. Harvey's oldest sibling gave up an activity after only 5 months; this isn't Alfie, who didn't try fencing.

7. Harvey's 12-year-old sibling tried an activity, which wasn't horse riding, for more than 3 months.

Sibling	Age

USA TODAY

	12	13	15	17	18	Baseball	Fencing	Horse riding	Kendo	Roller skating	3 months	5 months	6 months	9 months	10 months
Alfie															
Hayley															
Jessica															
Lewis															
Vicky															
3 months															
5 months															
6 months															
9 months															
10 months															
Baseball															
Fencing															
Horse riding															
Kendo															
Roller skating															

HE'S RIGHT, THERE'S NOTHING SPECIFIC ABOUT IT HERE

RULES OF FENCING

Activity	Duration

Red Handed

The notorious Hopkins Gang thought nobody noticed them as they assembled in disguise at 13 Bridewell Street preparing to rob the jewelry store next door. But the the cops already knew all about their plan, had the building under surveillance and at 3:05 p.m., moved in and arrested them all. Can you work out the nickname and surname of each gang member, when he arrived at number 13, and what disguise he wore?

Clues

1. Basher, whose surname isn't Briggs, made a not-very-successful attempt to disguise his huge frame as a nun.

2. Riley arrived at No.13 before McLaren, who was logged in by the watching detectives at 2:30 p.m.

3. Prof, who arrived at 2:00 p.m., wasn't the man disguised as a chef.

4. At 1:30 p.m. one of the gang members turned up dressed as a construction site laborer.

5. Tarzan Acroyd arrived 30 minutes after the man who was disguised as a businessman.

6. Hopkins, the gang leader, traveled to No.13 dressed as a motorcyclist in leathers and closed helmet; unfortunately, he can't ride a motorcycle, so had to go by taxi, arriving half an hour before Jelly, the explosives expert.

Nickname	Surname

	Acroyd	Briggs	Hopkins	McLaren	Riley	1:00 p.m.	1:30 p.m.	2:00 p.m.	2:30 p.m.	3:00 p.m.	Businessman	Chef	Laborer	Motorcyclist	Nun
Basher															
Fingers															
Jelly															
Prof															
Tarzan															
Businessman															
Chef															
Laborer															
Motorcyclist															
Nun															
1:00 p.m.															
1:30 p.m.															
2:00 p.m.															
2:30 p.m.															
3:00 p.m.															

Disorganized crime

Arrival time	Disguise

Guest List

Patrick is an egalitarian multimillionaire and loves to hold opulent parties throughout the spring and summer months at his home. But he doesn't just invite the glamorous and the famous, he notes the name of everyone who has knocked on his door since his last party to deliver a service, make enquiries, or complete a job for him, and sends them an invitation as well. Can you work out for each month the person who was unexpectedly invited and attended Patrick's party, how he briefly met the person, and who his guest came with?

Clues

1. Tommy, whose guest wasn't Sally, attended the party held in June.

2. Jackie attended the party with her husband Will; neither she nor Simone was the person who was invited to the July party after knocking on Patrick's door to ask about a missing cat.

3. During the recent election, Richie, a canvasser for the Environment Party, called at Patrick's door and later received a party invitation; he didn't attend with Aron or Sally.

4. The courier, who delivered a parcel of books to Patrick's house, took Brandon to the party, which wasn't in May; the guest who attended the party in May wasn't the one who carried out some garden maintenance work for Patrick.

5. Maddie accompanied an invited guest to a party in April.

6. Simone didn't go to Patrick's party in March and didn't go to a party with Sally.

Month	Guest

	Annette	Jackie	Richie	Simone	Tommy	Canvasser	Courier	Garden maintenance	Lost cat enquiry	Pizza delivery	Aron	Brandon	Maddie	Sally	Will
March															
April															
May															
June															
July															
Aron															
Brandon															
Maddie															
Sally															
Will															
Canvasser															
Courier															
Garden maintenance															
Lost cat enquiry															
Pizza delivery															

HOW DID YOU BECOME A MILLIONAIRE?

I HAVE MY KIDS TO THANK. BEFORE WE HAD THEM I WAS A BILLIONAIRE

Encounter	Companion

Clubland

Some of the nightclubs in Arlington are run by honest men, just out to make a fair profit—but some of them are run by outright criminals, who use them for purposes unconnected with their legitimate business. Five of the latter sort are going to be raided by the police tonight. Can you work out the name and address of each of these clubs, the name of the police officer leading the raid on it, and what the police will be looking for?

Clues

1. The Aztec Club, which is not in Lincoln Street, will be raided by one of the teams led by a sergeant, and the club in Walpole Lane will be searched for stolen goods; Inspector Harvey isn't taking his squad to either Lincoln Street or Walpole Lane.

2. The club where the police expect to find forged credit cards and the equipment for turning them out, the Equator Club, the club to be raided by Inspector Mullen and his men, and the club in Lincoln Street are four different establishments; Inspector Mullen isn't going to raid Foxx's.

3. The club called Mr. Hyde (after Dr. Jekyll's dark side), which is in Forsyth Street, is not the one where the police expect to find the cash stolen in a bank robbery yesterday morning.

4. Sergeant Pomeroy and his men are looking for drugs.

5. Sergeant Lyndon and his men will be raiding the club in Erskine Street.

6. Inspector Carter will be leading the raid on the Chicago Club.

Club	Address

	Buckland Street	Erskine Street	Forsyth Street	Lincoln Street	Walpole Lane	Insp. Carter	Insp. Harvey	Sgt. Lyndon	Insp. Mullen	Sgt. Pomeroy	Drugs	Forged cards	Guns	Stolen cash	Stolen goods
Aztec															
Chicago															
Equator															
Foxx's															
Mr. Hyde															
Drugs															
Forged cards															
Guns															
Stolen cash															
Stolen goods															
Insp. Carter															
Insp. Harvey															
Sgt. Lyndon															
Insp. Mullen															
Sgt. Pomeroy															

Police officer	Looking for

Dolphin Speak

Research at the Oceanic Biology Department at Florida University has finally made advances in deciphering the language of dolphins and Dr. Marie Negged has set sail to test out their theories. "Whistle, whistle, squeak," she broadcast through the underwater speaker, which she hoped was, "Hey guys, does anyone want to play?" What she actually said was "My hoping is for boys' toys," but it was intriguing enough to bring a pod of eight dolphins to find out what was going on. "I can call what's yours?" asked Marie. The dolphins, being intelligent creatures, understood and each gave their names. Can you name them? (Lefts and rights are from our point of view and, for clarity, dolphin 5 is in front of dolphin 1, 6 in front of 2, 7 in front of 3, and 8 in front of 4.)

Clues

1. Dolphins, it turns out, are named after the first things their parents see when the calf is born with an added poetic flourish. Seconds after dolphin 3 was born a tuna swam passed, providing the second part of their name.

2. The parents of dolphin 8 decided to call their calf Wise something, out of hope rather than expectation; dolphin 4 isn't the one whose parents chose the name Thoughtful (transcribed by Marie into her research log book as With a Cargo of Ideas) before the birth.

3. Marie pointed her microphone at the dolphin known to her friends as Eely but whose full name is Fearless Eel. "Squeaky, squeak, whistle, peep," she recorded and later translated as String of Bravery. Eely wasn't dolphin 1.

4. When one of these dolphins was only seconds old, a tiny shrimp dove into view—still, rules are rules—he is shown immediately right of the dolphin whose parents chose the first name Cultured and immediately behind the one named after an outcrop of coral; it was a quiet day in that particular area of the ocean.

5. The calf that was named after the sudden appearance of a shark (a rather scary moment) is immediately between the dolphin whose parents chose the name Dignified and the one who is called Peaceful, neither of whom was born when a squid wriggled by. Peaceful isn't numbered one higher than the dolphin known as Wandy after his Wandering first name.

6. The dolphin named Tranquil (translated by Marie as "Not bothered") is directly behind the one born just as a migrating salmon swam by on its long journey.

7. The dolphin born and named when a huge whale drifted into sight is facing right in the picture.

First names: Cultured; Dignified; Fearless; Peaceful; Thoughtful; Tranquil; Wandering; Wise
Second names: Coral; Eel; Salmon; Shark; Shrimp; Squid; Tuna; Whale

Starting tip: Work out after what sight dolphin 1 was named at birth.

Passage to San Guillermo

Late in the 1930s, a tramp steamer is on its way from New York to the little South American port of San Guillermo, with a full hold and mixed—indeed, very mixed—cargo and five passengers, each occupying one of the cramped and sordid cabins in the superstructure supporting the bridge. Can you fill in on the diagram the full name and occupation of the man traveling in each cabin?

Clues

1. Paul's cabin, which isn't number 3, is between Brett's and the one occupied by the gangster who, having murdered his gang-boss' rival, is fleeing retribution.

2. Mr. Stone is in cabin 1 and the novelist with ambitions to become a second Ernest Hemingway is in cabin 2.

3. Kevin McPhee's cabin is next to that occupied by the mercenary soldier of fortune on his way to fight in a revolution—any revolution.

4. Neither Brett nor his fellow passenger Mr. Walden has been sharing cabin 3 with the ship's supply of flour in sacks.

5. Jovanic's cabin is between McPhee's and that of the prospector who's on his way to South America to look for emeralds; the prospector is not the passenger cramped into cabin 4.

6. Gary, the jewel thief who managed to leave New York just one step ahead of the cops, is in the next cabin to Valdez.

First names: Brett; Gary; Kevin; Paul; Tom
Surnames: Jovanic; McPhee; Stone; Valdez; Walden
Occupations: gangster; jewel thief; novelist; prospector; soldier of fortune

Starting tip: Work out the number of the gangster's cabin.

Battleships

Do you remember the old game of battleships? These puzzles are based on that idea. Your task is to find the vessels in the diagram. Some parts of boats or sea squares have already been filled in, and a number next to a row or column refers to the number of occupied squares in that row or column. The boats may be positioned horizontally or vertically, but no two boats or parts of boats are in adjacent squares—horizontally, vertically, or diagonally.

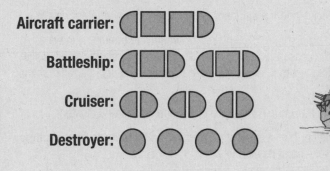

Aircraft carrier:

Battleship:

Cruiser:

Destroyer:

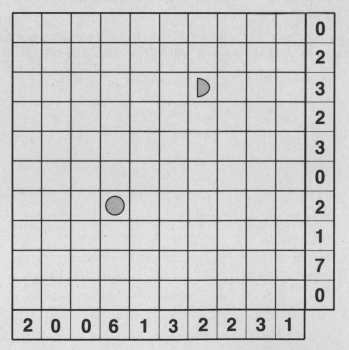

In the Year 2525

The new science fiction book *In the Year 2525* from publishers Aiger and Zevons is a collection of five novelettes on the common theme of life on Earth in the not too distant future, and for some reason none of them are very optimistic. Can you work out the name of each of the authors who has contributed to the book, the title of their story, and the problem which the story envisages confronting the world in the year 2525?

Clues

1. Mr. Rocklynne, Donald, and the author of *Endgame* are three different people.

2. Abigail's story depicts Earth in 2525 racked by worldwide famine, with wars being fought for the possession of the shrinking areas of fertile farmland, while Smith's has it falling victim to an unstoppable invasion by a very strange race of aliens.

3. Joanne, who wrote *The Horsemen*, doesn't have the last name Leinster.

4. *Dog Days*, which is not Rocklynne's story, features an Earth dying from the toxic and irreversible pollution of its air and water.

5. It was the author named Wells (no relation to the great H.G.) who wrote *Judgment*.

6. Michael Burrough's story isn't the one in which Earth's population is virtually wiped out by a man-made plague; neither of these stories is called *Red Sky*.

First name	Surname

	Burroughs	Leinster	Rocklynne	Smith	Wells	Dog Days	Endgame	Judgment	Red Sky	The Horsemen	Alien invasion	Famine	Nuclear war	Plague	Toxic pollution
Abigail															
Donald															
Joanne															
Michael															
Stephen															
Alien invasion															
Famine															
Nuclear war															
Plague															
Toxic pollution															
Dog Days															
Endgame															
Judgment															
Red Sky															
The Horsemen															

Title	Problem

Knights Out

It will come as no surprise to you to learn that the five Knock-Kneed Knights of King Arthur's Round Table were defeated ("walked over" might describe it better) in the first round of the annual Camelot Tournament, and so had plenty of time to order lunch at another kind of round table in the Blatant Beast Tavern. Can you fill in the name of the knight in each seat at the table and say what type of game dish, what sweetmeat, and what beverage each had for lunch?

Clues

1. One of the two knights who drank wine was seated immediately counterclockwise from a man who had a bird-based dish for lunch; Sir Coward de Custarde sat immediately counterclockwise of the man who ordered fruit comfits; Sir Timid de Shayke ate the meat of a bird and the knight who drank the spice-infused wine called hippocras ate the honeycakes.

2. The knight in seat B, whose first name didn't begin with S, ate either comfits or honeycakes while the other two knights whose name didn't begin with S ate neither of those items; the knight in seat D, whose first name did start with S, didn't eat either honeycakes or comfits while the other knight with S as his first name initial did partake in one of them; neither of the men sitting next to Sir Poltroon à Ghaste ate either comfits or honeycakes.

3. The knight in seat C, who ate the junket, did not drink any kind of wine; the man who ate grouse had a first name beginning with S, as did the one occupying seat E.

4. The knight who ate venison, who didn't drink any kind of wine and whose first name didn't begin with S, sat immediately counterclockwise of the one who had ordered roast boar; the man who drank hippocras sat immediately clockwise of Sir Spyneless de Feete.

5. Sir Sorely à Frayde, who didn't eat a bird-based dish, sat immediately clockwise of the man who ordered suckets (nuts dipped in hot honey) and immediately counterclockwise of the one who drank mead; the knight who drank ale was either first or last in the alphabetical list.

Knights: Sir Coward de Custarde; Sir Poltroon à Ghaste; Sir Sorely à Frayde; Sir Spyneless de Feete; Sir Timid de Shayke

Game: grouse; jugged hare; pigeon pie; roast boar; venison

Sweetmeats: comfits; honeycakes; junket; marchpane; suckets

Beverages: ale; cider; hippocras wine; Lyonesse wine; mead

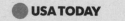

Under Wraps

Rachel emigrated to Australia a few years ago and recently returned to the US to visit her family and she brought everyone a present from Down Under. Can you work out for whom each present was intended, the main color of the wrapping paper, and the appropriately antipodean animal design on the gift tag?

Clues

1. Rachel brought a small dog basket for her sister Chloe's tiny puppy; the basket parcel didn't have a gift tag showing a koala or Tasmanian devil.

2. The present with a kangaroo design on its gift tag was for Ivan; this wasn't the boomerang, which was wrapped in silver paper, but wasn't intended for Eddie.

3. Rachel's gift for her mom Molly was wrapped in green paper.

4. The gift tag with a picture of a platypus was attached to the present wrapped in black paper.

5. The ornate tankard, which wasn't for Eddie, had a gift tag with a dingo design.

6. The red hoodie with the design of a wallaby, which wasn't for Ivan, wasn't wrapped in blue paper.

7. The present wrapped in white gift paper didn't have a gift tag with a picture of a Tasmanian devil.

Name	Present

	Boomerang	Clapsticks	Dog basket	Hoodie	Tankard	Black	Blue	Green	Silver	White	Dingo	Kangaroo	Koala	Platypus	Tasmanian devil
Chloe															
Eddie															
Fern															
Ivan															
Molly															
Dingo															
Kangaroo															
Koala															
Platypus															
Tasmanian devil															
Black															
Blue															
Green															
Silver															
White															

Color	Gift tag

Yummy Gummy

Gummy Cubs candy factory has five production lines, each creating one of their shaped candies. Workers are allowed to help themselves to one or two of the gummies as they roll off the production line—it's both a perk for the staff and an easy way to carry out quality control. Here we drop in at the factory and peer over the shoulders of five workers, one on each of the production lines. Can you fully identify each and say how many of what Gummy Cub shape he or she wolfed down during their shift?

Clues

1. The worker producing baby fox-shaped Gummy Cubs doesn't have a very sweet tooth, so their consumption over the eight-hour shift was a mere five.

2. Moira Stevens ate more Gummy Cubs than her fellow employee who was working on the baby-bear Gummy Cub production line, who was not called Reeves.

3. Onslow did not eat eight candies during his eight-hour shift.

4. It was the employee named Lawson who either munched the most Gummy Cubs or did most quality control, depending on your point of view; these weren't the candies molded to the shape of cute baby lions.

5. The employee molding baby pandas is named Hill; this isn't Shirley, who ate/tested 12 Gummy Cubs over the length of her shift.

6. Kevin spent his shift making baby tiger-shaped Gummy Cubs.

First name	Surname

	Bowman	Hill	Lawson	Reeves	Stevens	Bear	Fox	Lion	Panda	Tiger	5 Gummy Cubs	8 Gummy Cubs	12 Gummy Cubs	14 Gummy Cubs	18 Gummy Cubs
Anita															
Kevin															
Moira															
Onslow															
Shirley															
5 Gummy Cubs															
8 Gummy Cubs															
12 Gummy Cubs															
14 Gummy Cubs															
18 Gummy Cubs															
Bear															
Fox															
Lion															
Panda															
Tiger															

DAD, CAN I HAVE A PONY?

NO, WAIT FOR YOUR DINNER LIKE EVERYONE ELSE

Shape	Number

Close Encounters

Many people claim to have contact with aliens and other worlds, even people you might otherwise consider to be very sensible, level-headed people. Here are examples of five. Can you work out the occupation of each person, their strange extra-terrestrial claim, and the year in which it was made? Of course, none of these things actually happened, the people concerned were mistaken, confused, drunk, or dreaming—or so we are ensured by the powers that be . . .

Clues

1. Mrs. Sobers claims that her body was taken over by aliens, while the bus driver claims that his children are in fact aliens (oddly, they think the same about him).

2. Mr. Featon-Ground made the most recent claim; he is not a real estate agent (or he would have sold the alien that nice bijou property that had just come on the market).

3. Back in 2001, it was the doctor who reckoned to have had an alien encounter (the authorities put it down to a mix-up between sugar and tranquilizers in his morning coffee); the librarian made his or her claim four years after someone else said that they had been abducted by aliens and four years before Miss Clerehead told her story.

4. The sighting of alien spacecraft (described by the authorities as the inverted refraction of Venus though ice clouds) did not take place in 2009.

5. The person who claimed to have originally come from another planet made that claim in 2013.

6. Mr. Sayne is a teacher.

Year	Name

USA TODAY

	Miss Clerehead	Mr. Featon-Ground	Mr. Normhall	Mr. Sayne	Mrs. Sobers	Bus driver	Doctor	Librarian	Real estate agent	Teacher	Abducted by aliens	Body taken over	Children are aliens	From another planet	Saw spacecraft
2001															
2005															
2009															
2013															
2017															
Abducted by aliens															
Body taken over															
Children are aliens															
From another planet															
Saw spacecraft															
Bus driver															
Doctor															
Librarian															
Real estate agent															
Teacher															

Occupation	Claim

Sign In

Each row and column is to contain the digits 1-6. The given signs tell you if a digit in a cell is plus 1 (+) or minus 1 (-) the digit next to it. Signs between consecutive digits always work from left to right or top to bottom. Examples: $3 + 4$ or $\frac{2}{1}$ ALL occurrences of consecutive digits have been marked by a sign.

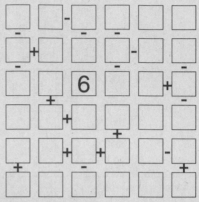

Killer Sudoku

The normal rules of Sudoku apply. In addition, the digits in each inner shape (marked by dots) must add up to the number in the top corner of that box.

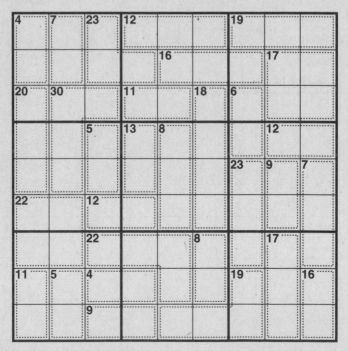

Model Members

Four members of the Georgetown Model Railway Club live along Railway Road in the town and have fairly large—and growing—layouts somewhere at their home. Can you work out at which number each club member lives, the location of their model railway, and the length of track it, so far, includes? (NB: Railway Road is numbered in the traditional way with odd numbers on one side and even on the other.)

Clues

1. Harold Sleeper lives at a lower number than the house where the layout is in the garage but a higher number than the one with the 55m display.

2. The layout in the guest bedroom is at a higher number than the longest track but a lower number than Jemima Syding's house, which is on the opposite side of the road to the 45m track but the same side as her fellow member whose layout is in the attic.

3. Imogen's layout is shorter than the track that runs around the inside of the shed but longer than the track at 23 Railway Road; Kenneth Halt doesn't live at 23 Railway Road and doesn't have a shed.

Members: Harold Sleeper; Imogen Poynts; Jemima Syding; Kenneth Halt
Locations: attic; garage; guest bedroom; shed
Lengths of track: 45m; 50m; 55m; 60m

No.7   No.12   No.16   No.23

Starting tip: Work out who lives at No.23.

Read and Rejected

The newly discovered manuscript of *Sloth and Slander* has been given to three Jade Austell experts to verify its authenticity. Sadly they found themselves unable to comply and labeled the manuscript a fake. Can you work out what style problem each expert singled out, and, more to the point, what item, not invented until long after Jade Austell's demise, appears in what chapter of the document?

Clues

1. Prof. Hound noted that the use of metaphor was very un-Austellish.

2. Prof. Ayne's concerns were confirmed when she read about a wireless in an earlier chapter than the one featuring the item pointed out by Prof. Legate.

3. Chapter 5 features Abigail making a telephone call; the expert who found an anachronistic item in chapter 2 wasn't the one who said the grammar wasn't up to Austell's usual standard, who wasn't the one who noticed the light bulb reference.

	Grammar	Metaphor	Punctuation	Light bulb	Telephone	Wireless	Chapter 2	Chapter 5	Chapter 8
Prof. Ayne									
Prof. Hound									
Prof. Legate									
Chapter 2									
Chapter 5									
Chapter 8									
Light bulb									
Telephone									
Wireless									

Expert	Style problem	Item	Chapter

Locker Fit

The diagram shows a block of lockers in the men's locker room at the Madison Gym. Can you fully identify and describe the men whose clothes are currently residing in each of the lockers numbered 1 to 4 while they work out?

Clues

1. The chef's day clothes are in the locker immediately above Melvin's.

2. Denzil's locker is the one immediately to the right of Fettle's.

3. The bank manager is using locker number 4.

4. Gareth's locker is in diagonal alignment with the one containing the lecturer's pants.

5. Kieron and the attorney, who work out together, have lockers on the same level.

6. Spry's locker is numbered one lower than Hardy's.

First names: Denzil; Gareth; Kieron; Melvin
Surnames: Fettle; Fitt; Hardy; Spry
Descriptions: bank manager; chef; attorney; lecturer

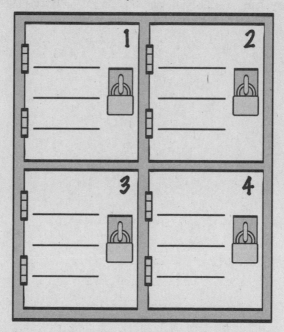

Starting tip: Begin by working out the first name of the man using locker 1.

Rose of Honor

The large and established nursery garden in Centerville has produced five beautiful hybrid rose shrubs this year, which have each been named in honor of five different local unsung heroes. Can you work out the name of each rose (which bears the first name of the hero), what its color is, why the rose has been named after the hero, and the month the rose shrub first came onto the market?

Clues

1. The orange rose is named Bonny.

2. The rose named Tessa has been on sale since April; this isn't the yellow one, which has been named after a police dog, who last year received a bravery award for saving the lives of his handler and another officer.

3. The rose shrub, which was neither the first nor the last one to be brought onto the market, has been named after Wesley, who has worked tirelessly over the years for the homeless, initiating many charity fundraising schemes.

4. One of the rose shrubs, which has been on sale since June, has been named after an athlete who won a bronze medal at the Olympics.

5. The lilac rose shrub, which isn't named Winston and hasn't been named after the swim coach, came onto the market at the end of March.

6. The red rose didn't first come onto the market in May.

Name	Color

	Lilac	Orange	Red	White	Yellow	Athlete	Charity work	Police dog	Retired politician	Swim coach	March	April	May	June	July
Bonny															
Sandy															
Tessa															
Wesley															
Winston															
March															
April															
May															
June															
July															
Athlete															
Charity work															
Police dog															
Retired politician															
Swim coach															

Reason	Month

The Drifters

The tiny Alaskan town of Wytout, home to only about 500 hardy souls, is no stranger to severe weather, and last weekend the only restaurant in town was almost buried under snow. The restaurant had taken reservations for a dozen families for dinner, but only five managed to make it through the blizzard. Can you work out how many members of each family there are, what method they used to get to the restaurant, and how long it took for them to make the journey?

Clues

1. The Evanses live closest of these five to the restaurant but it still took them 35 mins to make the journey.

2. The Carneys, who aren't the biggest family, live and work on a farm, so it wasn't too much of a stretch for them to clamber onto their tractor for the trip to the inn; they managed to get to the restaurant more quickly than the Green family did.

3. The family of three, which isn't the Dempsters or Greens, used their own pet huskies pulling sleds to get them to the restaurant.

4. One family donned snow shoes and trudged across deep snow for 46 mins to get to the restaurant; this wasn't the five-strong Franklin family.

5. The family of four, who didn't arrive in a motor vehicle, took 65 mins.

6. It wasn't the Dempster family that turned up on cross-country skis.

Name	Number

	Three	Four	Five	Six	Seven	Dog sled	4x4 truck	Skis	Snow shoes	Tractor	35 mins	42 mins	46 mins	65 mins	84 mins
Carney															
Dempster															
Evans															
Franklin															
Green															
35 mins															
42 mins															
46 mins															
65 mins															
84 mins															
Dog sled															
4x4 truck															
Skis															
Snow shoes															
Tractor															

NO, A SNOWMOBILE, NOT A SNOW MOBILE

Method	Duration

Haven't a Clue

Faith, an avid cryptic crossword solver, was very frustrated about not being able to complete the last clue in the recent crosswords she attempted in various puzzle mags and daily newspapers. Each one was a competition with a prize, but Faith missed out on the submission dates. Can you work out which clue remained unsolved in each magazine or newspaper's crossword, the prize on offer, and the latest submission date for entries?

Clues

1. Faith wasn't able to tackle 12 across in the *Daily News* puzzle.

2. The entry deadline for the crossword in the crossword magazine *Cross Swords* was June 14 and Faith managed to complete all its across clues.

3. Faith wasn't worried about missing out on the chance to win a pen set in one competition but was miffed that she wasn't able to solve its clue for 2 down.

4. One completed crossword had to be submitted by June 7 and the lucky winner would receive a book token.

5. Faith couldn't do 15 down for one crossword, which had to be submitted by June 23; this wasn't the one found in *Prize Puzzles* which offered a dictionary to the selected winner of their competition.

6. The deadline for the crossword in the *Daily Rag* wasn't in June and the prize offered wasn't the DVD.

7. The tricky 9 across clue, which wasn't in the puzzle for which the prize was a thesaurus, wasn't Faith's stumbling block in the competition to be sent by July 1.

Journal	Clue

	2 down	9 across	12 across	15 down	21 across	Book token	Dictionary	DVD	Pen set	Thesaurus	May 30	June 7	June 14	June 23	July 1
Cross Swords															
Daily News															
Daily Rag															
Monthly Teasers															
Prize Puzzles															
May 30															
June 7															
June 14															
June 23															
July 1															
Book token															
Dictionary															
DVD															
Pen set															
Thesaurus															

Prize	Date

Nice Ice

It may come as a surprise to learn that the Ancient Romans were often able to keep food cool by transporting blocks of compacted snow down from the hills in winter and storing it below ground in a house's cellar. Sent down below to collect some milk and something else for the family's needs, five clumsy servant-friends managed to take a tumble on a slippery patch and discovered when they were able to get up that what they'd been carrying had become mixed up with the snow, forming a not-unpalatable frozen dessert. Can you work out what type of liquid and solid ingredients each servant had been carrying and what he decided to call his newfangled icy treat?

Clues

1. The cherry-flavoured gelatum was named a Magnum—it came in rather a big bowl.

2. Hopelus called his discovery Muri, because he had to scrape most of it off the cellar walls; it wasn't the mixture of honey and asses' milk (a recipe pinched from the best-seller *The Cleopatra Collection*) originally intended for another servant's mistress' bathtub.

3. The servant who rolled a convenient sheet of parchment into a cone-shape, stuffed his mixture of creamy ice into it for ease of carrying and called it a Cornettum wasn't Gormlus; Euselus' new gelatum was based on sheep's milk.

4. Neither a dish of sliced lemons nor a bowl of goat's milk, which weren't in the same mixture, was in Cluelus' hands when he went head over heels into the snow.

5. Branelus was carrying a plate of chopped peaches when he slipped; neither he nor Gormlus was the servant who decided to call the icy mixture of the fruit he'd been carrying along with a jug of water Sorbum, to reflect his condition when he managed to stand up.

Servant	Flavor/fruit

	Cherry	Honey	Lemon	Peach	Strawberry	Ass	Cow	Goat	Sheep	Water	Cornettum	Magnum	Muri	Sorbum	Undulum
Branelus															
Cluelus															
Euselus															
Gormlus															
Hopelus															
Cornettum															
Magnum															
Muri															
Sorbum															
Undulum															
Ass															
Cow															
Goat															
Sheep															
Water															

Liquid/milk	Name

Pony Express

The Franklin area pony clubs' annual rally came to a tense finish this year, with five teams having the same total score. To sort things out, it was decided to run an activity race (for those of you who aren't into mounted games, it's the one where the riders jump off halfway along the course, run across five "stepping stones" which are usually upturned buckets, then vault into the saddle to finish the race) with one competitor from each team. Can you work out the name of each of the ponies, the full name of the young rider who rode it, and the name of his or her team?

Clues

1. None of the five riders had the same initials for their first name and surname.

2. Bonnie—and, of course, her rider—belonged to the team called St. Ursula's.

3. Edwin, who rode Muffin, wasn't the representative of the conservation-conscious Greenflyers.

4. Young Eppie rode for the Clopworthy and District Pony Club's own A-team, unimaginatively named CDPC-A.

5. Midnight (who was, of course, black) was not the rider named Jowle's pony, nor was he ridden by Joshua.

6. The pony club member named Mowis, who rode Samantha to victory in the race and won the rally for their team, wasn't Helen, who was the representative of the Round Up team.

7. Molly Algar was one of the competitors in the winner-takes-all tie-breaker.

Pony	First name

	Amanda	Edwin	Helen	Joshua	Molly	Algar	Eppie	Hugby	Jowle	Mowis	CDPC-A	Greenflyers	Round Up	St. Ursula's	Team Pegasus
Bonnie															
Lucky															
Midnight															
Muffin															
Samantha															
CDPC-A															
Greenflyers															
Round Up															
St. Ursula's															
Team Pegasus															
Algar															
Eppie															
Hugby															
Jowle															
Mowis															

Surname	Team

Private Hire

Five residents living in Station Road, an easy five-minute walk from Fairview railway station, have taken the advantage of living there to rent out their driveways for parking to daily commuters, who are trying to avoid both the difficulty of finding a space and the exorbitant charges. Can you work out which family lives at which house, the commuter who hires their driveway during the day, and the make of automobile he or she leaves there?

Clues

1. Mrs. Dawson owns the Anda 1.4, which isn't parked on the drive at a double-figure-numbered house and isn't parked where the Peters live.

2. Miss Benson's automobile can be seen in the drive of 14 Station Road, which isn't where the Browns live.

3. Mr. Child uses the Ericsons' drive from 8 a.m. to 6 p.m., which doesn't belong to house No.6; he doesn't own the Gastral 1.6, which is parked in the drive of house No.9.

4. The Stone family, which doesn't reside at either No.2 or No.6, has a Matrix Saloon parked in their driveway during the working day.

5. The Garrets live at No.11; they don't have a Solstice XS parked on their driveway.

6. Mr. Andrews doesn't drive a Vocus Wagon.

House	Commuter

	Brown	Ericson	Garret	Peters	Stone	Mr. Andrews	Miss Benson	Mr. Child	Mrs. Dawson	Mr. Edison	Anda 1.4L	Gastral 1.6L	Matrix Saloon	Solstice XS	Vocus Wagon
No.2															
No.6															
No.9															
No.11															
No.14															
Anda 1.4															
Gastral 1.6															
Matrix Saloon															
Solstice XS															
Vocus Wagon															
Mr. Andrews															
Miss Benson															
Mr. Child															
Mrs. Dawson															
Mr. Edison															

ROMEO, ROMEO, WHEREFORE ART MY ALFA ROMEO?

Owner	Car

Tsarina Ballerina

A short way along Greenville's Fonteyn Street is a set of double doors with a brass plate that says Tsarina Ballerina that leads to a small studio where Valentina Ballerina teaches ballet in the Russian style. This Saturday morning she's in a bad mood, as each of her seven young students were late for their 11 a.m. lesson, a crime that could only be exceeded by turning up without the correct equipment, which they've all also done, having forgotten their ballet shoes. Can you say how late was each of the student ballerinas, what they were doing that made them late enough to forget their shoes, and the footwear they were wearing when they arrived and are now still wearing? (We've drawn each of the girls barefooted, so feel free to sketch their shoes when you know what's what. Lefts and rights are from our point of view.)

Clues

1. Emmalina Ballerina, Valentina refers to all her students in this way, was in such a rush she forgot her ballet shoes and is now doing her exercises in her yellow rubber boots; she arrived one minute later than the girl who is dancing in her sneakers, who isn't Wilhelmina Ballerina.

2. The girl who had spent a happy hour kicking piles of leaves, who wasn't Philippina Ballerina, had also been wearing rubber boots but had had enough time to pull them off and slip on her flip-flops, but not quite enough time to remember her ballet shoes.

3. Angelina Ballerina was late back from walking the family dog Nureyev; Evangelina Ballerina, who is one of the three girls wearing boots of some kind, crept into the dance studio four minutes late hoping, but failing, to avoid the stern stare of Valentina.

4. The ballerina who arrived two minutes late, who isn't wearing loafers, had been playing on the swings in the park and is shown immediately right of the girl who had been helping with the gardening before getting ready for dance class; both of the immediate neighbors of the girl wearing loafers arrived later than she did.

5. The girl who is dancing in her Ugg boots was twice as many minutes late as the girl who spent a little too long playing on her new bicycle before leaving for dance class; the girl who had spent a pleasant hour in the sandpit in the park this morning isn't wearing any kind of boots.

6. The girl who arrived five minutes late is immediately right of the ballerina dancing in sandals and immediately left of the girl who had been picking mushrooms with her Dad; the mushroom picker isn't the girl in walking boots.

Lateness: 1 minute; 2 minutes; 3 minutes; 4 minutes; 5 minutes; 6 minutes; 7 minutes

Activities: gardening; kicking piles of leaves; picking mushrooms; playing on bicycle; sandpit in park; swings in park; walking dog

Shoes: flip-flops; loafers; rubber boots; sandals; sneakers; Ugg boots; walking boots

Thomasina Philippina Emmalina Angelina Katarina Evangelina Wilhelmina

Starting tip: Work out in what footwear Ballerina Evangelina is dancing.

Animal Magic

In yet another desperate attempt to instil some vestige of valor into the five Knock-Kneed Knights, Merlin cast a spell on each in turn, designed to turn them for 24 hours into a fierce animal, hoping that something would remain when they returned to normal human form. Even Merlin's magic proved inadequate, however, and the end product of each spell was assigned to the care of a lad from the Minstrel School in Camelot to look after until the effect wore off. Can you say in which order the knights were transformed into what, and name the apprentice minstrel who cared for him?

Clues

1. The spell which came closest to its intention was the one designed to produce a fighting bull, but the outcome was a little white one, and young Thomas, a steelier character than the knight, was inspired to compose a ballad on the subject of his charge.

2. Sir Sorely à Frayde became a chicken, rather than the fighting cock, in the spell immediately preceding the one affecting the knight tended by Elton, who was learning to play the clavichord.

3. Clifford, who had earned Merlin's approval by singing to the crowd at a jousting tournament when bad weather held up the proceedings, was given charge of the third spell's victim.

4. The fourth knight, who should have been transformed into an eagle, turned instead into a yellow wagtail.

5. Sir Timid de Shayke was the second knight to be subjected to Merlin's ministrations, while Sir Coward de Custarde was dealt with in a later spell than the one which produced a rabbit instead of the intended bull mastiff.

6. Frederick, a mercurial member of the minstrel's college, was assigned to look after the transmogrified Sir Spyneless de Feete, who was not the first to undergo Merlin's attentions.

7. The would-be tiger turned out to be a marmalade cat in the spell next, but one before that affecting Sir Poltroon à Ghaste.

Order	Knight

USA TODAY

	Sir Coward de Custarde	Sir Poltroon à Ghaste	Sir Sorely à Frayde	Sir Spyneless de Feete	Sir Timid de Shayke	Chicken	Little white bull	Marmalade cat	Rabbit	Yellow wagtail	Aled	Clifford	Elton	Frederick	Thomas
First															
Second															
Third															
Fourth															
Fifth															
Aled															
Clifford															
Elton															
Frederick															
Thomas															
Chicken															
Little white bull															
Marmalade cat															
Rabbit															
Yellow wagtail															

Transformation	Minstrel

Starlet Hopes

In the heyday of Hollywood, five aspiring actresses headed west to seek fame and fortune on the silver screen under romantic-sounding stage names. Can you discover in which year each arrived in Los Angeles, her home state and real name, and the name under which she found fame and fortune?

Clues

1. The girl who would become actress Sabrina Banks was born in Illinois, while Eunice Wigg hailed from New York.

2. The country girl from Ohio arrived in Hollywood in 1929 and soon found work in the burgeoning studios. She didn't choose the name Meryl Day.

3. Audrey Mullett arrived in Tinseltown the year before the girl from Louisiana, while the aspiring actress from Missouri arrived two years earlier than Simone Lamont was discovered.

4. The girl who would become Imogen Valentine arrived in 1930.

5. Hyacinth Mudge traveled west in 1932.

6. Grace Waghorn changed her name by dropping the "wag."

Year	Home state

	Illinois	Louisiana	Missouri	New York	Ohio	Janice Allibone	Hyacinth Mudge	Audrey Mullett	Grace Waghorn	Eunice Wigg	Sabrina Banks	Meryl Day	Grace Horne	Simone Lamont	Imogen Valentine
1929															
1930															
1932															
1933															
1934															
Sabrina Banks															
Meryl Day															
Grace Horne															
Simone Lamont															
Imogen Valentine															
Janice Allibone															
Hyacinth Mudge															
Audrey Mullett															
Grace Waghorn															
Eunice Wigg															

Real name	Screen name

Cheaper Chips

In the Silver Nugget Casino, one of the smaller, off-strip, and less glamorous establishments in the gambling resort of Los Fortune, five gamblers have sat down for a game of poker with affordable stakes and table limits. The first hand has been dealt and each player holds just one face card. Can you work out the profession of each stony-faced player, the face card held, and the amount of money each has brought to the table?

Clues

1. Donna Flinch, who is not the owner of the 6-to-12 grocery store, has a club picture card; the short-order chef at the Last Hope Diner has $50 in their pocket, but neither the chef nor the grocer has been dealt the king of diamonds.

2. Norah Clewes, the player with $60 to lose, the one holding the jack of spades, and the grocer are four different people.

3. Ted Pann isn't holding the jack of spades, but Luke Sterne has the jack of hearts.

4. The car mechanic at the Grease Elbow Garage has been dealt the queen of clubs.

5. The player with the king of clubs has brought the most money to play with.

6. Woody Le Blanc, who works at the Last Hand Undertakers, hasn't brought exactly $100 with him.

Player	Profession

	Car mechanic	Grocer	Plumbing contractor	Short-order chef	Undertaker	Jack of hearts	Jack of spades	King of clubs	King of diamonds	Queen of clubs	$50	$60	$75	$100	$120
Donna Flinch															
Luke Sterne															
Norah Clewes															
Ted Pann															
Woody Le Blanc															
$50															
$60															
$75															
$100															
$120															
Jack of hearts															
Jack of spades															
King of clubs															
King of diamonds															
Queen of clubs															

BUT WHAT USE IS ONE WHEEL? NOW YOU'LL HAVE TO INVENT THE REST OF THE CASINO

Picture card	Amount carried

Battleships

Do you remember the old game of battleships? These puzzles are based on that idea. Your task is to find the vessels in the diagram. Some parts of boats or sea squares have already been filled in, and a number next to a row or column refers to the number of occupied squares in that row or column. The boats may be positioned horizontally or vertically, but no two boats or parts of boats are in adjacent squares—horizontally, vertically, or diagonally.

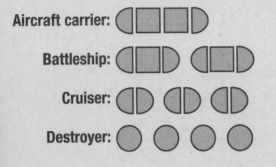

Aircraft carrier:

Battleship:

Cruiser:

Destroyer:

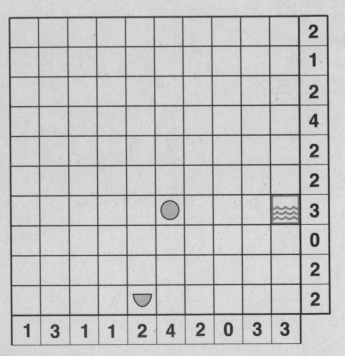

USA TODAY

The Movie Mob

The picture below is the opening shot of the new movie *Mobsters*, a comedy set in Prohibition New York. As the camera swings down and circumnavigates, we see four mob bosses discussing business. Can you name each man, work out his nickname and the area of New York he considers his patch, and discover which one, having transgressed some unwritten law, doesn't survive the meeting and is played by a bit actor who has only the one line "So wad I do?"

Clues

1. "Diamonds," his favored loot, is seated immediately counterclockwise of Al Feloni, the mob boss from Queens.

2. The mobster in seat 4 is the notorious Vito DeLinqui, and the character in seat 3 will be dead by the end of this first scene.

3. "Uncle" is in charge of operations in Greenwich Village; Jo "Boots" Villani—something to do with concrete—isn't the mob leader for Little Italy.

4. One mobster is seated between the gangster nicknamed "Shark" and the Brooklyn gang boss, who was immediately counterclockwise of Tommy Racketti.

Mobsters: Al Feloni; Jo Villani; Tommy Racketti; Vito DeLinqui
Nicknames: Boots; Diamonds; Shark; Uncle
Districts: Brooklyn; Greenwich Village; Little Italy; Queens

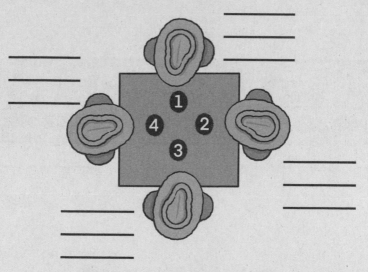

Starting tip: Work out Al Feloni's nickname.

There Were Ten in a Bed . . .

. . . and the little one said, "Roll over, roll over." And they all rolled over and one by one they all fell out in numerical order, starting with number one. From the clues, can you work out the names of the ten bedfellows?

Clues

1. Ray, Kay, and Fay fell out in that order, but none of them fell out immediately after the other. Ray was not the first to be dislodged and Fay was not the last one left in the bed.

2. Meg fell out immediately after Bob and immediately before Tom, whose position was numbered half that of Sue, who was next to fall after Pam, who fell out somewhat earlier than Lee, who rolled over and out before Dan.

Names: Bob; Dan; Fay; Kay; Lee; Meg; Pam; Ray; Sue; Tom

Starting tip: Find out who fell out first.

Logi-5

Each line, across and down, is to have each of the letters A, B, C, D, and E, appearing once. Also, every shape—shown by the thick lines—must also have each of the letters in it. Can you fill in the grid?

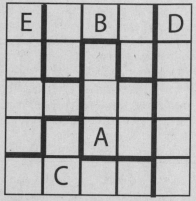

Sudoku

Complete this grid so that each column, each row, and each marked 3 X 3 square contains each of the numbers 1 to 9.

		6	5	3			1	
	4	1			6	8		
2	5			8		1		4
7	1			4		5		3
	6	2			5	4		
		8	7	2			9	

Pass the Chippes

Xander Chippes has run Chippes Industries for the past 40 years, expanding the company from a small chipboard manufacturer into many diverse areas all inspired by his family name. The chipboard business was closed a few years ago, but the five remaining arms of the company are thriving and the time has come for Xander to take a step away from the business and pass it on to his children, with himself remaining as Chairman. Can you work out the age of each of his five children, how they've been spending their time and earning a living so far, and the name and business sector of the division to which they have been appointed as Managing Director? (For clarity, Clinton and Eugene are Xander's only sons.)

Clues

1. Bernice Chippes is next older than the new Managing Director of the Chippesit division and next younger than her sister who has taken over the French fries manufacturing plant.

2. Daphne Chippes, who is now the MD at Chippeworld is more than two years older than her brother who is now in control of the chocolate chip manufacturing division which has lucrative deals with cookie and muffin companies.

3. Ariadne Chippes has been trying for a few years to launch a career as a singer but was still waiting for her big break; the new MD at the computer chips division has been scraping a living taking photographs, both paparazzi style and weddings.

4. The Chippeworx Managing Director is two years younger than the Chippes who is now in control of the golf club division, specializing in clubs for those tricky little shots not far from the green; the latter of these two hasn't been working as an assistant at a TV studio.

5. The Chippes who runs the Chippetts division, making gambling tokens for casinos, isn't the 26-year-old who has spent some time trying to make a splash as a clothes designer but creating nothing more than the odd ripple; the former clothes designer isn't Eugene.

6. The 28-year-old new MD of Chippestuff is not in charge of a division that manufactures an edible product.

Person	Age	Previous activity

	25 years	26 years	28 years	29 years	31 years	Aid worker	Clothes designer	Photographer	Singer	TV assistant	Chippesit	Chippetts	Chippestuff	Chippeworld	Chippeworx	Casino tokens	Chocolate chips	Computer chips	French fries	Golf clubs
Ariadne																				
Bernice																				
Clinton																				
Daphne																				
Eugene																				
Casino tokens																				
Chocolate chips																				
Computer chips																				
French fries																				
Golf clubs																				
Chippesit																				
Chippetts																				
Chippestuff																				
Chippeworld																				
Chippeworx																				
Aid worker																				
Clothes designer																				
Photographer																				
Singer																				
TV assistant																				

IT'S GOING TO BE THE NEXT BREAKTHROUGH. WE CALL IT THE MACROCHIP.

Business Name	Sector

All at Sea

In the Golden Age of Sail, five ships set off from Europe on intrepid voyages to far-flung destinations only to suffer misfortunes which have since drifted into legend and become metaphors for similarly calamitous situations. Can you find out the name of each vessel, in what year they set sail, the destination they never reached, and what befell them?

Clues

1. *Sisyphus* rammed a huge rock and was holed below the waterline five years after one vessel set sail for the Americas and five years before one crew were washed up on a deserted shore. The 1795 journey was bound for the Cape of Good Hope.

2. In 1800 one vessel was taken aback when a huge gust of wind slammed into the sails from the wrong direction and snapped the mainmast. This ship was neither *Icarus* nor the vessel bound for the East Indies. *Tantalus* left port ten years after one vessel keeled over.

3. It was not the 1790 voyage that was left high and dry when the ship beached and could not be re-floated. *Orpheus* was the last ship to sail but was not heading towards either of the Indies.

Name	Year

	1785	1790	1795	1800	1805	Holed below waterline	Keeled over	Left high and dry	Taken aback	Washed up	Americas	Antipodes	Cape of Good Hope	East Indies	West Indies
Icarus															
Nemesis															
Orpheus															
Sisyphus															
Tantalus															
Americas											
Antipodes											
Cape of Good Hope											
East Indies											
West Indies											
Holed below waterline						
Keeled over						
Left high and dry						
Taken aback						
Washed up						

WE BROKE NEW GROUND, PLANTED THE SEED, AND RE-INVENTED THE WHEEL. WE WERE AT THE CUTTING EDGE, WE BLAZED A TRAIL, AND PUSHED THE ENVELOPE...THEN WE RAN OUT OF METAPHORS

PROFITS

Misfortune	Destination

Chubby Felines

There's been much controversy recently about the huge bonus packages paid to executives of companies that are performing rather less than spectacularly. Below are the shameful details of five of them. Can you discover for which underperforming company each fat cat works, his post, and the amount each has been paid this year as a bonus?

Clues

1. Saul Meine's bonus package is $2 million more than the President of one of the other companies.

2. Phil Banks was not paid a bonus of $7 million and he's not his company's Chief Executive; neither he nor Robin Staff is the Financial Director who received $6 million in bonus shares.

3. Robin Staff does not work for Weir-Fayling; the executive from that company was paid less than the Managing Director of Pryce, Lowe, and Fawling.

4. Richie Guy received the largest bonus while the Detzer-Reisin executive picked up an $8 million bonus to his already sky-high salary.

5. Isaiah Payde works for Dunn Pawley.

Company	Name

	Isaiah Payde	Phil Banks	Richie Guy	Robin Staff	Saul Meine	$6m	$7m	$8m	$9m	$10m	Chairman	Chief Executive	Financial Director	Managing Director	President
Detzer-Reisin															
Dunn Pawley															
Pryce, Lowe, and Fawling															
Stocksdown															
Weir-Fayling															
Chairman															
Chief Executive															
Financial Director															
Managing Director															
President															
$6m															
$7m															
$8m															
$9m															
$10m															

Bonus	Post

Jack-o'-lanterns

Miranda and her friends have been busy carving pumpkin lanterns as Halloween decorations. From the clues, can you work out who carved each one? (For clarity, Miranda, Daisy, and Poppy are girls; the others are boys. Lefts and rights are as we look at the picture.)

Clues

1. Miranda's Jack-o'-lantern was smiling; Daisy's had a downturned mouth.

2. The pumpkins with circular eyes were both carved by boys and the ones with star-shaped eyes were sculpted by girls.

3. Frankie's lantern is not pumpkin A.

4. Dylan's creation has a boy's work on its left and a girl's on its right.

Names: Daisy; Dylan; Frankie; Jackson; Miranda; Poppy

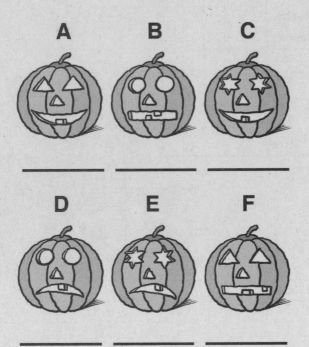

Starting tip: Pinpoint Daisy's pumpkin.

USA TODAY

Well Pressed

The picture shows four men who have just joined the US Navy in the early 1800s—but not voluntarily. They each had a few drinks too many and were picked up by the press gang in one of the inns in the harbor. Can you work out the full name of each man, and the occupation he pursued, before becoming an unwilling sailor? (Lefts and rights are from our point of view.)

Clues

1. The cobbler—well, ex-cobbler now—is immediately right of Henry.

2. John Horton, who is not figure A in the drawing, woke up with a sore head on the deck of the *USS Constitution*.

3. Samuel is immediately right of Mr. Markham, who until a short time ago was a pieman—and may well be sent to the galley.

4. Matthew was a groom, looking after the horses belonging to a wealthy local merchant; he is not Bacon, figure C in the drawing.

First names: Henry; John; Matthew; Samuel
Surnames: Bacon; Horton; Jones; Markham
Former occupations: cobbler; dairyman; groom; pieman

Starting tip: Work out Matthew's surname.

Prints Charming

Students from the Greenville School of Fashion have produced a set of dazzling fabrics and are displaying their creations, made up into garments of their own design, in a fashion show for charity. Can you work out the nature of the garment worn by each student model (we have drawn them all as dresses so as to not give the game away), the pattern it bears, and the background color?

Clues

1. The model wearing a garment printed with large pink peonies is directly behind the woman clad in a purple fabric and next in front of the one wearing a dress.

2. Layla is wearing a pattern on a red background; Olivia is sporting a pair of very bright pants.

3. The enormous passion flowers are adorning an outfit somewhere behind the one printed with gigantic pomegranates and somewhere in front of the garment resplendent with peacocks on a yellow background.

4. The model in the jacket is next behind the one in the garment printed with colossal poppies, which is not a coat.

5. Fiona is not wearing green and the fabric with the green background is not being worn by the model immediately behind the one with the poppy motif on her outfit.

Garments: blouse; coat; dress; jacket; pants
Patterns: passion flowers; peacocks; peonies; pomegranates; poppies
Backgrounds: green; orange; purple; red; yellow

Fiona　Layla　Olivia　Paula　Shania

Bridging the Gap

During the 18th century, bridge-builders across the world competed to see who could build the longest single-span bridge and claim the title of Top Bridgeman. Can you work out for each country the name of the river and of the architect for each of these five entries into that contest and say what span was achieved?

Clues

1. The names of the countries, rivers, and architects involved in the building of each particular bridge all have different initial letters.

2. The bridge built in Navonia is 5ft longer than the one designed by Baili, but the one over the Taber is shorter than both.

3. Neither the bridge designed by Archov nor the one over the Ghames is as long as the one in Cashenia.

4. The name of the architect who bridged the shortest span, which is not the one over the Bolta, is next alphabetically after the one responsible for the one over the Ghames.

5. Balonia's bridge, though longer than the one over the Rhane, is 5ft shorter than the one built by Gettova.

6. The bridge by Krosser is 5ft shorter than the one over the Nole but 5ft longer than the one in Greatovia; Voltski's bridge, which is not over the Rhane, is more than 5ft shorter than the one in Navonia.

Country	River

	Bolta	Ghames	Nole	Rhane	Taber	Archov	Baili	Gettova	Krosser	Voltski	105 feet	110 feet	115 feet	120 feet	125 feet
Balonia															
Barania															
Cashenia															
Greatovia															
Navonia															
105 feet															
110 feet															
115 feet															
120 feet															
125 feet															
Archov															
Baili															
Gettova															
Krosser															
Voltski															

Architect	Length

Tree Surgery

Five properties along Woody Avenue have, by coincidence this month, needed to call in one of the local companies of arborists to deal with a pressing problem on a specimen in their garden—with each, surprisingly perhaps, employing a different expert team. Can you assign each team to the number of the property concerned, identify which variety of tree they have been working on, and what the job has involved?

Clues

1. The beech has long graced the garden of a house numbered higher than where a dead tree needed to be cut down, but not as high as the property where Dr. Tree and his team were working on a maple.

2. A dangerously overhanging branch was removed by Trimms Ltd.

3. An ailing horse-chestnut had to be treated for an infestation of beetles; this was not the job for which the family at number 11 called Jack Lumber & Son, who also didn't have to remove a large fallen specimen blocking a front driveway.

4. Number 17 needed work done on a sycamore, but didn't engage Choppitt and Co. or A Cut Above, the latter of whom were called to a house numbered higher than the former.

5. The tree in the back garden of number 15 needed to be crown-lifted.

Arborists	House

	No.9	No.11	No.15	No.17	No.21	Beech	Evergreen oak	Horse chestnut	Maple	Sycamore	Crown-lift	Cut down dead tree	Dangerous branch	Remove fallen tree	Treat infestation
A Cut Above															
Choppitt & Co.															
Dr. Tree															
Jack Lumber & Son															
Trimms Ltd.															
Crown-lift															
Cut down dead tree															
Dangerous branch															
Remove fallen tree															
Treat infestation															
Beech															
Evergreen oak															
Horse chestnut															
Maple															
Sycamore															

HE'S NEVER BEEN ABLE TO STAND THE SIGHT OF SAP

Tree	Job

One-hit Backers

In the heyday of 1950s rock'n'roll, the following five singers each enjoyed just one big hit backed by their doo-wop-ing and sha-la-la-ing set of backing singers. Can you discover the name of the group that backed each singer, the title of their one and only hit, and the year it made the charts?

Clues

1. Bill Bounty and the Mutineers' big hit was not *You're My Baby*, while Johnny Day reached the charts in 1956 and then disappeared from public life.

2. Gene Goldman, who was not backed by the Songbirds, had his big hit after 1957; *Don't Say Goodbye* was the 1959 hit.

3. The Melodaires provided the backing dip-dee-dips for *Susie Do*, but neither they nor the Songbirds featured on the 1957 release.

4. Neither Frankie Lewis' song nor *Just One Kiss*, neither of which featured the Songbirds, was released in 1955.

5. Phil Nash's brief but successful flirtation with the charts wasn't in 1955.

6. The Highnotes sang the na-nana-nas and doodoo-dee-doos on the 1958 hit.

Singer	Backing group

	Heartbeats	Highnotes	Melodaires	Mutineers	Songbirds	1955	1956	1957	1958	1959	Don't Say Goodbye	Just One Kiss	River of Tears	Susie Do	You're My Baby
Bill Bounty															
Johnny Day															
Gene Goldman															
Frankie Lewis															
Phil Nash															
Don't Say Goodbye															
Just One Kiss															
River of Tears															
Susie Do															
You're My Baby															
1955															
1956															
1957															
1958															
1959															

Banana, nana, nana, nana, nana, nana, nana, nana, Batman.

Year	Big hit

Running Men

As Georgetown Mall prepares to opens its doors on the first day of its big sale, five men, who are looking a little disheveled after camping out overnight, are at the head of the line of bargain hunters. They each have their eye on a particular item and are limbering up for the sprint to the store in question. Can you discover which store each of them will be rushing toward as soon as the mall opens, the item he has set his heart on, and the percentage reduction being offered for the first few sold?

Clues

1. Scott will bolt through the doors of the mall the moment they are unbolted toward Barber and Groves, but not to snap up an item with a 50% reduction; Matt is after a piece of furniture, but not in the Lawton and Son's sale.

2. Bob is stretching his hamstrings in anticipation of his gallop to secure a bargain suit for work but Ryan is not after the shoes.

3. Keith, who won't be scampering towards Lawton and Son, isn't after a cheap pair of expensive shoes or the item with the 70% reduction, which also aren't shoes.

4. The item at Mitchells is marked at 45% off the normal price, but neither it nor the item at Lawton and Son is the set of golf clubs.

5. The bargain hunter who will be streaking towards Oakworld is hoping to secure a bargain-priced home-office desk.

6. The leather couch is in the sale at a massive 80% off the list price (although, to be honest, the list price was a bit extortionate).

Name	Store

	Barber and Groves	Lawton and Son	Mitchells	Oakworld	S and L	Desk	Golf clubs	Leather couch	Shoes	Suit	45%	50%	60%	70%	80%
Bob															
Keith															
Matt															
Ryan															
Scott															
45%															
50%															
60%															
70%															
80%															
Desk															
Golf clubs															
Leather couch															
Shoes															
Suit															

Item	Reduction

Weekend Working

Five pupils from Arlington High School have found themselves weekend work at stores in the town to earn some spending money. Can you work out the name of the store where each youngster works, what sort of establishment it is, and which street it's in?

Clues

1. The name of the shoe store, which isn't Jackson's, is longer than that of the store where Matt works at weekends.

2. Shane's weekend employment is at Marsh's.

3. Rachel works for the newsdealer over the weekend; the newsdealer is not the store known as Noble's of North Street.

4. Kirkby's is a sports store; it's not where Dawn works at weekends to bolster her finances.

5. Ann works in King Street over the weekend; the store's name is the same length as that of the store in the Market Hill.

6. The bakery is in East Street.

Name	Store

	Jackson's	Kirkby's	Lubbock's	Marsh's	Noble's	Bakery	Grocer	Newsdealer	Shoe store	Sports store	East Street	Friars Street	King Street	Market Hill	North Street
Ann															
Dawn															
Matt															
Rachel															
Shane															
East Street															
Friars Street															
King Street															
Market Hill															
North Street															
Bakery															
Grocer															
Newsdealer															
Shoe store															
Sports store															

Business	Address

Pulling Rank

The picture below shows the cab rank in New York one foggy winter's evening in 1892, with seven horse-drawn hansom cabs waiting for passengers to leave their restaurants and theaters to head for home. Can you fill in the name of the man driving each cab and his faithful horse?

Clues

1. The cab drawn by the horse called Bert is numbered one lower than the one driven by George Ford.

2. Cab 6 is pulled by a horse called Old King; neither of its immediate neighbors is drawn by Noddy.

3. The cab drawn by the mare called Venus is indicated by an even number two lower than the one driven by Wilfred Vine.

4. Tim Shaw is the driver of cab number 2.

5. The cab driven by Daniel Crick is not cab number 1, but is numbered lower than the one drawn by Molly.

6. The driver of cab 4 does not have a five-letter first name.

7. Harry Gable's cab, drawn by a horse called Zed, is numbered two lower than Robert Quayne's cab, which is next to the one pulled by Lincoln.

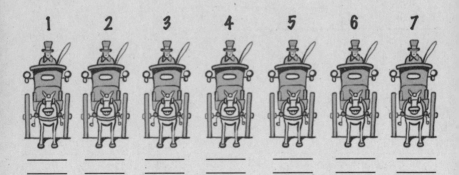

Domino Search

A standard set of dominoes has been laid out, using numbers instead of dots for clarity. Using a sharp pencil and a keen brain, can you draw in the lines to show where each domino has been placed? You may find the check grid useful— crossing off each domino as you find it.

0	4	4	6	3	4	2	3
1	5	3	3	3	3	1	6
1	2	1	6	5	5	1	0
6	4	0	0	4	2	5	0
3	4	6	2	0	2	1	6
6	1	0	5	5	0	5	6
2	5	3	2	4	2	1	4

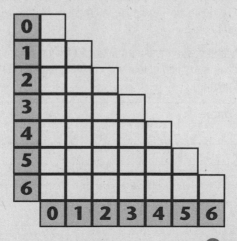

Star Hunting

Top Hollywood producer Harold J. Brassica has decided to make a film based on popular sword and sorcery fantasy heroine Shee-La the Golden, but has yet to choose a star to play the lead role. He wants a newcomer, someone who has not been in a movie before. Five such women are under consideration, but there are arguments for and against each of them. Can you work out the name of each of the five, her current occupation, the extent of her acting experience, and the drawback to giving her the role?

Clues

1. Kim La Veigh, who claims to have no experience at all, is not the heptathlete or the swimmer.

2. Neither Georgia Hart nor the woman whose acting experience stretches as far as playing a non-speaking part in one off-Broadway play is the former champion heptathlete, whose broad New York accent would need to be dubbed, as Shee-La has always been depicted as blonde and Scandinavian.

3. Tracey Urban, isn't the woman whose acting experience is limited to playing herself in a series of TV ads, and isn't the woman who is pregnant, so would need the filming to be completed in very short order.

4. The woman with some experience of theatrical work for children, who at 5 feet 2 inches is considered a little too short to play Shee-La and would require some clever camera work to make her look more statuesque, is not the swimmer who at one time held the world 200 meters freestyle record.

5. The model whose only acting experience was in her school play isn't Patsy Quinn, who has proved to be a little clumsy when required to do anything outside her professional competence—swinging a broadsword, for instance, or leaping into the saddle of a horse.

6. The movie stuntwoman who measures 5 feet 11 in her stockinged feet and who specializes in falling from high points and crashing through windows, isn't pregnant or clumsy.

Name	Occupation

	Circus acrobat	Heptathlete	Model	Stuntwoman	Swimmer	Children's theatre	None at all	One non-speaking part	Played self in TV ads	School play	Clumsy	New York accent	Pregnant	Squeaky voice	Too short
Andrea Berry															
Georgia Hart															
Kim La Veigh															
Patsy Quinn															
Tracey Urban															
Clumsy															
New York accent															
Pregnant															
Squeaky voice															
Too short															
Children's theatre															
None at all															
One non-speaking part															
Played self in TV ads															
School play															

Experience	Drawback

Pass the Parcel

Last week, five courier drivers turned up in Andover Road each with a parcel for one of the residents who, unfortunately, was not at home. Instead, the parcels, which were all one of very big, very heavy, or very big *and* very heavy, were given into the care of one of their neighbors to be passed on to the recipients when they returned. Can you work out at what house number each addressee lives, the name of the neighbor who took the parcel for them, and where the neighbor managed to find a space to accommodate it before passing it on?

Clues

1. Mrs. Kennedy lives at 9 Andover Road; her neighbor didn't put her heavy and bulky parcel in their garage, as, rather unusually, it was being used to house their car.

2. Mr. Norris' next door neighbor, who isn't Miss Flannagan, found a space in their conservatory for his large and cumbersome parcel.

3. Mr. Jarvis' parcel was taken by his neighbor Miss Isaacs; none of the neighbors accepted a parcel for an addressee, who had a family name with the same initial as theirs.

4. One courier spotted Mr. Granger cutting the hedge in his front garden, after getting no response from the occupants of No.11; Mr. Granger accepted a very large parcel for them.

5. Mr. Kirby has a large bathroom where a parcel he accepted, which wasn't for the addressee living at No.12, was able to fit.

6. A neighbor kept a parcel for the occupants of No.3 in their garden shed; it wasn't for Mr. Fletcher or Miss Holt, the latter of whom doesn't live at No.8.

7. Miss Nichols didn't put a parcel in her summerhouse because she doesn't have one.

Addressee	House

	No.3	No.8	No.9	No.11	No.12	Miss Flannagan	Mr. Granger	Miss Isaacs	Mr. Kirby	Miss Nichols	Bathroom	Conservatory	Garage	Shed	Summerhouse
Mr. Fletcher															
Miss Holt															
Mr. Jarvis															
Mrs. Kennedy															
Mr. Norris															
Bathroom															
Conservatory															
Garage															
Shed															
Summerhouse															
Miss Flannagan															
Mr. Granger															
Miss Isaacs															
Mr. Kirby															
Miss Nichols															

Neighbor	Place

Tennis Aces

Competition is fierce in the Greenville Open Tennis Champs this year, with the prestigious prize for the winner attracting players from the global circuit, as well as home-grown stars. Here we meet five top competitors fighting for their places in an early round, with greater or lesser success. With the matches played over three sets and the first player to win two sets winning, can you assign each player to his scores in each? (NB: Under early-round rules, when a match reaches 5-5 in a set players may either agree to opt for a tie-break straight away, or allow play to continue up to a maximum of 8-8 when a tie-break must be played. So we cannot know the exact number of games in the tie-break sets.)

Clues

1. Each match was played over the full three sets; the player who won his first set 6-4 also won his final set without a tie break.

2. There was one fewer game in Canadian hopeful Bernie Cereas' final set than in his other set played to a finish without a tie break.

3. Local hero Charlie Dedbotham's first two sets, neither of which involved a tie break, contained the same number of games in total.

4. U. Kannat, B. Cereas, and C. Dedbotham all lost their first set, with Thai star Upapan Kannat posting the worst score of the three.

5. Spanish ace Ernesto Sagrunta won two of his sets; Aleks Stitagen from the Ukraine lost two of his.

6. The player who lost the 2nd set on a tie-break went on to lose 2-6 in the third.

7. E. Sagrunta, who was the only player not to have been involved in a tie-break, lost fewer games in his final set than did U. Kannat.

Player	Set 1

	Set 1					Set 2					Set 3				
	Lost 1-6	Lost 2-6	Lost tie-break	Won 6-3	Won 6-4	Lost 2-6	Lost tie-break	Won 6-2	Won 6-4	Won tie-break	Lost 2-6	Lost 3-6	Won 6-1	Won 6-4	Won tie-break
A. Stitagen															
B. Cereas															
C. Dedbotham															
E. Sagrunta															
U. Kannat															
Set 3 — Lost 2-6															
Set 3 — Lost 3-6															
Set 3 — Won 6-1															
Set 3 — Won 6-4															
Set 3 — Won tie-break															
Set 2 — Lost 2-6															
Set 2 — Lost tie-break															
Set 2 — Won 6-2															
Set 2 — Won 6-4															
Set 2 — Won tie-break															

Set 2	Set 3

Ant Hill Mob

The ants from the hill are readying themselves for the first foray of the day and the first nine in line are ready to head out into the morning sun. Can you name each of them? (In our picture, the ants are numbered from the front of the line to the back, with number 1 leading the way.)

Clues

1. None of the ants is in the position it would have been in if they were arranged in alphabetical order—either ascending or descending.

2. Adam ant is immediately ahead of Fond ant and immediately behind Gall ant; Dorm ant is numbered twice that of Flip ant.

3. Fez ant, who isn't in last position in the line, and Seal ant are adjacent in the line; Boy ant is somewhere ahead of Sybil ant, who is in an odd-numbered spot somewhere ahead of Adam ant.

Ants: Adam; Boy; Dorm; Fez; Flip; Fond; Gall; Seal; Sybil

Starting tip: Work out which ant is in position 9.

Sign In

Each row and column is to contain the digits 1-6. The given signs tell you if a digit in a cell is plus 1 (+) or minus 1 (-) the digit next to it. Signs between consecutive digits always work from left to right or top to bottom. Examples: 3 + 4 or 2 ALL occurrences of consecutive digits have been marked by a sign.

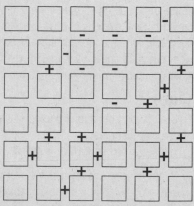

Sudoku

Complete this grid so that each column, each row, and each marked 3 X 3 square contains each of the numbers 1 to 9.

					9			5
4								
	2	6	8			1		4
	6			2	7	3		
		2	3		8	9		2
		9	4	5			6	
2		7			6	5	3	
								8
3			5					

Before the Pen

In the latest edition of *The Penman*, a quarterly magazine for writers of all sorts, the authors of five recent bestsellers reminisce about the jobs they held before becoming full-time professionals following their commercial successes. Can you work out each one's full name, in which genre they write their popular novels, and what occupation they followed before picking up their pens?

Clues

1. Brenda isn't the author named Wallace, whose war novels have become very popular just recently; the war novel author didn't work as a forensic scientist; neither Brenda nor Dave is called Gordon.

2. Penny, who writes fiendishly clever whodunnits, isn't McIlwain; McIlwain's first name appears later in the alphabetical list than that of the writer of wildly imaginative fantasy novels.

3. The author who now writes extremely funny humorous novels, who isn't Mike, was once a ferry boat captain on one of the Great Lakes; Jessica's surname is Del Rey.

4. Mike does not write science fiction.

5. The writer named Tiptree was once a flight attendant with a major international airline.

6. Dave was a sports teacher at a high school before putting down his referee's whistle and picking up his pen.

First name	Surname

	Del Rey	Gordon	McIlwain	Tiptree	Wallace	Fantasy	Humorous novels	Science fiction	War novels	Whodunnits	Ferry boat captain	Flight attendant	Forensic scientist	Teacher	Undertaker
Brenda															
Dave															
Jessica															
Mike															
Penny															
Ferry boat captain															
Flight attendant															
Forensic scientist															
Teacher															
Undertaker															
Fantasy															
Humorous novels															
Science fiction															
War novels															
Whodunnits															

WE LOVE YOUR USE OF WORDS, BUT WE'D LIKE YOU TO USE THEM IN A COMPLETELY DIFFERENT ORDER

EDITOR

Genre	Former job

Mosaic Mischief

Taking advantage of an unseasonable breakdown in their villa's bath house furnace, the bosses of our servant friends from Ancient Rome have made the most of the opportunity to upgrade the décor in each of the suite of rooms by installing some shiny new mosaic floors. As part of the decorating team, the servants have also taken their chance to add a little personal heart-felt touch to the design and, to finish things with a flourish, have each created an avatar-motif to sign their work. Can you uncover in which room of the baths each servant was working, the subject of the main design to which he contributed an extra little something, and the nature of his signature motif?

Clues

1. In the tepidarium (warm room), the mosaic depicting the great god Neptune was given its artist's own features.

2. One servant, working in the natatio (swimming pool), created an avatar of himself as a fisherman spearing a sea monster with a face more than somewhat reminiscent of his boss's; this wasn't Cluelus or Hopelus, the latter of whose mosaic of the Gorgon Medusa bore more than a passing resemblance to his boss's wife.

3. The mosaic of cavorting sea nymphs, signed romantically with a heart, which wasn't in the apodyterium (changing room), wasn't the work of Euselus, who was renovating the mosaic in the caldarium (hot room).

4. The mosaic of an octopus enveloping a strangely familiar couple in its fearsome tentacles wasn't the work of Gormlus or signed with a spiral shell.

5. Branelus signed his artwork with the letters BF, standing for Branelus Fecit— made by Branelus—although his colleagues had no trouble finding an alternative meaning for them.

Servant	Room

	Apodyterium	Caldarium	Natatio	Palaestra	Tepidarium	Dolphins	Medusa	Neptune	Octopus	Sea nymphs	BF	Fisherman	Heart	Shell	Ship
Branelus															
Cluelus															
Euselus															
Gormlus															
Hopelus															
BF															
Fisherman															
Heart															
Shell															
Ship															
Dolphins															
Medusa															
Neptune															
Octopus															
Sea nymphs															

Main design	Signature motif

Straight and Narrow

On the wall of the Greenville Agricultural Society's meeting room there is a fading photo of a plowing contest from the early 1900s. Can you name the man who had been allocated each of the areas lettered A to F in the photo, name the horse that he partnered in the contest, and work out the order in which they were placed by the panel of judges?

Clues

1. The strip plowed by George and his elderly mare Judy was adjacent to the one plowed by the eventual winner of the competition.

2. The horse named Brownie can been seen plowing furrow E; he and his plowman partner, who wasn't Harry, didn't finish as high as the pair that includes the horse named Caesar.

3. Aaron and the man who partnered Punch on an adjacent strip were both awarded an odd-numbered placing.

4. The entrant given strip B to plow was placed sixth, but only because there was a large stone just under the surface causing a kink in the furrow.

5. Sam was given fifth place, but Tom was not placed second, nor was that position gained by the plowman whose "one-horse" power was being supplied by Hector.

6. Billy was allocated strip D for the competition.

7. Goliath, who did not pull the plow along strip F, helped to earn fourth place for the man whose plow he pulled; the name of the competitor who finished just ahead of him is listed in an even-numbered position in the alphabetical list.

Names: Aaron; Billy; George; Harry; Sam; Tom
Horses: Brownie; Caesar; Goliath; Hector; Judy; Punch
Positions: first; second; third; fourth; fifth; sixth

A B C

D E F

Starting tip: Work out in what position Aaron finished.

Paradisus Lost

Four young female/male couples decided to go on vacation together and booked a cut-price deal at the Hotel Paradisus in Cancun. Can you connect each of the pairings, say into which room each was originally placed, and why they complained and demanded, unsuccessfully, a room swap? (The hotel room numbers start with the floor number, so room 318 is on the third floor.)

Clues

1. "Our room has no view," complained Yves, who isn't in a couple with Deborah, "we need to move." "Yes, it does," replied the hotel manager, "It has a very clear view of the water treatment plant."

2. "And our room is far too noisy," added Bridget, "it's right next to the nightclub." "And so very convenient to get back late at night," suggested the hotel manager.

3. "And we'd like to move from room 318," added a third voice from the crowd now surrounding the manager's desk, "the air conditioner is broken." "It isn't broken," said the hotel manager, "it has been disabled to keep the noise down late at night."

4. "There's no fence on our balcony," said one vacationer, "it's just a ledge." "It's not a ledge," said the hotel manager, "it's an infinity balcony, like those infinity pools." The person complaining here wasn't Zack, who had been allocated room 412.

5. Claudia and her boyfriend Xavier were in a room on the floor one above Abigail's room.

Woman	Man

	Xavier	Yves	Will	Zack	Room 216	Room 318	Room 412	Room 514	Air con. broken	Balcony unfenced	Noisy	No view
Abigail												
Bridget												
Claudia												
Deborah												
Air con. broken												
Balcony unfenced												
Noisy												
No view												
Room 216												
Room 318												
Room 412												
Room 514												

Room	Reason

Carnival Fun

Miranda's mother has taken Miranda and four of her friends to the carnival. Each has been given a ticket for the ride of their choice and a dollar to spend on whatever other amusement they want. Can you find out what ride each child chose, what they spent their dollar on, and how much cash they had left at the end of the day? (NB: Miranda and Daisy are girls; the others are boys.)

Clues

1. Daisy is always encouraged to eat healthily, so naturally she headed straight for the cotton candy stall with her dollar. Neither she nor the child who dared the Ferris wheel ended up with $0.50 left over.

2. One of the boys had a ride on the rollercoaster. Another was so dizzy after his ride that he didn't want to eat or play anything and still had his dollar at the end of the day.

3. The child who played the slot machine explained that they had won a few and lost a lot and borrowed a bit from Miranda's mum and were down to minus $0.64.

4. Jackson went on the ghost train but didn't gamble on the hook-a-duck and ended the day with more cash than Dylan but less than Frankie. Miranda spent all her money but won an enormous teddy bear.

5. The child who chose a ride on the Rotor ended up with more cash than the one who took a spin on the carousel.

Child	Ride

	Carousel	Ferris wheel	Ghost train	Rollercoaster	Rotor	Cotton candy	Hook-a-duck	Nothing	Rifle range	Slot machine	-$0.64	$0.00	$0.50	$1	Teddy bear
Daisy															
Dylan															
Frankie															
Jackson															
Miranda															
-$0.64															
$0.00															
$0.50															
$1															
Teddy bear															
Cotton candy															
Hook-a-duck															
Nothing															
Rifle range															
Slot machine															

HALL OF MIRRORS

OH, COME ON, ARNOLD, LET YOURSELF GO

Amusement	Change

Saving the Planet

The new team-based, on-line strategy game *Battle for the Earth* pits a team of eleven players against alien enemies bent on taking over the Earth. The game starts as the first alien ship lands. One player is nominated the leader and sets the strategy and gives instructions for each player to follow. They all then do their thing and meet up later to see how the strategy panned out, who survived, and whether or not the Earth is now in the hands of ET and his friends. In this game, Dominic has been made captain and is setting out his strategy and orders, which involves his 10-person team working in five pairs to attack the aliens who are beginning to leave their ship. Can you work out who is to do what and where?

Clues

1. "Right," began Dominic, turning to his first pair, "you two get as close as you can under cover and report to me on the enemy's movements. Now, Ellis, you take Sean with you when you go."

2. "Right, listen, Frankie. Don't go anywhere near the river but keep in radio contact with Regan and her partner as they circle round. Also check in with Cassidy, who'll be cutting off their retreat and Brett and his pal, who'll be busy elsewhere . . . "

3. "Now Brett, you and your partner get up that hill on the left, but make sure you don't make a sound; leave the diversionary tactics to someone else."

4. "Blake, I want plenty of covering fire, understand?"

5. "Remember, Hayden, leave the others to take out the enemy."

6. "Finally, you two stay down by the river and watch as the other two cut off their retreat. Clear? Right, go!"

First partner	Second partner

	Cassidy	Hayden	Madison	Regan	Sean	Circle round	Get close	Hill on left	Hill on right	River	Create diversion	Cut off retreat	Give cover	Report movements	Take out enemy
Blake															
Brett															
Ellis															
Frankie															
Mason															
Create diversion															
Cut off retreat															
Give cover															
Report movements															
Take out enemy															
Circle round															
Get close															
Hill on left															
Hill on right															
River															

DOGS HOME

They came in peace but chose their landing site poorly.

Destination	Order

Hitting the Wrong Note

The slapdash servants from Ancient Rome have decided to raise their profiles and add to their skills a little by taking up a musical instrument—although there is mostly an ulterior motive behind this, as well. Can you match each servant to his chosen instrument, say why he really decided to try to learn it, and what soon led to the idea having to be abandoned?

Clues

1. Gormlus bought a second-hand tibia (flute), but hadn't decided to learn it in order to impress anybody specific.

2. Neither Euselus, who didn't abandon his instrument in a huff after a row with his teacher about practicing, nor Branelus, was the servant whose instrument was stolen (actually by some of his fellow servants, fed up with the noise).

3. The servant who hoped to play the cornu (horn) but had to give up, having failed to get a single note out of it for a whole month, wasn't hoping to impress his latest girlfriend.

4. Cluelus was eager to hit the big time by joining the famous local band Calidissimi Peperoncini, but not on the cithara (a type of harp); one of his colleagues was trying to cadge a few denarii by playing for tips by performing in the street when he was arrested by Prefect Crassus for causing a nuisance in a public place.

5. Hopelus, clumsy as ever, broke his instrument; he wasn't the servant intending to learn the hydraulis, or water organ, to play Nero's famed example housed in one of the forum temples.

Servant	Instrument

	Cithara	Cornu	Hydraulis	Tibia	Tympanum	Impress girlfriend	Impress boss	Join band	Play in temple	Playing for tips	Arrested	Broke it	Failed to play it	Row with teacher	Stolen
Branelus															
Cluelus															
Euselus															
Gormlus															
Hopelus															
Arrested															
Broke it															
Failed to play it															
Row with teacher															
Stolen															
Impress girlfriend															
Impress boss															
Join band															
Play in temple															
Playing for tips															

Ambition	Drawback

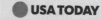

Hello, Wee Ones!

It's Halloween and these five toddlers are being taken down the road by their parents to meet some friendly neighbors and perhaps get a few candies. From the clues, can you find out the name of each little child, the costume they are wearing (we have drawn them all as ghosts so as not to give the game away), the receptacle they are carrying in which to stash their candy, and the number of candies each has managed to stash? (Rosie and Polly are the only girls; lefts and rights are from our point of view.)

Clues

1. The little boy in his astronaut outfit, who is directly left of Tommy and immediately right of the child who has the most candies, is using his space helmet to collect his loot. The child dressed as a mermaid is in a position numbered twice that of Polly, who isn't wearing the pirate outfit.

2. Freddy is wearing a firefighter's uniform and carrying his toy fire truck, as well as his candy collecting receptacle. The child next right to him is collecting candies in their mom's handbag.

3. Rosie, who has garnered 11 candies, is at one end of the row and the toddler who is optimistically carrying a bucket is at the other end.

4. Child 4, equipped with a plastic bag, has collected fewer candies than the children on either side of him or her, but more than Freddy.

Children: Bobby; Freddy; Polly; Rosie; Tommy
Costumes: astronaut; firefighter; mermaid; pirate; witch
Containers: bucket; handbag; plastic bag; pumpkin; space helmet
Candies: 8; 9; 10; 11; 12

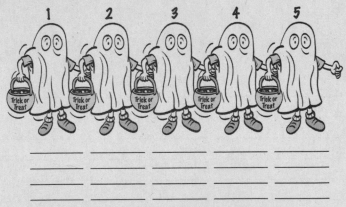

Starting tip: Work out where Rosie is standing.

Battleships

Do you remember the old game of battleships? These puzzles are based on that idea. Your task is to find the vessels in the diagram. Some parts of boats or sea squares have already been filled in, and a number next to a row or column refers to the number of occupied squares in that row or column. The boats may be positioned horizontally or vertically, but no two boats or parts of boats are in adjacent squares—horizontally, vertically, or diagonally.

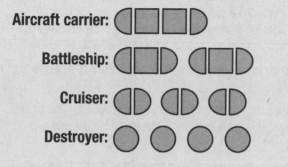

Aircraft carrier:

Battleship:

Cruiser:

Destroyer:

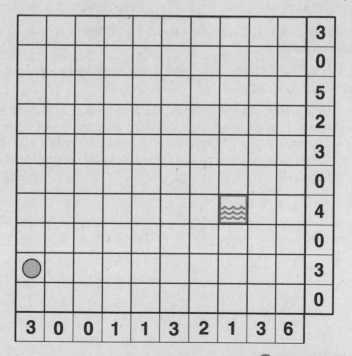

Land of Nod

The picture below shows El Presidente of the Republic of San Guinari waiting to meet with his cabinet, who, contrary to what you might think, are not a bunch of yes men. None of them is brave enough to speak and has to make do with enthusiastic nodding. Can you fill in the title, name, and cabinet role of each of the men at the table (apart, of course, from El Presidente himself, who also retains Defense, public order, and electoral oversight under his own control)?

Clues

1. The General (an army officer) will be sitting directly opposite the Minister of Finance, Miguel Zorra, whose job is to keep money rolling into the country's exchequer and El Presidente's personal account—for safe keeping, of course.

2. Brigadier Jacobo Rata (an air force officer) will sit at the Minister of Justice's left hand.

3. The Professor's seat at the cabinet table is numbered one lower than that of the Minister of Trade, whose main responsibilities are bribery and corruption—encouraging them, of course.

4. The Minister of Home Affairs, who always sits on the right of Rafael Arafia, bears the title of Doctor—he holds a degree in musicology, bought from the Internet.

5. The man who will be nodding eagerly in seat 4 is the Admiral (a naval . . . —no, forget I mentioned it).

6. Seat 6 is reserved for Felipe Bicho; Tadeo Gusano doesn't have seat 3, nor is his seat next to Emilio Culebra.

7. Seat 1 belongs to the Minister of Culture, who is responsible for censorship of San Guinari's TV and radio networks and newspapers—and movies and posters and people talking in public; the man in seat 5 is not the Minister for Foreign Affairs, who is sitting on the same side of the table as the Colonel (a Secret Police officer).

Titles: Admiral; Brigadier; Colonel; Doctor; General; Professor
Names: Emilio Culebra; Felipe Bicho; Jacobo Rata; Miguel Zorra; Rafael Arafia; Tadeo Gusano
Ministries: Culture; Finance; Foreign Affairs; Home Affairs; Justice; Trade

Starting tip: Work out the Ministry run by the man in seat 5.

 **USA TODAY** 163

Digging Out

During WWII, the prisoners of war in the German camp Stalag Tyte are attempting to tunnel their way to freedom, and five escape routes are currently under construction. Can you work out from which hut each tunnel starts, where its entrance is hidden, the officer in charge of each, and its current length?

Clues

1. The tunnel from Hut A, which is an odd number of yards long, is longer than the one that starts under the stove, which isn't 65 yards long.

2. The tunnel from Hut K is under the direction of Squadron Leader Digwell and is shorter than the one being dug from Hut C; Captain Burrows' tunnel, which so far reaches 218 yards, starts from neither Hut C nor Hut F; Hut F's tunnel is not the shortest.

3. The length of Hut C's tunnel is greater than the total of the length of the one being dug by Major Warren and the one from the latrine; the latrine tunnel is not being supervised by Lieutenant Trowell.

4. One tunnel begins behind a cupboard in Hut D.

5. The tunnel being dug beneath the steps of one of the huts is not the longest.

6. The entrance to Squadron Leader Shovell's tunnel is hidden under a bed.

Hut	Where hidden

	Back of cupboard	Beneath hut steps	In latrine	Under bed	Under stove	Capt. Burrows	Sqn. Ldr. Digwell	Sqn. Ldr. Shovell	Lt. Trowell	Major Warren	22 yards	65 yards	176 yards	218 yards	341 yards
Hut A															
Hut C															
Hut D															
Hut F															
Hut K															
22 yards															
65 yards															
176 yards															
218 yards															
341 yards															
Capt. Burrows															
Sqn. Ldr. Digwell															
Sqn. Ldr. Shovell															
Lt. Trowell															
Major Warren															

Leader	Length

Jupiter's Feast

It's mid-September and Ancient Rome is enjoying the Ludi Romani festival in honor of the city itself. One of the highlights is the Epulum Iovis, a feast prepared for the gods when Jupiter invites his extended family to enjoy a delicious banquet. The images of the gods are set around a table and priests serve them rich courses (helping them to consume the feast as proxies). Our five under-achieving servant friends have been roped in to help prepare the banquet and are determined that the priests aren't going to have it all to themselves. Can you say which god each servant was attending, to which priest he was assigned, and how he managed to nab himself a goodly helping of the fare? (For clarity, Juno and Minerva are goddesses.)

Clues

1. Cluelus explained to his priest-in-charge that the portion with which he'd arrived at the table looked particularly meager—indeed, half eaten—because the deity he was looking after had revealed they were on a diet.

2. The servant who claimed that Vulcan, the god of fire, really enjoyed his food burnt to a crisp and thus unidentifiable was not Branelus, who was serving another male deity overseen by priest Perspex.

3. Minerva, goddess of arts and crafts, was being attended by Euselus; it wasn't her feast that was spilt all over priest Circumspex when the servant "accidentally" caught his tunic on a table leg, thereby disguising which tasty morsel was missing.

4. Suspex was overseeing the meal for Mars, the god of war.

5. Priest Prospex was in charge of ensuring a goddess enjoyed her feast; Hopelus' patron deity was male, and so was the god who had apparently decided to turn vegan that day, explaining of course why the peacock casserole brought by the servant concerned was suspiciously peacock-free.

Servant	God

	Mars	Mercury	Minerva	Juno	Vulcan	Circumspex	Inspex	Perspex	Prospex	Suspex	Allergic	Burnt food	On diet	Spilt	Vegan
Branelus															
Cluelus															
Euselus															
Gormlus															
Hopelus															
Allergic															
Burnt food															
On diet															
Spilt															
Vegan															
Circumspex															
Inspex															
Perspex															
Prospex															
Suspex															

Priest	Ruse

Going Nuts

Oliver Sward is lucky enough to have a large garden with flower beds, borders, and a wooded area at the bottom, but his pride and joy is his lawn. So this time of year is a struggle for him as the local squirrel population likes to bury their winter stores in that green area, leaving small bare patches. Can you work out what nut each of the squirrels shown here has buried where in Oliver's lawn? (Lefts and rights are from our point of view.)

Clues

1. The squirrel who has buried a hazelnut is immediately left and on the same side of the tree trunk as the one who has been digging by the potting shed, but on the other side to the squirrel who has hidden a beechnut.

2. The squirrel who brazenly dug a hole right in the middle of Oliver's lawn is perched next to the tree trunk on the same side as the one who buried a nut by the pond; Skippy isn't fond of chestnuts and never stores them away.

3. The squirrel who has secreted a nut by the greenhouse is next right to the one who has been collecting and burying pine nuts; Bushy buried a nut near the rose bed.

Nuts: acorn; beechnut; chestnut; hazelnut; pine nut
Locations: greenhouse; middle of lawn; pond; potting shed; rose bed

Starting tip: Work out where Chippy has been digging.

Domino Search

A standard set of dominoes has been laid out, using numbers instead of dots for clarity. Using a sharp pencil and a keen brain, can you draw in the lines to show where each domino has been placed? You may find the check grid useful—crossing off each domino as you find it.

0	2	4	6	2	3	4	0
1	4	3	3	5	6	5	1
2	4	1	0	0	2	4	6
2	6	3	5	2	1	1	1
3	5	5	2	3	6	5	1
4	6	0	2	0	6	4	3
3	5	5	0	4	1	0	6

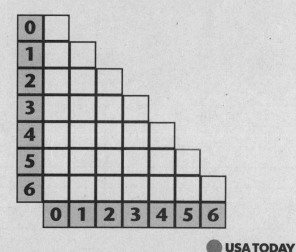

Art Felt

Fairview's Museum of Modern Art specializes in contemporary art, and below are details of upcoming main featured works. Can you discover the artist and the title of the sculpture to be seen each month, and find what each comprises?

Clues

1. August's featured sculpture is a composition of car tires, commenting on the "circular nature of recycling," apparently, but not assembled by Connor Cheatham.

2. *Nimbus*, by Patience Thynne, can be seen the month after the cinder block construction which evokes, according to the pamphlet, the "impermanent quality of permanence."

3. The chrome spirals—inspired by the never-ending climb to perfection, or perhaps a corkscrew—are the featured exhibit the month after Ida Grant's piece, and the month before the sculpture entitled *Retribution*.

4. *Silence* will be on display in October.

5. The title of Gerda Weld's iron rod sculpture (designed to be displayed for many years to represent the inevitability of decay as it rusts, and provide Gerda with a regular royalty payment) does not begin with the letter S.

6. *Northern Sky* comprises pebbles in liquid.

Month	Artist

  **USA TODAY**

	Connor Cheatham	Ida Grant	Adam Pyle	Patience Thynne	Gerda Weld	Nimbus	Northern Sky	Retribution	Sands of Time	Silence	Cinder blocks	Car tires	Chrome spirals	Iron rods	Pebbles in liquid
August															
September															
October															
November															
December															
Cinder blocks															
Car tires															
Chrome spirals															
Iron rods															
Pebbles in liquid															
Nimbus															
Northern Sky															
Retribution															
Sands of Time															
Silence															

Title	Description

Veg Revolt

Alice and Mike have five children between them and, whereas Mike mostly cooks the evening meals, last week Alice took over in the kitchen, as Mike was ill in bed with man flu. On each of the five days, one of the children left a portion of vegetables that wasn't liked and perhaps didn't go too well with the main dish. Can you work out the day of the week each child left a portion of vegetables on their plate, what the main dish was, and the vegetable that was served with it? (For clarity: the root veg are beets, parsnips, and rutabaga.)

Clues

1. Lewis left the root vegetable he didn't like on Tuesday.

2. Freddie didn't like the rutabaga, which wasn't served with the breaded cod or veggie burger.

3. It was when they had the salmon fillets, which wasn't on Thursday, that Amy left the vegetables, which weren't parsnips.

4. A serving of vegetables was left after eating macaroni and cheese on Monday.

5. It wasn't Neville who left the brussels sprouts, which were served up with the prawn stir fry.

6. Fava beans were included in the Friday evening meal, which wasn't a fish dish.

Day	Child

	Amy	Daisy	Freddie	Lewis	Neville	Breaded cod	Macaroni and cheese	Prawn stir fry	Salmon fillets	Veggie burgers	Beets	Brussels sprouts	Fava beans	Parsnips	Rutabaga
Monday															
Tuesday															
Wednesday															
Thursday															
Friday															
Beets															
Brussels sprouts															
Fava beans															
Parsnips															
Rutabaga															
Breaded cod															
Macaroni and cheese															
Prawn stir fry															
Salmon fillets															
Veggie burgers															

YOUR FATHER AND I HAVE DECIDED WE SHOULD EAT MORE VEGETABLES.

I CAN HELP WITH THAT. YOU CAN HAVE MINE.

Dish	Vegetable

Counted Out

Young Oscar spent an afternoon in his bedroom excitedly counting the contents of his large and full piggy bank. His savings of $67.20 was to provide him with some spending money for the summer vacation with his family. As he counted the money, members of his family interrupted him for one reason or another, and each time he would have to start all over again. Can you work out the order each family member interrupted Oscar, why they knocked on his bedroom door, and where he reached with his counting?

Clues

1. Oscar had reached $15 when he was interrupted by his dad Michael, who wasn't the interrupter who handed him the phone with his grandmother on the other end, or the one who came to let him know that his favorite TV program was about to start.

2. Oscar's eldest sister Marie was the last person to interrupt him; he hadn't at that point reached a figure that was a whole number of dollars.

3. His youngest sister Ellen insisted he join in the hunt for the gerbil, which had made a dash for it when its cage was left open for cleaning; this disruption came later than the one instigated by Oscar's mom Charlotte, who didn't interrupt as Oscar's counting reached $48.

4. The second interruption came when someone asked Oscar if he wanted a cup of coffee.

5. Just as he counted $37 the door opened and he was reminded that it was his turn to walk the dog; this wasn't the third interruption.

6. On the fourth interruption, which wasn't by his brother Stanley, Oscar had managed to get to $56.40; Stanley hadn't come to remind him to watch his favorite TV program.

Order	Interrupter

	Charlotte	Ellen	Marie	Michael	Stanley	Coffee made	Hunt for gerbil	Phone call	TV program	Walk the dog	$15	$37	$48	$53.50	$56.40
First															
Second															
Third															
Fourth															
Fifth															
$15															
$37															
$48															
$53.50															
$56.40															
Coffee made															
Hunt for gerbil															
Phone call															
TV program															
Walk the dog															

Reason	Sum

Snapping the Celebs

Pic Schuter is a celebrity photographer who works at LA airport snapping famous faces on incoming flights. During the midday period, five arrivals are expected at quite close intervals, so he is hoping that there won't be any delays to throw off his tight schedule. Can you say from which country each celebrity is arriving, and at what airport gate and time they are due to appear?

Clues

1. The hotel magnate, due to arrive at Gate 9, was on a later flight than the one with the actress flying in from Italy, but an earlier flight than the one due to dock at Gate 6, which wasn't arriving from Slovakia.

2. Pic's itinerary was thrown a curve ball when the flight from Ireland, which was supposed to land next before that of the tennis star, was delayed and ended up docking at Gate 12 at the same time as that of the tennis star landed; fortunately the gates were only two numbers apart.

3. The celebrity chef was due in at 12:40 p.m., but not from Sweden; the flight from Sweden was due in earlier than the politician was meant to arrive.

4. The plane docking at Gate 10 wasn't bringing the earliest of Pic's targets; the flight from Cyprus wasn't the last to land.

Celebrity	Country

	Cyprus	Ireland	Italy	Slovakia	Sweden	Gate 6	Gate 9	Gate 10	Gate 12	Gate 14	11:40	12:10	12:40	13:40	14:10
Actress															
Chef															
Hotel magnate															
Politician															
Tennis star															
11:40															
12:10															
12:40															
13:40															
14:10															
Gate 6															
Gate 9															
Gate 10															
Gate 12															
Gate 14															

PHOTOGRAPHER

We specialize in portraits or, for the technologically proficient "yousies."

Gate	Due time

What a Shower

Bathroom product developers O-So-Fresh have been working on a new range of fruit-based shower gels, which they have started to roll out to a number of trial outlets. Can you sort out the color of each of the enticingly named products and which two fruit essences—strangely, not necessarily related to the color—each contains?

Clues

1. By an amazing feat of relevance (or perhaps just lucky coincidence), the Blueburst gel is in fact colored blue; it's not the product that combines the delicious scents of peach and watermelon, which isn't colored green.

2. Summerset gel contains essence of strawberry.

3. Disconcertingly, the gel that contains more than a hint of lime is colored orange.

4. Including cranberry juice in the Fruitfool gel was one of the development team's cleverer ideas; it isn't the red product, which less appropriately has lemon as one of its ingredients, but doesn't include any orange essence and isn't called Wellnow.

5. The green gel doesn't contain any banana essence.

Name	Color

	Blue	Green	Orange	Red	Yellow	Cranberry	Lime	Mango	Orange	Peach	Banana	Lemon	Raspberry	Strawberry	Watermelon
Blueburst															
Cloudchaser															
Fruitfool															
Summerset															
Wellnow															
Banana															
Lemon															
Raspberry															
Strawberry															
Watermelon															
Cranberry															
Lime															
Mango															
Orange															
Peach															

Energy saving tip: How to stop your kids spending too long in the shower.

BATES MOTEL

First fruit	Second fruit

Battleships

Do you remember the old game of battleships? These puzzles are based on that idea. Your task is to find the vessels in the diagram. Some parts of boats or sea squares have already been filled in, and a number next to a row or column refers to the number of occupied squares in that row or column. The boats may be positioned horizontally or vertically, but no two boats or parts of boats are in adjacent squares—horizontally, vertically, or diagonally.

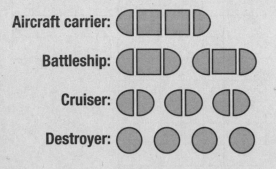

Aircraft carrier:

Battleship:

Cruiser:

Destroyer:

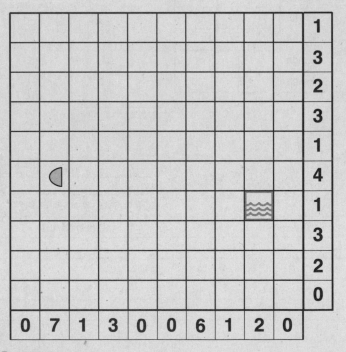

Americans Abroad

The University of Yakford in the UK has an exchange agreement with Harvale University in the US, and currently there are three visiting American academics. Can you determine in which department each US visitor works, the month in which they arrived, and the main reason they are doing the exchange?

Clues

1. The academic who has joined the History Dept. is researching the individuals who sailed on the *Mayflower* for a book they are writing.

2. Dr. Hancock has joined the Yakford Physics Dept. and arrived before Prof. Franklin; the new member of the Mechanical Engineering Dept. arrived in January.

3. Dr. Bartlett hasn't traveled to Yakford to take up a teaching assignment.

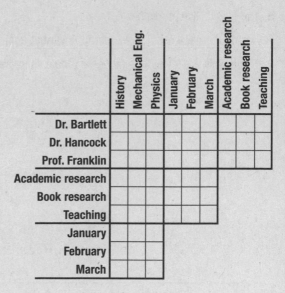

Name	Department	Arrival	Reason

Gnomes and All

The first five houses along the northern side of Jim Craque Avenue each have small front yards, but each yard contains a number of ornamental stone figures. Can you name the family living in each house and say how many of which type of figure their respective front yards boast?

Clues

1. The Wimseys have more figures in their front yard than their neighbors in the property on the lower-numbered side, but fewer than the number of gnomes in the other neighboring yard.

2. The Masons' fairies outnumber by one the ornaments in the front yard of number 1.

3. The dogs are fewer in number than the figures at number 3.

4. The Stones are the proud owners of just three ornaments.

5. The Lovetts live at number 7.

6. Just four ornamental figures adorn the yard at number 9.

7. The rabbits are fewer in number than the cats in the next-door yard.

House No.	Family

	Deckham	Lovett	Mason	Stone	Wimsey	2 figures	3 figures	4 figures	5 figures	6 figures	Cats	Dogs	Fairies	Gnomes	Rabbits
No.1															
No.3															
No.5															
No.7															
No.9															
Cats															
Dogs															
Fairies															
Gnomes															
Rabbits															
2 figures															
3 figures															
4 figures															
5 figures															
6 figures															

Scientist looking for the G-gnome

Number	Figures

The Haunted *Oyster*

The Black Oyster, a pirate ship from the great age of Caribbean piracy has been restored and preserved as a tourist attraction at Fort Willoughby in Florida. Over the years, a number of witnesses have experienced supernatural phenomena while taking the guided tour. Can you work out the name and description of each witness, what they saw or heard, and where they saw or heard it?

Clues

1. The attorney had an experience when the tour was at the fo'c'sle; the person who heard ghostly voices somewhere was not Perry Riordan, whose experience was by the ship's wheel.

2. The person who saw the lookout climbing the rigging towards the crow's nest wasn't the tour guide; Holly Jurado, who isn't the former naval petty officer who now works as a charity fundraiser, wasn't the one who saw a ghostly pirate parrot; nor was the parrot specter spotted by the attorney.

3. Velda Young saw a wounded pirate with a bandage round his head—but she could also see right through him; it wasn't on the poop deck that one person saw the pirate captain with a hook for one hand and a patch over his eye.

4. The engineer who heard ghostly voices wasn't Holly Jurado, who is not a attorney.

5. Kent Larsen is a police officer from Alabama who was in Fort Willoughby on vacation with his family.

Name	Occupation

	Attorney	Engineer	Fund raiser	Police officer	Tour guide	Heard voices	Saw lookout	Saw captain	Saw parrot	Saw wounded pirate	Fo'c'sle	Poop deck	Rigging	Ship's hold	Ship's wheel
Boyce Cramer															
Holly Jurado															
Kent Larsen															
Perry Riordan															
Velda Young															
Fo'c'sle															
Poop deck															
Rigging															
Ship's hold															
Ship's wheel															
Heard voices															
Saw lookout															
Saw captain															
Saw parrot															
Saw wounded pirate															

Experience	Location

Tricky Snaps

Petra's family came to visit her last month. Her brother Jake is a keen photographer and was eager to take snaps of the family. The clicking began almost as soon as the family arrived and ventured into Petra's garden for a cold drink, but members of the camera-shy family, including herself, have developed techniques for avoiding being snapped. Can you work out in what order he tried to photograph each one of the family, how each person avoided this, and what it was that was in the background?

Clues

1. Jake tried to take a photo of Grandad Arnold when he was sitting on the deck.

2. Dad Nick had been wearing his broad-brimmed straw hat ever since getting out of the automobile and he strategically adjusted the brim from time to time to avoid Jake's lens; he wasn't by the apple tree when Jake tried to photograph him.

3. The third person Jake attempted to snap carried a golf umbrella as a parasol, which once opened was very easy to hide behind.

4. One person, who wasn't the first targeted through Jake's viewfinder, ducked out of sight by rolling out of the hammock just in time; this wasn't Deanna who was the fourth person to avoid the camera.

5. The second person toward whom Jake aimed his camera, who wasn't Fiona or Nick, was standing by a vegetable plot.

6. Petra didn't use a book as a handy hiding spot.

Order	Name

	Arnold	Deanna	Fiona	Nick	Petra	Book	Brimmed hat	Ducked	Hands	Umbrella	Apple tree	Deck	Hammock	Pond	Vegetable plot
First															
Second															
Third															
Fourth															
Fifth															
Apple tree															
Deck															
Hammock															
Pond															
Vegetable plot															
Book															
Brimmed hat															
Ducked															
Hands															
Umbrella															

CAMERA SHY
SELFIE TAKER

Method	Background

Models

In the height of summer, five models are sweltering under the photo studio lights as they model warm garments for the winter collections to be featured in issues of magazines later in the year. From the clues, can you work out which fashion house each mannequin works for and the color and material of the garment each is modeling?

Clues

1. Tara, whose full name is Tara Laura Lay, is a model for Moonshine. Lara's pink outfit was not designed by Mermaid and Marshmallow was not the designer of the legendary fleece in, of course, gold.

2. Neither Cara's costume nor Dara's woolen outfit was the work of Marbles. Zara was a mannequin for a sophisticated fashion house, which wasn't Mermaid, and she never wears silver, gold, or fake fur.

3. Moochy's seasonal offering is crafted from top-quality leather. The name of its wearer is earlier in the alphabetical list than that of the woman modeling the purple garment, which was not the creation in fake fur, who is herself earlier in the alphabetical list than the mannequin from the House of Marshmallow.

Model	Fashion house

	Marbles	Marshmallow	Mermaid	Moochy	Moonshine	Black	Gold	Pink	Purple	Silver	Fake fur	Fleece	Leather	Mohair	Wool
Cara															
Dara															
Lara															
Tara															
Zara															
Fake fur															
Fleece															
Leather															
Mohair															
Wool															
Black															
Gold															
Pink															
Purple															
Silver															

Color	Material

Going for a Paddle

The final race of an international championship is the 1km kayak race, and as we join it, it's entering the final 100m. Can you fully identify the man in each of the kayaks numbered 1 to 6 and say which country he represents? (For clarity, the lane numbers are written on the kayaks and their current positions are given.)

Clues

1. Neither Neville Langtry nor the Scottish kayaker is paddling in first or last position and neither is in a lane adjacent to either side of the course (that is, lanes 1 and 6).

2. England is represented in the race by Mr. Baldwin; he is paddling in the position immediately behind the South African representative, but somewhere ahead of Marlon.

3. Mr. Pearson's kayak is immediately ahead of Mr. Scott's; Mr. Scott isn't Will.

4. Craig is the Australian competitor; at the moment he is immediately ahead of Rupert.

5. Mr. Collier is lying second as the kayakers paddle past the 100m to go sign.

6. The Canadian competitor is lying fourth at this stage of the race and tiring fast.

7. Jeff is currently hanging on to third place.

First names: Craig; Jeff; Marlon; Neville; Rupert; Will
Surnames: Baldwin; Collier; Gregson; Langtry; Pearson; Scott
Countries: Australia; Canada; England: New Zealand; Scotland; South Africa

Second

Fifth

First

Fourth

Sixth

Third

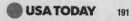

New Skills

At Centerville Prison, five inmates are about to be released, having paid their debts to society. During their time in prison, they each learned a new skill, three useful for a crime-free life but two not so good. Can you work out the skill each has learned, the crime of which they were convicted, and the number of months they were sentenced to serve? To protect identities, the inmates are known by the numbers allocated to them when they first arrived at the prison.

Clues

1. Prisoner 397 learned the art of picking pockets.

2. Prisoner 523 was sentenced to six months.

3. The arsonist, who wasn't sentenced to 18 months, learned the skills of forgery from a fellow inmate.

4. The person convicted of being disorderly was sentenced to eight months.

5. The prisoner sentenced to 15 months developed baking skills from working in the prison kitchen; this wasn't Prisoner 124, who had been convicted of burglary but who didn't learn Mandarin.

6. Both prisoner 418, who didn't learn Mandarin, and prisoner 649, who wasn't convicted of vandalism, served sentences longer than a year.

Inmate	New skill

	Baking	Cabinet making	Forgery	Mandarin	Pick pocketing	Arson	Burglary	Dangerous driving	Disorderly conduct	Vandalism	6 months	8 months	12 months	15 months	18 months
Prisoner 124															
Prisoner 397															
Prisoner 418															
Prisoner 523															
Prisoner 649															
6 months															
8 months															
12 months															
15 months															
18 months															
Arson															
Burglary															
Dangerous driving															
Disorderly conduct															
Vandalism															

WHO WOULD YOU LIKE ME TO SIGN IT FROM?

FORGERY MADE SIMPLE

BOOK SIGNING

Crime	Duration

If Not In . . .

Will Bringett is a courier for the online store Zambezi.com and has only four deliveries left on his round today. Can you work out the recipient's name for each of the parcels arranged in delivery order in the back of Will's truck, their street address and the location Will has been instructed to leave the parcel if no one is at home?

Clues

1. The parcel addressed to Mr. Hooper will be delivered next, after the one addressed to Sunny Lane that will be left in the shed if there's no answer at the door.

2. The box for Mr. Smith will be delivered some time before the one that may well end up being left in the greenhouse.

3. The second parcel to be delivered is addressed to a house in King Row.

4. The third delivery comes with the instruction to leave it with a neighbor if there's no one home at the delivery address.

5. Mrs. Angel, who doesn't live in Middle Street at present, has asked for her parcel to be left in her garage if she's not in when Will calls.

Recipients: Mrs. Angel; Mrs. Frost; Mr. Hooper; Mr. Smith
Streets: King Row; Middle Street; Sunny Lane; Stable Hill
Locations: garage; greenhouse; neighbor; shed

First   Second   Third   Fourth

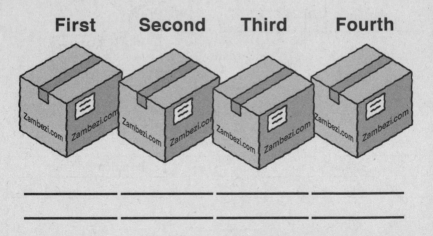

Starting tip: Work out which parcel is addressed to Sunny Lane.

Wardrobe Choice

Contrary to popular opinion, Santa doesn't only have a red and white outfit. Hanging in his wardrobe are six of various color combinations. Can you work out the color of the cloth and fur of each of them (and color them in if you have a set of crayons on hand) and say which, after consideration, he has selected for this year's rounds?

Clues

1. No suit has the same color cloth and fur.

2. The green cloth, which isn't matched with the white fur, is numbered twice that of the green fur; Santa's choice for this year is not directly above the green cloth and not directly below the green fur.

3. The red cloth isn't part of suit 3 and isn't matched with the yellow fur; the blue fur is not part of suit 5; the gray cloth has an even number; the chosen suit for this year is not directly above the gray cloth and not immediately left of the gray fur.

4. The yellow cloth is directly below the white fur and immediately right of the red fur; the blue cloth is somewhere to the left of the blue fur in the wardrobe; Santa's outfit for this year is not immediately left of the blue fur.

Cloth: blue; green; gray; red; white; yellow
Fur: blue; green; gray; red; white; yellow

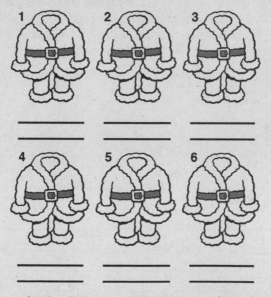

Starting tip: Work out the cloth color for suit 3.

McGann's Gun

Marshal Gus McGann was the lawman in Paradise Valley in Arizona from 1870 to 1890 and, despite being undersized, underweight, and short-sighted, he made a reasonably good job of it. Using his brain over brawn policy, he brought a large number of notorious criminals to justice, preferring to catch the bad guys at a disadvantage rather than get into a gunfight. In 1878, for instance, he arrested five men who had been wanted for some time. Can you work out each outlaw's name and crime and say where and in which month Marshal McGann arrested him?

Clues

1. The man arrested at the card table in October—he looked down at the royal flush he held and looked up again into the muzzles of Marshal McGann's shotgun—wasn't the gunman Rio Pike.

2. Zeb Young was arrested in December of 1878.

3. The rustler was arrested earlier in 1878 than Marty Lock; neither of these two was the man the Marshal locked up in February.

4. The bank robber was enjoying a bath at Fantoni's Barber Shop and Bath House, laying back smoking a cigar and planning how to spend his loot, when Marshal McGann broke the bad news that he was under arrest.

5. Buck Akins was arrested—he was not only in bed but he was asleep until the Marshal put the handcuffs on him—in the same quarter of the year as another outlaw was arrested in the livery stable, where he had just unsaddled his horse and so had both hands full when McGann called on him to surrender.

6. The gunrunner, who wasn't Deke Carroll, was arrested in June 1878.

Outlaw	Crime

	Bank robber	Gunman	Gunrunner	Rustler	Train robber	At card table	In bar	In bath	In bed	In stable	February	March	June	October	December
Buck Akins															
Deke Carroll															
Marty Lock															
Rio Pike															
Zeb Young															
February															
March															
June															
October															
December															
At card table															
In bar															
In bath															
In bed															
In stable															

Place of arrest	Month

Quest in Venice

Every now and then my friend Alex accompanies me on a city break, and to make exploration a bit more fun and see more of the district, one of us sets the other a challenge to follow a set of clues to end up at a final destination where the other is waiting, having booked a nice meal as a reward. This year we visited Venice and it was Alex's turn to set me the challenge. She gave me the first clue and left five others in envelopes, each with what might be a piece of graffito written on the front, around the city. Can you identify the writing on each envelope, to where the clue led me, and by what means of transport I reached each one?

Clues

1. I found the envelope reading Beware of the Doge on the famous glass-making island of Murano and set off in pursuit of the next destination on one of the vaporetto public water-buses.

2. My excursion by gondola, which wasn't to the location where I discovered an envelope with an inscription reading Iago Hearts Des, took place later in the sequence than the visit to the location where I found the envelope Mariners Wanted, Apply M. Polo.

3. My trip to the Rialto Bridge took place some time after I'd discovered the legend Tadzio Was Here, which itself was found some time before I visited St. Mark's Square, which wasn't the fourth stop on my quest.

4. A trip across the Grand Canal on one of the ferries known as a traghetto led me to my third cryptic message.

5. I found the envelope inscribed My Other Attorney is a Portia sometime before I made a journey on foot to the Doge's Palace, but after I had a trip to the Lido, for which I didn't hire a private boat.

Order	Envelope

	Beware of Doge	Iago Hearts Des	Mariners Wanted	My Other Attorney	Tadzio Was Here	Doge's Palace	Lido	Murano	Rialto Bridge	St. Mark's Square	Gondola	Hired boat	Traghetto	Vaporetto	Walking
First															
Second															
Third															
Fourth															
Fifth															
Gondola															
Hired boat															
Traghetto															
Vaporetto															
Walking															
Doge's Palace															
Lido															
Murano															
Rialto Bridge															
St. Mark's Square															

Location	Transport

Santa at Sea

The late 15th century was a boom time for explorers and many great discoveries were made by intrepid voyagers. But not all sea-going captains and crews were so intrepid or so honest. In the early months of 1465, five dishonorable captains persuaded five different royal patrons to sponsor them for a voyage of discovery, having no intention of going anywhere uncharted. Can you work out the name of the captain of each of these five vessels, the country whose royal patronage he managed to obtain, the month in which he and his crew returned from their journey, what they claimed to have found, and where they had been hiding for the few months of their "exploration"?

Clues

1. The ship that slipped quietly into the Black Sea and sailed around in circles while the captain and crew counted the cash they had secured from their backers is shown in the diagram immediately left of the ship sponsored by the Italian state and immediately right of the ship under the command of Captain Tourrite.

2. The *Santa Almira*, which wasn't the first ship to return from its expedition and wasn't commanded by Captain Walter Pedlar, sailed in circles in a "sea" for a few months; the *Santa Eloise* returned next after the ship whose captain claimed to have found the West Pole.

3. The *Santa Bonita* sailed back into its home port in December 1465; the ship paid for from the coffers of the Count of Holland arrived back from its venture one month before the captain who claimed to have sailed so far he saw the edge of the world.

4. The ship sponsored by France, which arrived back next after the *Santa Cristina*, wasn't the one sailed by Sir Francis Gander, who claimed he had discovered the center of the world.

5. The *Santa Cristina* was sponsored by King Cristian of Denmark, hoping for a big return on his investment; the ship sponsored by the Portuguese royals is shown immediately right of the one that sailed south along the coast of West Africa into the Southern Atlantic.

6. The ship that limped slowly back into port in November 1465 is shown immediately left of one whose captain saw a small eddy and decided it must have been water pouring through a hole in the seabed.

7. The *Santa Eloisa* sailed in tight circles in the North Sea keeping a wary eye for other ships that might recognize her; Captain Brausch didn't command either of the ships at the end of the row.

Captains: Capt. Brausch; Capt. Gander; Capt. Gonzales; Capt. Pedlar; Capt. Tourrite

Countries: Denmark; France; Holland; Italy; Portugal

Months: August; September; October; November; December

Claimed discoveries: center of the world; edge of the world; hole in the seabed; new continent; West Pole

Hiding location: Black Sea; Mediterranean Sea; North Atlantic Ocean; North Sea; South Atlantic Ocean

| Santa Almira | Santa Bonita | Santa Cristina | Santa Dominga | Santa Eloisa |

Starting tip: *Work out which country provided the funding for the voyage of the Santa Bonita.*

Still Lifers

Pockson Haddock runs the Still Life painting class at Fairview Art School and has been casting a critical but friendly eye over the submissions from five of his eager students for the new term. Can you name each of his students and say what subject they chose, in which medium they worked, and what comment Pockson somewhat generously made?

Clues

1. The pencil sketch by Delia d'Auber wasn't the offering Pockson described as an "unlucky choice," on the basis that its purported subject of a dragonfly had flown off at the wrong moment, resulting in a picture of a rather bare twig.

2. One student presented a wax crayon picture of her husband on a couch, declaring that life didn't come much stiller than that . . . for hours on end.

3. Simone Smeare's submission was not the picture of the boiled egg; neither her picture nor the rather unimaginative attempt at a vase was the offering declared to "need refining."

4. The only word Pockson could find to describe Paula Pastell's effort was "unusual."

5. The painting done in oils and pronounced a "creditable effort" wasn't the vase or Tammy Tempera's depiction of a fishbowl, which wasn't drawn in charcoal.

Artist	Subject

	Boiled egg	Dragonfly	Fishbowl	Husband	Vase	Charcoal	Oils	Pencil	Watercolor	Wax crayon	Creditable effort	Has potential	Needs refining	Unlucky choice	Unusual
Delia d'Auber															
Leona Lande-Scaype															
Paula Pastell															
Simone Smeare															
Tammy Tempera															
Creditable effort															
Has potential															
Needs refining															
Unlucky choice															
Unusual															
Charcoal															
Oils															
Pencil															
Watercolor															
Wax crayon															

Medium	Comment

Cracking Up

Among the many marvelous gadgets endorsed by celebrity chef Hector Ramsay is this range of nutcrackers, each aimed at a specific nut and incorporating a feature of a household tool that can sometimes be resorted to in a nut-cracking emergency. You need to find the name of each nutcracker, its additional feature, and the kind of nut on which it works best. Can you crack it?

Clues

1. The device that uses spannerism to crack almonds is next right of the one that relies on pliersaction for its effect.

2. The Shellraiser makes short work of hazelnuts. It is somewhere right of the nutcracker that incorporates hammerology.

3. There is more than one place between the Kernelator with the built-in vise device and the brazil breaker, which is not the Nutworker.

Nutcrackers: Crackomatic; Kernelator; Nutworker; Shellraiser
Features: hammerology; pliersaction; spannerism; vise device
Best for: almonds; brazils; hazelnuts; walnuts

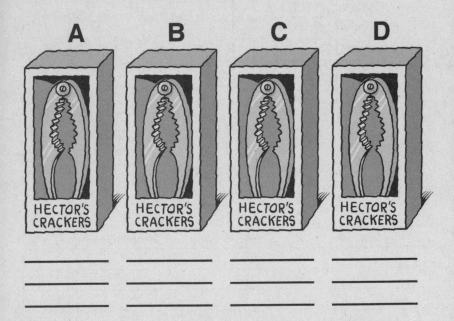

Starting tip: Work out which cracker cracks brazils and then place it in the line-up.

Logi-5

Each line, across and down, is to have each of the letters A, B, C, D, and E, appearing once. Also, every shape—shown by the thick lines—must also have each of the letters in it. Can you fill in the grid?

Killer Sudoku

The normal rules of Sudoku apply. In addition, the digits in each inner shape (marked by dots) must add up to the number in the top corner of that box.

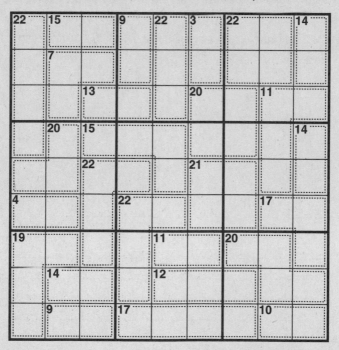

House Hunters

Real estate agent Selwyn Holmes has five appointments to show prospective purchasers around five properties that he currently has on his books. Can you discover the times of his appointments, the address of each property, the name of the prospective buyer, and the feature of his property that he will be stressing to them?

Clues

1. Selwyn's first appointment is at the property with the three en-suite bathrooms, which isn't in Bear Lane.

2. At midday he has an appointment with Mr. and Mrs. Hawkes, followed at 1 o'clock by a visit to Grove Close, where the potential customer is not Mr. Jackson.

3. Mr. Jackson isn't looking at the house distinguished by its surviving original features.

4. Holmes' appointment at Southfields is an hour later than his meeting with Mr. and Mrs. McDonald, and an hour before he shows someone round the house with the large solid oak kitchen.

5. Miss Cole will be shown the extensive views from the property that she is interested in.

6. Mr. and Mrs. Hall have made an appointment to look round the property in Broadlands.

Time	Address

	Bear Lane	Broadlands	Grove Close	Linden Drive	Southfields	Miss Cole	Mr. and Mrs. Hall	Mr. and Mrs. Hawkes	Mr. Jackson	Mr. and Mrs. McDonald	Double garage	En-suite bathrooms	Extensive views	Original features	Solid oak kitchen
10 a.m.															
11 a.m.															
12 noon															
1 p.m.															
2 p.m.															
Double garage															
En-suite bathrooms															
Extensive views															
Original features															
Solid oak kitchen															
Miss Cole															
Mr. and Mrs. Hall															
Mr. and Mrs. Hawkes															
Mr. Jackson															
Mr. and Mrs. McDonald															

AND IT'S IDEALLY POSITIONED FOR THE GOLF COURSE

FOR SALE

Purchasers	Feature

Five Children and IT

It is the school's summer break and Moz the Boss, the immediate supervisor of TechCorp's junior IT team, has brought her brood of five children into work and asked her underlings to look after them. "They have some really interesting project ideas," she told her staff, "I am sure you can help them." Can you work out the name and age of each child, the team member to whom they had been assigned, and the unrealistic project they needed help with?

Clues

1. One of the five-year-old twins was entrusted to the care of Caz, who was not minding the child who had heard that diamonds were formed from carbon under pressure and was trying to make their own by stamping on pencils. Jez was minding the child who had rescued one of the pencils and wanted it adapted so that anything they drew would come to life.

2. Bill, who had pulled up one of the carpet tiles and reckoned it could be converted into a flying carpet with a few technological adjustments, is younger than Amber but older than Sunshine. Lolly is seven. Neither she nor Amber wants help with making a robot horse they can ride.

3. Kez was entrusted with the oldest child. Baz's charge is one year older than Moondown, who isn't being minded by Caz, and one year younger than the kid who wants to become invisible.

Child	Age

	5 years	5 years	6 years	7 years	9 years	Baz	Caz	Daz	Jez	Kez	Diamonds	Flying carpet	Invisibility	Magic pencil	Robot horse
Amber															
Bill															
Lolly															
Moondown															
Sunshine															
Diamonds															
Flying carpet															
Invisibility															
Magic pencil															
Robot horse															
Baz															
Caz															
Daz															
Jez															
Kez															

Minder	Idea

Monstrous

Over the years, horror movies have produced many memorable monsters—versions of Frankenstein, vampires, and mummies—and small independent Ivywood studios hopes to cash in on that legacy. Below are some details of five new horror movies whose directors hope that their monsters will be equally memorable. Can you work out for each movie, the name or description of its monster, the name of the actor who plays the monster, and the name of the director who designed the monster's appearance?

Clues

1. The leading monster in *The Pit* is a seven-foot, exoskeletal, tentacled bloodsucker called, for some reason, the Alien Angel.

2. It's not *Monsteropolis* which stars acknowledged monster specialist Dan Chaney as its leading—well, monster, of course.

3. The monster in *Shock After Shock*, who (or which) is played by Emily Donner and was designed by a director whose first name and surname initials come from the same half of the alphabet, is not called The Faceless Killer—who looks like a very large, tough ape-man with no—but I expect you've already worked that bit out.

4. Glen Ogle suffered many hours in the make-up artist's chair and wore a lot of prosthetics to play the monster designed by director Gus Hoch.

5. Jay Kingston, who plays the Croc Man—a cross between a crocodile and a man, but less handsome than either—doesn't appear in *Heartquake*, which features a monster designed by Ivywood veteran Count Roden, a bloated, slime-dripping batrachian with no redeeming features whatsoever, was created by director Josie Royce but doesn't feature in *Anomaly*.

6. Count Roden, a bloated slime-dripping batrachian with no redeeming features whatsoever, was created by director Josie Royce but doesn't feature in *Anomaly*.

Movie title	Monster

	Alien Angel	Count Roden	Croc Man	Faceless Killer	Stalker	Dan Chaney	Emily Donner	Glen Ogle	Jay Kingston	Tania Strange	Eddie Gold	Gus Hoch	Josie Royce	Meg O'Brian	Riley Palmer
Anomaly															
Heartquake															
Monsteropolis															
Shock After Shock															
The Pit															
Eddie Gold															
Gus Hoch															
Josie Royce															
Meg O'Brian															
Riley Palmer															
Dan Chaney															
Emily Donner															
Glen Ogle															
Jay Kingston															
Tania Strange															

Actor	Director

French Connection

Interpot, the international police division that focuses on marijuana smuggling, has put together an operation called Operation Grass Skirt that requires a squad of five French-speaking volunteers from different forces to go undercover in Marseilles. Can you work out the details of the five individuals who have volunteered—their names, nationalities, former police specialities, and reasons for volunteering?

Clues

1. Chris Brookes, who is English, was never a member of the Vice Squad and is neither the man who volunteered in order to avoid an internal investigation by his own force nor the man whose boss gave him the stark choice of volunteering for Operation Grass Skirt or being sacked.

2. The Swiss volunteer was formerly a member of Geneva's Murder Squad; Jules Lebrun is not the Canadian Mountie who was born in Quebec.

3. The Belgian police officer from Antwerp, who volunteered for Operation Grass Skirt because he wanted a change of scenery and weather, didn't belong to his force's Robbery Squad.

4. The Organized Crime specialist who volunteered because he had got so involved with the mob that he had been made the subject of an internal investigation is not from France.

5. Etienne Delacroix volunteered for Operation Grass Skirt because he's desperate for promotion and has tried everything else.

6. Armand Bonvin served for the last decade in his force's Robbery Squad.

Name	Nationality

	Belgian	British	Canadian	French	Swiss	Car Crime	Murder	Organized Crime	Robbery	Vice	Avoid ex-spouse	Avoid investigation	Avoid sacking	Wanted a change	Wants promotion
Armand Bonvin															
Chris Brookes															
Etienne Delacroix															
Jules Lebrun															
Olivier St. Michel															
Avoid ex-spouse											
Avoid investigation											
Avoid sacking											
Wanted a change											
Wants promotion											
Car Crime						
Murder						
Organized Crime						
Robbery						
Vice						

Speciality	Reason

PC Ballets

Not even the highly traditional world of ballet can totally afford to ignore the conventions of the modern world, and the five celebrated divas below are each currently finding themselves appearing in a well-known score, whose story has been updated to fit in with our more enlightened and politically-correct times. Can you assign each star to her current ballet, and name its composer and the prestigious theater where the show is being performed?

Clues

1. Marcie Hussle is in *The Nutstacker*, a magical tale of night-time adventures around the supermarket shelves, which is not by Leo Beliebes; Marcie is not appearing at the Storbury Opera House, which is staging a work by Serge Nokofiev.

2. *Sleeping Person*, a non-judgmental score by Mikhail Klunka, is not the ballet showcasing Hannah Vacherin at the Chester Arts Center.

3. Felicia Makeover is dancing a work by Pyotr Teesonsky; *The Differently Attractive Sisters*, the well-known Cinderella story retold from the perspective of the misunderstood underdogs, is not the ballet being staged in Storbury.

4. Rising star Frasquita Cornward is not appearing in the ever-popular ballet now re-imagined to eliminate accusations of elitism and renamed *Duck Pond*.

5. Tickets are sold out at the Madison Odeon for the exciting new gender-fluid romance *Romeo & Julian*.

6. Edith Eve is not the featured composer at the Stoneville Arena.

Dancer	Ballet

	Duck Pond	Nutstacker	Romeo & Julian	Sleeping Person	The ... Sisters	Beliebes	Eve	Klunka	Nokofiev	Teesonsky	Chester Arts Center	Clinton Garden Bowl	Madison Odeon	Stoneville Arena	Storbury Opera House
Felicia Makeover															
Frasquita Cornward															
Hannah Vacherin															
Marcie Hussle															
Margery Cascayde															
Chester Arts Center															
Clinton Garden Bowl															
Madison Odeon															
Stoneville Arena															
Storbury Opera House															
Beliebes															
Eve															
Klunka															
Nokofiev															
Teesonsky															

ELECTROCORP

Suppliers of Parasols, Telescopes, Party Planners, And Disco Lights

WE CAN'T BLAME THE SUNSHINE, THE MOONLIGHT, OR THE GOOD TIMES. WE HAVE TO BLAME IT ON THE BOOGIE.

Composer	Theater

Cluney Tunes

Simon Cluney started out as a TV actor, but over the last 30 years he's become a TV institution—so much so that he's not only the star of his present series *Mustang Jack* (his character is Jack Moran, a vet with twin obsessions—the Wild West and solving crimes) but he's also the executive producer and directs some of the episodes, and has taken advantage of that to cast various of his relatives in small roles. Can you work out which character was played by a relative in each of the first five episodes of the latest series, the name of that relative, and his relationship to Simon?

Clues

1. Simon's stepson, who played Dr. Jones, an eye-witness to a crime, appeared in a later episode of *Mustang Jack* than Gary Jones.

2. David Cluney, Simon's nephew, who did not play Jean, the French barman (you were wondering about that, I bet), appeared in the episode before the one in which a member of the Cluney family appeared as Sergeant Wood, the cop who actually made the arrest.

3. Larry Cluney appeared in an earlier episode than Wayne Rovik—which, like Gary Jones, is an adopted screen-name. (Possibly, you were wondering about that, too.)

4. John Cluney, who is not Simon's son by his first wife, actress Sheena Kaye, was cast as "Ginger," a carnival worker; he didn't appear in episode 1 or episode 5.

5. Episode 2 featured a non-acting member of the Cluney family in the minuscule role of Store Worker—all he had to do was look up and smile and managed it perfectly in only 11 takes.

6. Simon's brother, whose name is not Larry, appeared in episode 3.

Episode	Role

	Dr. Jones	Ginger	Jean	Sergeant Wood	Store Worker	David Cluney	Gary Jones	John Cluney	Larry Cluney	Wayne Rovik	Brother	Cousin	Nephew	Son	Stepson
Episode 1															
Episode 2															
Episode 3															
Episode 4															
Episode 5															
Brother															
Cousin															
Nephew															
Son															
Stepson															
David Cluney															
Gary Jones															
John Cluney															
Larry Cluney															
Wayne Rovik															

Relation	Relationship

Witches' Brew?

Last fall, Eddie decided to begin brewing some wine but wanted some help with the initial, labor-intensive stage. With Halloween imminent, he hit upon the idea of persuading his two children and three of their friends to help out while he took a more supervisory role. He took his five brewing bins, disguised them as witches' cauldrons, labeled them, and told the children they were making magic potions. Can you work out the age of each young witch, the name Eddie gave to each of the potions, and eventual wines that each young witch mixed with and in what order he and his friends drank the wine after it was eventually bottled and left to age for a few months?

Clues

1. The second wine that was tried, which wasn't Bony Finger or Witch's Warts, was the one that Tamsin had helped with.

2. Florence mashed the contents of one cauldron that Eddie had labeled Gory Gizzard.

3. The young witch who began the creation of Toads and Tails was six years old.

4. The wine labeled Blood Sucker, with its very dark burgundy color from the blackberries, was first to be tried; this wasn't brewed by Grace or Jody, the latter of whom was the seven-year-old.

5. The wine made from the mixture that the nine-year-old, who wasn't Grace, stirred together was the last lot to be drunk.

6. Amy wasn't the ten-year-old, who didn't start the wine that was fourth in line to be tested and drunk; Witch's Warts wasn't the third wine to be tried.

Witch	Age

	Six	Seven	Eight	Nine	Ten	Blood Sucker	Bony Finger	Gory Gizzards	Toads and Tails	Witch's Warts	First	Second	Third	Fourth	Fifth
Amy															
Florence															
Grace															
Jody															
Tamsin															
First															
Second															
Third															
Fourth															
Fifth															
Blood Sucker															
Bony Finger															
Gory Gizzards															
Toads and Tails															
Witch's Warts															

Witch's Cauldron Restaurant
MENU

WHEN SHALL WE THREE MEET AGAIN
IN THUNDER, LIGHTNING, OR CHOW MEIN... $11.50

DOUBLE, DOUBLE, TOIL, AND TROUBLE
FIRE BURN AND CAULDRON BUBBLE TEA... $3.50

ADDER'S FORK AND BLINDWORM'S STING
LIZARD'S LEG AND BUFFALO WINGS ... $9.75

WHEN THE HURLY BURLY'S DONE,
WHEN THE BATTLE'S HOT CROSS BUN ... $4.60

Wine	Order

Animal Magnetism

Once upon a time, not so long ago, in the far away land of Alysia, five young goatherds each fell in love with different young shepherdesses. Can you match the loving couples and say how many goats or sheep each had charge of?

Clues

1. The boy with 16 goats courted the lass with 29 sheep to look after.

2. Francis, who had fewer than 20 goats, was in amorous pursuit of Mary, who had more sheep than Phyllida to tend.

3. Garth had the flock of goats next smaller than Ralph's.

4. Clarissa fell in love with the goatherd who had only 10 goats, but a smile to die for.

5. Lucy was the shepherdess with 37 sheep; her swain had an even number of goats.

6. Seth, who had more goats than Thomas, courted the damsel whose flock numbered exactly 30, who was not Dorinda.

Goatherd	Shepherdess

	Clarissa	Dorinda	Lucy	Mary	Phyllida	10 goats	16 goats	18 goats	22 goats	25 goats	26 sheep	29 sheep	30 sheep	37 sheep	43 sheep
Francis															
Garth															
Ralph															
Seth															
Thomas															
26 sheep															
29 sheep															
30 sheep															
37 sheep															
43 sheep															
10 goats															
16 goats															
18 goats															
22 goats															
25 goats															

IT'S NOT THAT I LOSE THEM, IT'S JUST THAT I FALL ASLEEP WHEN I COUNT THEM.

Goats	Sheep

Battleships

Do you remember the old game of battleships? These puzzles are based on that idea. Your task is to find the vessels in the diagram. Some parts of boats or sea squares have already been filled in, and a number next to a row or column refers to the number of occupied squares in that row or column. The boats may be positioned horizontally or vertically, but no two boats or parts of boats are in adjacent squares—horizontally, vertically, or diagonally.

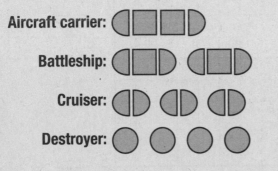

Aircraft carrier:

Battleship:

Cruiser:

Destroyer:

										0
										0
										6
										0
										5
										1
										0
										3
									■		4
										1
0	0	3	3	1	6	0	3	1	3	

Fireworking It Out

Max Tempest is celebrating July 4 with some spectacular fireworks. He's bought four "barrage" fireworks that can be set off in sequence with one lighting. Can you name each display firework shown, say what it does, and how much it cost?

Clues

1. Screaming Angel will do its thing some time after the Roman candle display but some time before the least expensive firework.

2. The words on the side of Comet's Revenge describe it as a fountain of shooting stars but doesn't explain why the comet is so vengeful.

3. Earthquake was priced at $4 less than the firework that sends up a cloud of crackling sparklers but which isn't the firework called Saturn Starburst which will take over immediately after the display and noise of the shooting explosions is over.

4. The third firework is the most expensive.

Firework: Comet's Revenge; Earthquake; Saturn Starburst; Screaming Angel
Type: cracking sparklers; Roman candles; shooting explosions; shooting stars
Prices: $23; $25; $27; $29

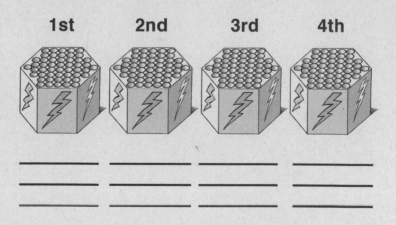

| 1st | 2nd | 3rd | 4th |

Starting tip: Work out in what order the $23 firework will burst into life.

Classical Catalog

The celebrated contemporary Russian composer Ivanic Inos took time from his busy performing schedule last week to delight a gathering of his fans at the Chester Arts Center. After a short performance, he took part in a question-and-answer session about some of his most popular works, all given dedications to cities that have played a major part in his career. Can you work out in which year each type of piece was written, how long it lasts, and to which city it is dedicated?

Clues

1. Ivanic informed his eager audience that his favorite of his dedicated compositions, although not the longest, was the concerto dedicated to his home city of Moscow.

2. The 38-minute work is a homage to his adoptive city of London and was written four years after his étude.

3. The city to which Ivanic dedicated his most recent composition is Prague where he first found fame; this work lasts 10 minutes longer than his sonata.

4. The cantata is a shorter piece than his symphony, which was written in 2008.

5. The work which lasts a short (but delightful) 20 minutes was composed sometime after the piece dedicated to Paris, where he met the brilliant pianist who was to become his wife.

Year	Piece

	Cantata	Concerto	Étude	Sonata	Symphony	20 mins	30 mins	38 mins	40 mins	55 mins	Berlin	London	Moscow	Paris	Prague
2000															
2004															
2008															
2013															
2018															
Berlin															
London															
Moscow															
Paris															
Prague															
20 mins															
30 mins															
38 mins															
40 mins															
55 mins															

Length	City

Lost and Found

Young Jamie has just started his new job as a coat check attendant at the highly rated, immensely popular and ferociously expensive restaurant, The Chubby Mallard. Nervously he took coats and other items from five self-important and rude customers who flung them at him as they arrived and refused to take the coat check ticket which would have made finding the correct items at the end of the evening much easier than it was. Can you work out the ticket number Jamie tried to hand each customer, the item that the customer hurled in his direction, and the number of minutes it took for him to find it again when the diner was leaving?

Clues

1. Jamie tried to give Miss Kendal ticket number 51; the item she tossed at him, which wasn't the waterproof jacket, took fewer than 15 minutes to find.

2. Mr. and Mrs. Selby were two of the last diners to leave the restaurant, so there was only a small pile of unlabeled items in the coat check and Jamie's search for Mr. Selby's item took just six minutes.

3. The brimmed hat that Jamie caught as it was thrown in his direction Frisbee-style belonged to Mrs. Wallace; this wasn't the item that should have been labeled with ticket 62, which took 12 minutes to find among all the other unlabeled items.

4. Jamie attempted to give ticket number 29 to the customer who almost speared him with a carelessly slung black umbrella.

5. The red gilet, which didn't belong to Mr. Pickering, took ten minutes to find at the end of the evening but wasn't the item to which Jamie attempted to assign the numbers 38 or 51.

Customer	Number

	No.23	No.29	No.38	No.51	No.62	Black umbrella	Brimmed hat	Green overcoat	Red gilet	Waterproof jacket	3 minutes	6 minutes	10 minutes	12 minutes	15 minutes
Miss Joyce															
Miss Kendal															
Mr. Pickering															
Mr. Selby															
Mrs. Wallace															
3 minutes															
6 minutes															
10 minutes															
12 minutes															
15 minutes															
Black umbrella															
Brimmed hat															
Green overcoat															
Red gilet															
Waterproof jacket															

Item	Minutes

A Good Mix

For their daughter's wedding, Mr. and Mrs. Mingle have arranged the reception seating plan to give a good mix of people at each table, ensuring that there's at least one of the groom's and bride's relations on each table, together with a young friend of the happy couple. Can you work out which two relations and friend are on each table?

Clues

1. The bride's Grandma and groom's Uncle Henry are on a table numbered one less than the one where Uncle Frank is sitting.

2. The groom's Auntie Brenda and friend Linda are on a table numbered one less than the one where Grandad is sitting; Grandad is not on the same table as the groom's Uncle Tommy, and the latter is not on table 4.

3. Janet is on table 6 with a relation of the groom whose first name is longer than that of the groom's relation sitting at Mark's table.

4. The bride's Auntie Eileen is on the same table as Ryan, which is not table 3.

5. Uncle Bob is not on the same table as Harriet.

6. Cousin Lou is at table 5.

Table	Bride's relation

	Auntie Eileen	Cousin Lou	Grandad	Grandma	Uncle Frank	Auntie Brenda	Cousin Charles	Uncle Bob	Uncle Henry	Uncle Tommy	Harriet	Janet	Linda	Mark	Ryan
Table 3															
Table 4															
Table 5															
Table 6															
Table 7															
Harriet															
Janet															
Linda															
Mark															
Ryan															
Auntie Brenda															
Cousin Charles															
Uncle Bob															
Uncle Henry															
Uncle Tommy															

Groom's relation	Friend

Arts Knight

After a series of particularly embarrassing lily-livered escapades, King Arthur sent the five friends, the Knock-Kneed Knights of the Round Table to a top Camelot psychiatrist in an attempt to improve their courage rating. The expert advised each patient to write about a noble knight rescuing a maiden in distress, and then to try to think and act as his hero would have done when faced with a difficulty. Dutifully, each composed a work of a different genre, featuring a noble knight and a distressed maiden. Can you work out all the details?

Clues

1. The ballad entitled *Sir Noblesse Oblige* did not feature the damsel named Melisande.

2. Sir Audace was the hero who sprang from the quill of Sir Sorely à Frayde; this was not in the novelette, in which the heroine was Eleanor.

3. Sir Purefoy was not a character in the play produced by one of the pusillanimous five.

4. The short story was written by Sir Timid de Shayke.

5. Gwendoline did not appear in the work by Sir Coward de Custarde.

6. The work by Sir Poltroon à Ghaste features Cassandra being rescued by a noble knight but Sir Poltroon, well known for being the worst poet in Camelot and for many miles around, didn't write a ballad or an epic poem.

7. In one work, the fair maiden Liliane was rescued by brave Sir Paladin.

Author	Work

	Ballad	Epic poem	Novelette	Play	Short story	Sir Audace	Sir Noblesse	Sir Paladin	Sir Purefoy	Sir Valiant	Cassandra	Eleanor	Gwendoline	Liliane	Melisande
Sir Coward de Custarde															
Sir Poltroon à Ghaste															
Sir Sorely à Frayde															
Sir Spyneless de Feete															
Sir Timid de Shayke															
Cassandra															
Eleanor															
Gwendoline															
Liliane															
Melisande															
Sir Audace															
Sir Noblesse															
Sir Paladin															
Sir Purefoy															
Sir Valiant															

The Lady of the Swiss Lake

Hero	Heroine

Running Wild

Leading zoologist Davina Charles has made a documentary film about her latest expedition to the economically poor but wildlife-rich Tufab region of the African republic of Acirfa, taking her team and the film crew out on each day of one week to a particular location in pursuit of an endangered species. Can you work out where she went each day, what creature she was looking for, and how many specimens of the creature she was able to find and photograph?

Clues

1. On the Thursday of the filmed week, Davina was looking for the spider-lizard (very much like any other lizard except it has eight legs); this was later in the week than the trip to Mount Lunku, where she found just three specimens.

2. Neither Monday's trip nor the one in pursuit of the rainbow parrot involved a mountain, and both of these trips found fewer specimens than did the one to Mount Borri.

3. The expedition to the D'Kuna Forest was the day after Davina's team scaled Mount Borri.

4. Davina and the film crew found more specimens of the ding-bat than of the creature she looked for in the Gwangi Valley.

5. The copper monkey, which takes its name not from its color but from the strange helmet-shaped protrusion on top of its head and its constant cry of "allo, allo, allo," lives only in the trees of the Sporo Plain.

6. Only two specimens of the creature being sought on Wednesday were sighted; in contrast, Davina and her team managed to photograph and film nine specimens of the whistling hog.

Day	Area

	D'Kuna Forest	Gwangi Valley	Mount Borri	Mount Lunku	Sporo Plain	Copper monkey	Ding-bat	Rainbow parrot	Spider-lizard	Whistling hog	2	3	6	8	9
Monday															
Tuesday															
Wednesday															
Thursday															
Friday															
2															
3															
6															
8															
9															
Copper monkey															
Ding-bat															
Rainbow parrot															
Spider-lizard															
Whistling hog															

Creature	Number

Ssnake Charmers

At the Georgetown Snake Sanctuary, Sselina's latest batch of eggs have hatched and the young snakelings are coming along well. Can you name each of them as they line up for their weekly photograph? (Lefts and rights are from our point of view.)

Clues

1. Ssam is somewhere left of Ssue (who is posing between two male snakes) but somewhere right of Ssonia, who is somewhere left of Ssid but somewhere right of Ssuky, who isn't two places left of Ssid.

2. Ssaul is in an odd-numbered position but isn't an immediate neighbor of Ssonia.

3. Ssara's number in the picture is twice that of Ssal's; Ssara is immediately right of Sstan, whose other immediate neighbor is also female; Ssal is immediately right of a male snake but somewhere left of Sseb, who isn't immediately next to Ssue.

4. Both end positions are taken by female snakes.

Females: Ssal; Ssara; Ssonia; Ssue; Ssuky
Males: Ssam; Ssaul; Sseb; Ssid; Sstan

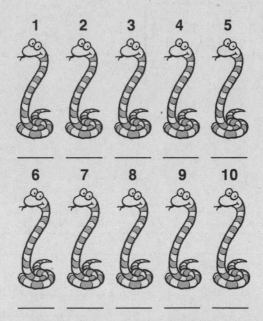

Starting tip: Name the snake in position 10.

Flower Power

Six young girls whose names harmonize better than their voices have decided to form a band. Can you work out the name of the wannabe in each position and the instrument they hope to learn to play? (We've shown them all as guitarists, so as not to give the game away. Lefts and rights are from our point of view.)

Clues

1. Lily expects to be a virtuoso on the trumpet if she ever gets her hands on one. She is next left to the girl who already owns a flute and hopes to work out how to play it one day, whose position is numbered twice that of Rose, who isn't the wannabe keyboardist or bass guitarist.

2. The wannabe keyboard player is next right of the would-be drummer, neither of whom is Daisy who is further right than both. Violet is at position 4 and is planning to learn to play a guitar of some sort. Iris is at one end of the line.

Girls: Daisy; Iris; Lily; Poppy; Rose; Violet
Instruments: bass guitar; drums; flute; keyboards; lead guitar; trumpet

Starting tip: Name the girl in position 2.

What the Flock?

In years gone by, large flocks of sheep were looked after by hardy shepherds who suffered the vagaries of the weather along with their flocks. Five such men are listed here. Can you discover the meadow in which each shepherd tends to his flock, the number of sheep in his flock, and the name of his only companion, his trusty and faithful sheepdog?

Clues

1. Job Herdin worked on Badleigh Meadow, but his sheepdog wasn't Dan; Jacob Ramm wasn't the shepherd on Staggerdon Meadow and his flock numbered more than 100.

2. Ben and his boss led their flock across Tripton Meadow, but neither this flock nor the one tended to by the shepherd on Staggerdon Meadow had the fewest number of sheep.

3. Neither Bob, nor the dog working with Isaiah Hills, looked after 70 sheep or worked on Staggerdon Meadow.

4. Esau Craggs had a flock of 80 sheep; Phil Penn didn't look after a flock of exactly 70.

5. Jem the sheepdog helped to look after the largest flock.

6. The flock of 105 sheep grazed the slopes of Alldown Meadow.

Shepherd	Fell

	Alldown Meadow	Badleigh Meadow	Rosen Meadow	Staggerdon Meadow	Tripton Meadow	50 sheep	70 sheep	80 sheep	105 sheep	110 sheep	Ben	Bob	Dan	Jem	Pip
Esau Craggs															
Isaiah Hills															
Jacob Ramm															
Job Herdin															
Phil Penn															
Ben															
Bob															
Dan															
Jem															
Pip															
50 sheep															
70 sheep															
80 sheep															
105 sheep															
110 sheep															

Apps for Shepherds

Ewe Tube

Fleece Book

Online Gambolling

Sheep	Sheepdog

Bio Logical

Sturm and Drang Ltd., a publishing house specializing in autobiographies, has purchased manuscripts from five men describing their lives in excruciating detail. Can you work out each man's full name, the profession he followed and from which he has recently retired, freeing him to document his times, and the title he has given his book?

Clues

1. Neither Anthony nor the man named Blackburn, whose book is called simply, if a little arrogantly, *Chosen*, ever served in the armed forces.

2. Tom, whose surname isn't Warwick, isn't the author of *Four Seasons*, who isn't the retired Army officer.

3. The first name of the heart surgeon who has entitled his autobiography *So Little Time* is one letter shorter than Tonbridge's.

4. Gordon, who was not the Navy officer, doesn't have seven letters in his surname.

5. Paul had been manager of half a dozen sports teams before his retirement, while Mr. Lancing has won two Oscars as a film director and likes to tell people all about it.

6. The author of *Man Bites Dog* isn't Mr. Farnham.

First name	Surname

	Blackburn	Farnham	Lancing	Tonbridge	Warwick	Army officer	Film director	Heart surgeon	Navy officer	Sports manager	Chosen	Four Seasons	Jack of Diamonds	Man Bites Dog	So Little Time
Anthony															
Gordon															
Nigel															
Paul															
Tom															
Chosen															
Four Seasons															
Jack of Diamonds															
Man Bites Dog															
So Little Time															
Army officer															
Film director															
Heart surgeon															
Navy officer															
Sports manager															

AUTOBIOGRAPHY

The stories are real but the names have been changed

SOLD OUT

The stories are false but the names are real

Occupation	Title

Driven to Destruction

The following details relate to the final race in last night's demolition derby racing event at the Dayton Oval—a dirt track with a few rickety temporary stands that has been fabricated on wasteland. Five cars were involved: can you work out the number of each car, the make of chassis upon which each was based, the name of the driver, and the name each had given to his car?

Clues

1. Isadora Stallon was at the wheel of car 7.

2. The bonnet and top of car 5 was daubed with the name *Red Devil*, but neither it nor car 10 was driven by ace driver Tilly Brakes.

3. Rex Carr was driving *Black Magic* (it was black and would need the help of something magical if it was to make it to the second lap), but it wasn't car 20 or the car based on the skeleton of an old Jeep.

4. The number on the Ram was ten higher than that of the car named *Hell on Wheels*.

5. Justin Bitts's car had a higher number than the Volkswagen that had been named *Firestorm*.

6. Des Troy's car was based on a Ford chassis but had so many dents it was only just recognizable as a car.

Car number	Chassis

	Dodge	Ford	Jeep	Ram	VW	Des Troy	Isadora Stallon	Justin Bitts	Rex Carr	Tilly Brakes	Black Magic	Firestorm	Greased Lightning	Hell on Wheels	Red Devil
Car 5															
Car 7															
Car 10															
Car 15															
Car 20															
Black Magic															
Firestorm															
Greased Lightning															
Hell on Wheels															
Red Devil															
Des Troy															
Isadora Stallon															
Justin Bitts															
Rex Carr															
Tilly Brakes															

I DON'T LIKE THE LOOK OF THE OPPOSITION

Demolition derby

Driver	Car name

Secret Identities

Among the passengers on the Associated Amalgamated Airways (AAA) late-night flight to John F. Kennedy Airport were five who were traveling onwards from New York to other destinations in the USA but who were not what they seemed. Can you work out the name and job which each of these people (or, in some cases, "people") claimed, their final destination, and who or what they really were? (Babs and Jessica are female identities, the other three are male.)

Clues

1. The alien is carefully disguised, but if you look very closely you can still make out the outline of the third eye in the middle of its forehead; it's an advance scout for the invading forces of the Micovan Horde, but is not heading for Memphis—so at least Graceland is safe for now.

2. The man heading for Pittsburgh is an industrial spy, out to steal the secrets of a newly developed piece of electronic equipment.

3. The traveler pretending to be an attorney, who is actually Europe's top hired killer on "business" in the US, is not the man—well, at least he seems to be a man—traveling to Minneapolis using a passport in the name of Terry Wiles.

4. The passenger heading for St. Louis really is a TV critic—but not just a TV critic.

5. The traveler using the name Babs Curry is a qualified dentist, among other things; she—well, at least she seems to be a she—isn't on the way to Atlanta.

6. Gary Hearn's passport says he's a 35-year-old Englishman, but actually he's a 300-year old Transylvanian vampire—so you know why he's taking the night flight; Sean Tallis isn't the passenger described as an engineer.

Name	Occupation

	Attorney	Dentist	Engineer	Pilot	TV critic	Atlanta	Memphis	Minneapolis	Pittsburgh	St. Louis	Alien	Hired killer	Industrial spy	Jewel thief	Vampire
Babs Curry															
Gary Hearn															
Jessica Kay															
Sean Tallis															
Terry Wiles															
Alien															
Hired killer															
Industrial spy															
Jewel thief															
Vampire															
Atlanta															
Memphis															
Minneapolis															
Pittsburgh															
St. Louis															

Destination	Secret identity

Sylvia's Mother

Last Saturday Sylvia's elderly mother was admitted to Clinton Hospital for tests. Sylvia visited her mom on the five subsequent days but, not wanting to pay the exorbitant $10 per half day hospital parking fees, came up with a money-saving plan. Being a keen and fit walker, she drove to a nearby location, where parking was much more reasonable, and walked from there to the hospital. Can you work out where she parked on each occasion, how far she walked to the hospital, and how much she saved herself in parking fees?

Clues

1. Sylvia parked at the gym on Monday where she saved more than she did Sunday, when she had walked 750 yards from the parking lot to the hospital.

2. On one of the days, which wasn't on Thursday, she parked at the Majestic Hotel and saved $7.30. The hotel isn't 900 yards from the hospital.

3. Another time, Sylvia walked 500 yards from the parking lot at the shopping mall to the hospital.

4. Sylvia saved $6.80 by walking a distance of 600 yards to the hospital from where she had left her car.

5. She saved $7.60 on Wednesday when she parked further from the hospital than the swimming pool.

Day	Facility

	Bar	Gym	Hotel	Shopping mall	Swimming pool	500 yards	600 yards	750 yards	900 yards	1,400 yards	$6.65	$6.80	$7.00	$7.30	$7.60
Sunday															
Monday															
Tuesday															
Wednesday															
Thursday															
$6.65															
$6.80															
$7.00															
$7.30															
$7.60															
500 yards															
600 yards															
750 yards															
900 yards															
1,400 yards															

Distance	Saving

Altared Arrangements

Madison's quite a large town and most Saturdays there are weddings going on at many of its assorted churches. But last Saturday, five weddings that should have taken place didn't. Can you work out which bride should have married which groom at which church—and the reason why the wedding did not take place?

Clues

1. Grace Hall wasn't the bride whose groom was arrested because of unpaid fines when he arrived at the church, nor was she the bride who should have been married at St. Mary's church but was in the City Hospital being treated for injuries sustained in a bachelorette party escapade.

2. Carol Bell should have been married at St. Paul's church, but not to John Impey.

3. Kay Lane should have married Ben Crabtree on Saturday; the woman who should have been married at Hart Road Baptist Church, whose first name begins with a vowel, was due to wed Ian Johnson.

4. Ellen French had an attack of cold feet so icy she fled, passport in hand, to the airport.

5. The groom who fled the night before his wedding, finally giving way to his fear of commitment, who was neither the man who should have been married at Parkside Church nor the man who should have married Grace Hall, wasn't named Robin Shaw.

6. Tim Vance's wedding had to be postponed because of bats in the belfry—or, to be more specific, to the contamination of the church by droppings from the bats living in the tower, causing the church to be closed for public health reasons.

Bride	Groom

	Ben Crabtree	Ian Johnson	John Impey	Robin Shaw	Tim Vance	Hart Rd. Baptist	Parkside Church	St. Francis RC	St. Mary's	St. Paul's	Bats in belfry	Bride fled	Bride in hospital	Groom arrested	Groom fled
Carol Bell															
Ellen French															
Grace Hall															
Kay Lane															
Olive Price															
Bats in belfry															
Bride fled															
Bride in hospital															
Groom arrested															
Groom fled															
Hart Rd. Baptist															
Parkside Church															
St. Francis RC															
St. Mary's															
St. Paul's															

Church	Reason

Paranoica Pioneers

A recent book tells for the first time of the work of the top-secret Triple-0 Department of the Paranoica Secret Service, the largest and most intrusive in the world. Tracing its creation to about half an hour after the coup that brought the recent administration to power, the book names the first eight agents who passed the rigorous Snooping Course, numbered in the order in which they were recruited, and who are now revered as pioneers. Can you work out the name and pre-coup occupation of each of the Triple-0 agents whose pictures adorn the wall of the Secret Service HQ? (As you might imagine, the author is currently spending some time at the Secret Service headquarters—he may be there for a while.)

Clues

1. Valerie Deighton, a one-time junior civil servant from the Ministry of Pensions, was one of the first four recruits to the Triple-0 Department, as her identification number testified.

2. Desmond Childers, revered in Secret Service circles for his "Spy on your neighbor" initiative, was 0006.

3. Edmund Ambler, whose is revered for informing on every member of his family including his unborn daughter while his wife was expecting, was recruited next after the former forensic psychologist.

4. Sebastian Le Queux, who wasn't 0001, was recruited to the Service some time before Frederick Gardner.

5. The former university historian's identification number was two higher than that of Charlotte Fleming, whose Secret Service number ended in an even digit.

6. Monica Buchan was recruited next but one after the teacher who began their Secret Service career by arresting the entire teaching staff from their previous place of employment and most of the pupils (only those who were away sick that day remained at large).

7. Rowena Maugham wasn't the journalist, whose former colleagues were easy meat and were soon rounded up and despatched to re-education camps; the journalist was second to be recruited and had a shorter first name than agent 0003.

8. The former socialist politician and agitator had a Triple-0 number one higher than that of the linguist formerly employed by the Paranoica Museum in the ancient language section.

Names: Charlotte Fleming; Desmond Childers; Edmund Ambler; Frederick Gardner; Monica Buchan; Rowena Maugham; Sebastian Le Queux; Valerie Deighton

Previous occupations: broadcaster; civil servant; historian; journalist; linguist; politician; psychologist; teacher

Starting tip: Begin by positioning Charlotte Fleming.

Skeery Spectres

Skeery Castle, home of the MacGhast family, has stood on a rocky island in Scotland's Loch Tartarus since the 15th century, and parts of the original structure still survive, although subsequent generations of MacGhasts have added much. Among the things they have added are five ghosts who haunt the parts of the castle where they died. Can you work out each ghostly MacGhast's nickname, the form his ghost takes, the room he haunts, and the date of his death?

Clues

1. The ghost that manifests itself in the Gallery is that of the MacGhast who died there in 1535 after being poisoned by his cousin and heir.

2. Angus MacGhast, known, quite justifiably, as Angus the Bad, is not the invisible phantom who throws things around, which is not the ghost of the man who died from his battle wounds in the Blue Room in 1469 or the one who expired in the Library, murdered by his long-suffering wife.

3. Duncan the Sinner, whose ghost is invisible but screams, died in an earlier century than, but not the one immediately before, the MacGhast whose death occurred in the Music Room, possibly from natural causes but also possibly smothered with a pillow.

4. Mungo the Wicked died in 1681, but not in the Master Bedroom.

5. Lachlan the Diabolic died in the Library in the century following the death of Hamish the Vile—if you're getting the impression that these MacGhasts weren't nice people, you're not wrong.

6. The ghost which appears as a skeletal figure is that of the MacGhast who died in 1744.

7. The MacGhast whose ghost appears as a shadowy, cloaked figure is not the one who shot himself (probably) to avoid arrest and public disgrace in 1873.

MacGhast	Ghost

	Headless figure	Invisible (screams)	Invisible (throws)	Shadowy figure	Skeletal figure	Blue Room	Gallery	Library	Master Bedroom	Music Room	1469	1535	1681	1744	1873
Angus the Bad															
Duncan the Sinner															
Hamish the Vile															
Lachlan the Diabolic															
Mungo the Wicked															
1469															
1535															
1681															
1744															
1873															
Blue Room															
Gallery															
Library															
Master Bedroom															
Music Room															

Room	Death

Spare Room

Only one of the five homeowners in Deddenned Drive, a quiet cul-de-sac, uses their garage for the purpose for which it was intended. Can you work out the name of the family at each house, the use to which they have put their garage, and the color of its door? (NB: the houses are arranged in a horseshoe shape with the houses numbered sequentially around it.)

Clues

1. Mr. Jones, whose garage door isn't navy blue, controversially uses his garage to protect his car from the elements.

2. The Franklins, whose garage door is bright green, live next door to a family who have converted their garage into an office; this isn't the Reillys, who don't live at 5 Deddenned Drive.

3. The Saunders live at No.4.

4. The family at No.2 use their garage as a gym; their garage door isn't navy blue or red.

5. The garage at 1 Deddenned Drive, which isn't the one set up as a workshop with benches, power tools, and toolboxes, has a black door.

6. The white garage door, which isn't at Nos. 3 or 5, is no longer opened as it holds back piles of junk that would tumble out onto the drive if released.

House	Family

	Carlson	Franklin	Jones	Reilly	Saunders	Car	Gym	Junk room	Office	Workshop	Black	Green	Navy blue	Red	White
No.1															
No.2															
No.3															
No.4															
No.5															
Black															
Green															
Navy blue															
Red															
White															
Car															
Gym															
Junk room															
Office															
Workshop															

IT'S OK DEAR, I'VE FOUND THE GARAGE DOOR REMOTE

Function	Color

Progressive Disorders

Five reformed 1970s prog-rock bands have recently all had internal disputes over various issues. This has caused one member from each to storm off in a huff and form a splinter group, which he has given an optimistic designation, asserting his version of the band's precedence over that of his remaining colleagues. Can you work out which musician from each group has broken away, what superior designation he claims for his break-away band, and what was the reason that brought about the acrimonious split?

Clues

1. Exodus' veteran singer Lee Giddy has split with his erstwhile bandmates, but has not declared his new incarnation of the band to be the One and Only.

2. One spin-off group on the circuit is now known as The Genuine GPI, but they're not the outfit formed by a disgruntled lead guitarist or bass player; the bass guitarist was unimpressed with the musical direction his former colleagues seemed to be taking.

3. Appropriately enough, the argument that caused one member to leave Queen Scarlet was caused by a dispute over payment of royalties; the player instigating the split is not the unhappy keyboardist who has declared his new group to be the Official line-up.

4. Tickets will not be available anytime soon for the Authentic versions of either Gush or Exodus, as no such bands exist—yet.

5. The group torn apart by management issues has not resulted in their drummer storming out and forming a rival version; Maybe's troubles have not been caused by either type of guitarist.

6. The leader of the band now touring as the Real manifestation claims the split was due to "creative differences" with his old colleagues.

Band	Musician

	Bass guitarist	Drummer	Keyboardist	Lead guitarist	Singer	Authentic	Genuine	Official	One and Only	Real	Creative differences	Management issues	Musical direction	Personality clashes	Royalty payments
Exodus															
GPI															
Gush															
Maybe															
Queen Scarlet															
Creative differences																
Management issues																
Musical direction																
Personality clashes																
Royalty payments																
Authentic																
Genuine																
Official																
One and Only																
Real																

Designation	Reason

Misses Right

The proliferation of internet dating sites has persuaded five single men to sign up in the hope of finding Miss Right. Can you work out to which site each man sent his signing on fee, the name of the woman with which its algorithm has matched him, and the venue for their first meeting?

Clues

1. Neil signed up with Heart2Heart.com, but didn't meet Jill Ryatt as a result; Donna Rite went with one of the five to the theater, but not through Heart2Heart or Overture.com.

2. Mark didn't use Solemates.com and didn't have a dinner date; the possible Miss Right who was taken to dinner wasn't Gina Wright.

3. Karl took his prospective new partner to a concert.

4. One of the men met Sandy Write through Keydate.com.

5. The new QPid.com member took his companion to the cinema.

6. When Joe arranged to meet Laura Wryte through his chosen agency, they agreed to meet at the train station before going on to their venue.

Man	Agency

	Heart2Heart.com	Keydate.com	Overture.com	QPid.com	Solemates.com	Donna Rite	Gina Wright	Jill Ryatt	Laura Wryte	Sandy Write	Bar	Cinema	Concert	Dinner	Theater
Joe															
Karl															
Mark															
Neil															
Ralph															
Bar															
Cinema															
Concert															
Dinner															
Theater															
Donna Rite															
Gina Wright															
Jill Ryatt															
Laura Wryte															
Sandy Write															

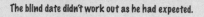

The blind date didn't work out as he had expected.

Miss Right	Venue

Equus October

In Ancient Rome, this month sees the traditional chariot race where eager teams compete for the honor of beating their rival sponsors (the men of the Subura and the Via Sacra team are the biggest rivals) and carrying off the pennant by arriving first back at the Trigarium—the main training ground. An exciting, if rather chaotic, time is had by all apart from, rather unfortunately, the leading horse of the victorious team, who ends up being sacrificed and then displayed in triumph at its sponsors' HQ. The servant friends have each been called in to help with their boss's favorite team, so can you identify the name of the chariot squad, the district its sponsors represent and where on the course they all came to grief . . . nobody's fault in particular, of course?

Clues

1. The squad who had the doubtful honor of enjoying the services of Branelus were known as the Fulmina (lightning bolts).

2. Neither the Veloces (swifties) nor the team employing Cluelus were the unlucky competitors whose chariot came detached from its horses at the corner of the Circus Flaminius, thanks to a carelessly fastened harness.

3. The Suburani were pinning their hopes this year on the Corusci (flashes); they didn't have reason to investigate the loose axle which caused Gormlus' squad's chariot to disintegrate in front of the Temple of Mars.

4. The debacle that befell the men of the Via Recta district's chariot took place outside the Temple of Neptune; Hopelus wasn't working for the Suburani faction.

5. Team Scintillae (sparks) weren't the charioteers who came closest to winning, actually reaching the Trigarium . . . before "someone" over-excitedly leapt out and caused the horses to bolt in the opposite direction.

6. It was the Pennipedes (winged feet) who came a cropper when a wheel fell off near the Temple of the Castors; they weren't the charioteers sponsored by the men of the Via Lata, or the Via Sacra, who were temporarily employing Euselus.

Servant	Chariot squad

	Corusci	Fulmina	Pennipedes	Scintillae	Veloces	Praetoriani	Suburani	Via Lata	Via Recta	Via Sacra	Circus Flaminius	Temple/Castors	Temple/Mars	Temple/Neptune	Trigarium
Branelus															
Cluelus															
Euselus															
Gormlus															
Hopelus															
Circus Flaminius															
Temple/Castors															
Temple/Mars															
Temple/Neptune															
Trigarium															
Praetoriani															
Suburani															
Via Lata															
Via Recta															
Via Sacra															

Sponsors	Accident site

Getting Alarmed

Angie is getting a bad name for herself at her local shopping mall, but through no fault of her own. Over five months earlier this year she bought five garments from five of the boutiques in the mall and on each occasion set the alarms ringing and security staff running when she left the store, as the security tag had not been removed or neutralized. Can you work out the name of the store where she bought each garment that was still tagged, its cost, and in what month the incident occurred?

Clues

1. Angie's purchase of a pair of jeans from PJ Fashions wasn't in July; the jeans were more expensive than the item she purchased in May.

2. She bought an item and spent ten minutes having her bags searched by the security staff at JD Gear in August.

3. Angie didn't buy the dress or sneakers from the security conscious MC Highstreet, where she had to produce a receipt for $49.95 after being stopped as she was wandering out of the store.

4. Angie's new jacket, which cost $57.99, wasn't bought from HF Store or KR Trends; nor was KR Trends the store from which she bought her dress.

5. In February, Angie's bags were searched by one security woman while another scanned her receipt showing a purchase for $54.50.

6. Angie bought her shoes in April; her new sneakers didn't cost $34.99.

Store	Garment

	Dress	Jacket	Jeans	Shoes	Sneakers	$34.99	$49.95	$54.50	$57.99	$62.50	February	April	May	July	August
HF Store															
JD Gear															
KR Trends															
MC Highstreet															
PJ Fashions															
February															
April															
May															
July															
August															
$34.99															
$49.95															
$54.50															
$57.99															
$62.50															

Cost	Month

What a Picture

The last race at Arlington Park produced a photo finish as shown below. Can you name the horses placed in each position and their jockeys and say what colored silks the jockeys were each wearing?

Clues

1. Sandpiper was placed immediately in front of the horse ridden by Luke Grenfell, who was riding in the black and blue colors.

2. King's Ransom was ridden by Marvin Gale, whose riding colors were not pink and white.

3. Conor O'Brien's horse finished with a higher placing than Jackie Moran's.

4. The jockey of the horse which came in third was in the red and orange colors.

5. The race was awarded to Brooklyn by a short head when the judges had studied the photograph.

Horses: Blue Streak; Brooklyn; King's Ransom; Sandpiper
Jockeys: Conor O'Brien; Jackie Moran; Luke Grenfell; Marvin Gale
Colors: black and blue; pink and white; red and orange; yellow and green

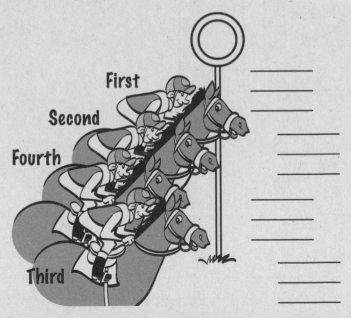

First
Second
Fourth
Third

Starting tip: Begin by working out where Sandpiper finished.

Sign In

Each row and column is to contain the digits 1-6. The given signs tell you if a digit in a cell is plus 1 (+) or minus 1 (-) the digit next to it. Signs between consecutive digits always work from left to right or top to bottom. Examples: 3 + 4 or 2 ⁻ 1 ALL occurrences of consecutive digits have been marked by a sign.

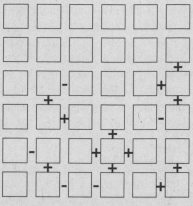

Sudoku

Complete this grid so that each column, each row, and each marked 3 X 3 square contains each of the numbers 1 to 9.

							5	1	
			8			3		9
	9			2			8	6
6				8				
9	5				7	1		
	1		2				6	
1	3							
		6	1	4		8		
4		8		5	2			

Les Chevaliers

When six champion knights from Lutetia, on the European mainland, visited Camelot to participate in a tournament, they insisted on making a ceremonial entrance to the city, fully-armored and with banners flying, and the picture below is a representation of the recently discovered tapestry that was created to record the event. Can you fill in each knight's name and cognomen (that's the second part of his name), and the name of his horse, or cheval, as it was known in Lutetian? (For clarity: chevalier 1 is directly ahead of chevalier 4, 2 is directly ahead of 5 and 3 directly ahead of 6; chevaliers 2 and 3 are riding side by side as are 5 and 6.)

Clues

1. The knight known as le Sauvage rode somewhere ahead, but not directly ahead, of the man called le Rouge mounted on Le Gris, who was not numbered 2 and who did not enter Camelot directly behind or directly ahead of his knightly companion le Chevalier Giraud.

2. Le Chevalier Vesey l'Estocade fought Sir Lancelot in the tournament and, predictably, lost.

3. Le Chevalier Aubin, whose horse was called Maraudeur, rode into Camelot directly behind the knight mounted on Guerrier.

4. Knight 3 was le Chevalier Levric, who was not le Sauvauge; Flamme is indicated by a higher number.

5. The man known as de la Lance, who was later defeated with the lance by Sir Galahad, entered Camelot directly behind le Chevalier Hugues; the man bearing the cognomen des Roches rode beside one of his fellow knights.

6. Knight 6, who was not le Chevalier Thibaut, bore the cognomen le Borreau.

7. Knight 1 was mounted on Fureur; Licorne's rider was not knight 2.

First names: Aubin; Giraud; Hugues; Levric; Thibaut; Vesey
Cognomens: de la Lance; de l'Estocade; des Roches; le Borreau; le Rouge; le Sauvage
Horses: Flamme; Fureur; Guerrier; Le Gris; Licorne; Maraudeur

Starting tip: Work out the name of knight 2's horse.

Sitting Pretty

In the last quarter of the 19th century, many famous romantic and sentimental paintings were produced by leading New York artists, and several unknown models found their faces becoming equally well-known when they provided inspiration for the paintings. Can you work out in which year each artist produced which painting and the name of the girl who posed for each?

Clues

1. Claude Middleton produced his painting in the 1890s, but it wasn't entitled *Eternal Hope*.

2. Morag Kennedy posed on a windy hillside for the 1884 work, which wasn't painted by Alfred Jenkins, whose work dates from later than *Queen Guinevere*.

3. Fanny March posed for *Bluebells* among a field of bluebells which was painted more than seven years earlier than Montague Hope's *Constance*.

4. Herbert Ballard didn't paint *Queen Guinevere*.

5. Rosie Tranter, who was painted perched upon a rock looking out to sea, wasn't the model for *Spring Dream*.

6. Edith Howard was painted by Angus Dunn as she sat on the banks of a tranquil lake.

Year	Artist

	Herbert Ballard	Angus Dunn	Montague Hope	Alfred Jenkins	Claude Middleton	Bluebells	Constance	Eternal Hope	Queen Guinevere	Spring Dream	Lily Gough	Edith Howard	Morag Kennedy	Fanny March	Rosie Tranter
1878															
1884															
1886															
1893															
1895															
Lily Gough															
Edith Howard															
Morag Kennedy															
Fanny March															
Rosie Tranter															
Bluebells															
Constance															
Eternal Hope															
Queen Guinevere															
Spring Dream															

Picture	Model

Carnival Crime

Five police officers each found themselves in demand on a different night of the Springfield carnival, and each made a successful arrest. Can you say on which evening each officer was in action, to what attraction in the carnival they were called, and what crime they tackled?

Clues

1. Saturday night saw one officer called to separate participants in a brawl between local feuding families; this took place after Sgt. Ningall sorted out an incident at the Big Wheel.

2. Sgt. Lowe was in action on Thursday, but not at the Ghost Train.

3. The incident at the Rifle Range, which wasn't attended by Sgt. Trunchan, took place more than a day later than the night the pickpocket was arrested by Sgt. Sorliss.

4. The arrest of a drunk did not take place on either the Ghost Train or the Bumper Cars, and none of these three incidents occurred on the last night of the carnival, which wasn't when Sgt. Collaham was on duty.

5. A successful stake out of the Fortune Teller's tent resulted in the interception of a fortune in stolen diamonds.

Evening	Police officer

	Sgt. Collaham	Sgt. Lowe	Sgt. Ningall	Sgt. Sorliss	Sgt. Trunchan	Big Wheel	Bumper Cars	Fortune Teller	Ghost Train	Rifle Range	Assault	Brawling	Drunk	Pickpocket	Stolen gems
Wednesday															
Thursday															
Friday															
Saturday															
Sunday															
Assault															
Brawling															
Drunk															
Pickpocket															
Stolen gems															
Big Wheel															
Bumper Cars															
Fortune Teller															
Ghost Train															
Rifle Range															

GHOST TRAIN

We'll scare you half to death!
Third ride free

Attraction	Crime

Local Menu

Five well-traveled friends are eating dinner and reminiscing about occasions on their adventures when bravado, curiosity, or politeness obliged them to eat a creature they wouldn't normally select from the chiller section at the supermarket. Can you work out in what year each friend visited a particular country and the creature they found on their plate or in their bowl? (Carol and Kate are women; the others are men.)

Clues

1. It was in Australia of course that one diner, who wasn't Kate, ate a witchety grub.

2. One friend tackled the snake two years after one man dined on an electric eel that had been caught (very carefully) that morning, but some time before Alex found a whole octopus lurking in his soup.

3. In 2010 one woman ate a sea urchin as part of what the chef called his "Sea Spectacular." Kate, who did not go anywhere in 2014, has never visited Japan and, listening to her dining companion who has, is now not sure she ever wants to go there.

4. Carol, who didn't eat the snake, traveled to Mauritius two years before Greg's adventure, which was earlier than someone visited China. In 2018 one of the friends had a wonderful vacation in Korea—apart, that is, from one rather exacting evening meal.

Year	Person

	Alex	Carol	Greg	Kate	Phil	Australia	China	Japan	Korea	Mauritius	Eel	Octopus	Sea urchin	Snake	Witchety grub
2010															
2012															
2014															
2016															
2018															
Eel															
Octopus															
Sea urchin															
Snake															
Witchety grub															
Australia															
China															
Japan															
Korea															
Mauritius															

Country	Creature

Pod Casting

It's the last day of term for the pupils at the Moby School of Whales and the youngsters are eager to set off on vacation with their parents. Can you name each of the whales shown here, say in which subject they excelled this term, and work out where they will be heading for their vacation? (Left and rights are from our point of view; Chic, Flick, Nic, and Vic are females, the other four are male whales.)

Clues

1. In the diagram, Moby Mick, who isn't immediately left of the whale vacationing in the ocean near California, is numbered half that of the male whale who is going to the seas off South Africa for their vacation; Moby Nic (short for Nichola), who is looking to the left in the picture, isn't heading for a vacation in the balmy waters off Costa Rica.

2. Moby Flick (Felicity to her parents) is in the back row immediately to the left of the whale who excelled at plankton identification this term; the whale who came top of the class in tail slapping will spend their vacation demonstrating that skill in the seas off Mexico; Moby Vic (or Victoria, when her parents are annoyed with her) is numbered three higher than the whale who came top in the singing class.

3. Whale number 8 in the picture is female; the whale who came top of the class in krill recognition is male and is in the other row to the whale who is heading for California first thing in the morning and who is numbered two higher than the female whale who will be going with her parents to seas off Colombia.

4. The parents of whale 2 have been planning their imminent vacation to New Zealand for a few months; those of whale 3 have been beaming with pride that their offspring has topped the class in deep diving.

5. Moby Rick is looking directly at the tail of the whale who will be visiting the Pacific Ocean around Hawaii this year, who wasn't the whale who aced the swimming course; Moby Slick is at one end of one of the rows but isn't next to the whale who topped the swimming class with their impressive dolphin kick and rather unconventional backstroke.

6. Moby Chic, short for Chiquita, has a number two times that of the whale who excelled at the rather show-offy skill of breaching; Moby Ahab (whose parents somewhat misunderstood the naming memo) is looking directly at the face of the whale whose excellent blowhole control put them at the top of that class.

Whales: Ahab; Chic; Flick; Mick; Nic; Rick; Slick; Vic

Excelled subjects: blowhole control; breaching; deep diving; krill recognition; plankton identification; singing; swimming; tail slapping

Vacation spots: Alaska; California; Colombia; Costa Rica; Hawaii; Mexico; New Zealand; South Africa

Starting tip: Work out the name of whale 6.

Lost in Translation

Since moving into a new home a few months ago, Tim has needed to assemble flat-pack furniture on a regular basis. The assembly instructions for each product had been translated into many languages, including English, from their original language but often lacked the clarity Tim would have liked. Fortunately, he has some multilingual friends on whom he could call for help. Can you work out which month he bought which product, the original language of the instructions, and the friend who helped with their translation? (NB for clarity: Beverly, Ellen and Jayne are female and Curtis and Lennie are male.)

Clues

1. The flat pack for the kitchen cart was bought in March; it isn't the item with which Lennie had lent a linguistic hand.

2. Luckily for him, Tim's girlfriend works as a French translator and was able to help him build the cocktail cabinet by reading the instructions; the cocktail cabinet wasn't bought in May.

3. Ellen's helpful translations enabled Tim to assemble the bunk beds.

4. Tim's friend Curtis, who doesn't know any German, was available when Tim needed help with assembling the product he bought in January; this wasn't the bedside cabinets, which were bought earlier in the year than the bunk beds.

5. Jayne's dad is Japanese and she grew up being able to speak and write the language.

6. In April, Tim received some assistance from a family friend, whose university degree is in Italian.

Month	Product

	Bedside cabinets	Bunk beds	Cocktail cabinet	Kitchen cart	Wardrobe	French	German	Italian	Japanese	Spanish	Beverly	Curtis	Ellen	Jayne	Lennie
January															
February															
March															
April															
May															
Beverly															
Curtis															
Ellen															
Jayne															
Lennie															
French															
German															
Italian															
Japanese															
Spanish															

Flat-pack assembly made easy

Language	Friend

Robin the Rich

Following the discovery of a medieval document the *Sunnandaeg Tidings Ryche Lyste*, it turns out that Robin Hood and his Merry Men were not as charitable as they are depicted in legend and, while robbing the rich, singularly failed to keep to the second half of that well-known epithet. Indeed, they lived out their lives in great comfort, occupying the top five positions in the wealth league. Can you discover the order that the former outlaws appear in the list, the name of the estate, and the number of acres each has bought with the accumulated plunder?

Clues

1. Robin himself is only third in the list (the full epithet should be "steal from the rich and fritter away quite a lot of it on wine, women, and song"—Lady Marion was pretty high maintenance), while the former outlaw immediately above him in the list has an estate of 700 acres.

2. Will Scarlet is in the position immediately above the occupant of Pillidge Castle; the latter is wealthier and has more land than Much the Miller's Son.

3. Little John lives in luxury in Swagley Castle, but he has fewer than 1,000 acres.

4. The owner of Boodle House is in fifth place having lost quite a lot of money digging a moat that had to be filled in again when its building permit was revoked; Boodle House is not owned by Much.

5. Friar Tuck's estate extends to 1,000 acres.

6. Looton Manor stands in 900 acres, but isn't owned by the wealthiest of the five.

Position	Outlaw

	Friar Tuck	Little John	Much the …	Robin Hood	Will Scarlet	Boodle House	Dunrobin Hall	Looton Manor	Pillidge Castle	Swagley Castle	700 acres	800 acres	900 acres	1,000 acres	1,100 acres
First															
Second															
Third															
Fourth															
Fifth															
700 acres															
800 acres															
900 acres															
1,000 acres															
1,100 acres															
Boodle House															
Dunrobin Hall															
Looton Manor															
Pillidge Castle															
Swagley Castle															

Estate	Acres

One Page

Teller.com is a website catering for, according to its home page, "creative people who have a story to tell but nowhere to tell it," and has just announced the winners of its annual one-page writing contest. Can you work out the details of the five winners—the writer's name, and the title and length of the story?

Clues

1. First prize didn't go to Cliff Parks' 500-word story; the second-place story was only 400 very carefully chosen words long.

2. *Performance*, the story of an actress' final but very short cameo role, won third prize.

3. Darren Quayle's fifth-placed story was not *Sunday Dinner*.

4. *All About Alan*—fortunately there isn't a great deal about Alan, so it all fits on one page—received the prize one place ahead of that awarded to Ann Norton's story, which is longer than *Sunday Dinner*.

5. Beth Oliver's *Museum Piece*, the story of an extraordinary (and extraordinarily brief) love, is less than 550 words long.

6. The 550-word story is *Last Resort*, a story of a forgotten beach resort town where not much happens, luckily.

Position	Writer

	Ann Norton	Beth Oliver	Cliff Parks	Darren Quayle	Edna Roberts	All About Alan	Last Resort	Museum Piece	Performance	Sunday Dinner	400 words	450 words	500 words	550 words	600 words
First															
Second															
Third															
Fourth															
Fifth															
400 words															
450 words															
500 words															
550 words															
600 words															
All About Alan															
Last Resort															
Museum Piece															
Performance															
Sunday Dinner															

Title	Length

Saintly Lessons

School inspectors are at work in five schools ensuring the quality of the education being provided, which involves sitting in on and observing certain lessons. Can you discover the name of the principal at each school being inspected and the lesson being inspected by the inspector at each school?

Clues

1. Mrs. Sterne is the inspector at Mr. Mortense's school, which is dedicated to a saint whose name begins with the letter M.

2. Mrs. Gaunt is observing a Music lesson in a school dedicated to a saint whose name is one letter shorter than that of Mrs. Fretwell's school.

3. The History lesson, which is not being observed by Mr. Checkley, is not taking place at St. Michael's.

4. The Drama lesson is being evaluated at St. Peter's, while Mr. Stark is the inspector working at St. Matthew's.

5. The English lesson is being observed in Miss Trembull's school and Mr. Edge is principal at St. Martin's.

6. St. Bernadette's is not the school being inspected by Mr. Cavill or the one where the Math lesson is being observed.

School	Principal

 USA TODAY

	Mr. Edge	Mrs. Fretwell	Mr. Mortense	Miss Pannick	Miss Trembull	Mr. Cavill	Mr. Checkley	Mrs. Gaunt	Mr. Stark	Mrs. Sterne	Drama	English	History	Math	Music
St. Bernadette's															
St. Martin's															
St. Matthew's															
St. Michael's															
St. Peter's															
Drama															
English															
History															
Math															
Music															
Mr. Cavill															
Mr. Checkley															
Mrs. Gaunt															
Mr. Stark															
Mrs. Sterne															

Inspector	Lesson

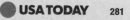

Hollywood Hats

Back in the 1930s, in Hollywood as in most places, every well-dressed man wore a hat of some kind and any screenwriter worth his or her salt would describe their leading man's headwear as an integral part of his character. The movies described were no exception. Can you work out which movie was made in which year, name its male star, and describe his headgear?

Clues

1. *She Fell for Him* was released in 1934.

2. *Coming Home* was released later than the film starring C-list actor Gene Parker and sometime before the movie whose hero always wore a trilby, even at dinner.

3. Royston Wallace, the star of many unremarkable western movies, rode into the sunset wearing the Stetson he had sported throughout the film.

4. The top hat was worn throughout the movie released in 1935.

5. The derby was worn by the hero of *What's Cooking?*, even when he was cooking.

6. Clark Maybank starred as a constantly be-hatted man in the movie *City Life*, which was released earlier than the movie in which a stylish fedora was sported by a much less stylish leading man.

7. Victor O'Sullivan's movie was released the year before *Stepping Out*.

Year	Movie

	City Life	Coming Home	She Fell for Him	Stepping Out	What's Cooking?	Clark Maybank	Gene Parker	Jefferson Rodgers	Royston Wallace	Victor O'Sullivan	Derby	Fedora	Stetson	Top hat	Trilby
1931															
1932															
1933															
1934															
1935															
Derby															
Fedora															
Stetson															
Top hat															
Trilby															
Clark Maybank															
Gene Parker															
Jefferson Rodgers															
Royston Wallace															
Victor O'Sullivan															

YES, IT'S A LOVELY TEN-GALLON HAT. BUT YOU'VE ONLY GOT A FIVE-PINT HEAD

Hero	Hat

Don and Dusted

The reality TV series *The Trainee* took five hopefuls from their everyday jobs and gave them the chance to train for a high-powered post in a large company. Their progress was monitored by well-known and outspoken business guru Donny Drump, who each week barked, "You're dumped!" to one of the candidates, eventually leaving one to take up their new lucrative position. Can you work out the age of each contestant, his or her previous background, the department of the company to which each was allocated as a trainee, and, finally, which one was successful?

Clues

1. One of the five, who was over 25, took a break from their gardening trade to become a trainee in the Human Resources department of the large company.

2. Elwyn Post was a student, but wasn't the youngest of the five.

3. The oldest candidate, who was not Hope Smee, worked as a trainee in the Marketing department.

4. Dwight Mann was the Sales trainee, but wasn't the trainee on a break from the catering job; the caterer was ejected by Donny at the end of episode 3 with the words, "You couldn't sell a carrot to a rabbit. You're dumped!" He may be a business guru, but he often has a great turn of phrase.

5. Marcus Best was neither the caterer nor the Logistics trainee, but he was sacked early on with the phrase, "You couldn't sell a parasol in a desert. You're dumped!"

6. Guy Keene, the 27-year-old, was thrown out with the phrase, "You couldn't sell a sprat to a penguin. You're dumped!"; the 28-year-old contestant went back to their personal trainer job.

Name	Age

	23	24	27	28	30	Cab driver	Caterer	Gardener	Personal trainer	Student	Accounts	HR	Logistics	Marketing	Sales
Marcus Best															
Guy Keene															
Dwight Mann															
Elwyn Post															
Hope Smee															
Accounts															
HR															
Logistics															
Marketing															
Sales															
Cab driver															
Caterer															
Gardener															
Personal trainer															
Student															

Background	Training post

Domino Search

A standard set of dominoes has been laid out, using numbers instead of dots for clarity. Using a sharp pencil and a keen brain, can you draw in the lines to show where each domino has been placed? You may find the check grid useful—crossing off each domino as you find it.

0	2	3	5	0	3	3	5
1	5	4	5	4	4	6	0
3	1	1	2	5	3	0	2
4	5	6	4	1	0	5	0
6	6	4	2	3	0	2	4
1	6	1	2	5	2	1	4
3	3	6	1	6	2	0	6

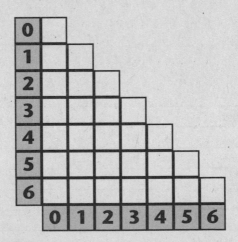

USA TODAY

Let's Face It

Artie Chuter runs a drawing class for amateur artists. This evening, he has arranged for poser Ed Moddle to visit the class to demonstrate a range of expressions for the students to capture and has given each student a set of part-empty faces for them to fill in the eyebrows, eyes, and mouths as Ed poses. Can you work out in what order Ed made his expressions and, if you're feeling artistic, draw them in?

Clues

1. Ed put on an angry face two expressions after he looked bored; he was surprised more than one expression after he looked tired and sometime before he appeared happy, which was sometime after his angry act, which wasn't his third expression.

2. Ed's puzzled face, which was in an odd-numbered position in his sequence of expressions, was immediately after he looked sad and immediately before he looked scared; Ed didn't portray sadness immediately after he did tiredness.

3. Ed neither began nor ended his range of expressions with a thoughtful face, which wasn't immediately after he looked bored and wasn't his second face.

Expressions: angry; bored; happy; puzzled; sad; scared; surprised; thoughtful; tired

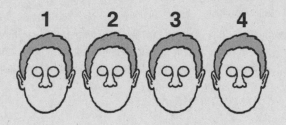

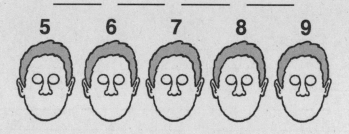

Starting tip: Work out with what expression Ed finished his demonstration.

● USA TODAY   287

The MeCam

The MeCam is the latest must-have gadget. Primed with the skills of the world's top photographers and armed with an inventory of the user's interests, it will automatically photograph anything interesting you encounter on your travels and post it to the social media account of its choice, leaving you free to concentrate on your phone, fitness tracker, and smart watch. These five women were each wandering through Central Park on the way to somewhere else. Can you work out where each woman was going, what her MeCam photographed on the way, and the website it sent the photo to?

Clues

1. The woman walking her dog had to wait for a moment while her MeCam captured an image of her dog. This was not Brenda, who was not the young woman whose MeCam took a picture of herself looking particularly lovely but did not post it to MyFace; nor was Brenda the unlucky walker who fought off a mugger while her MeCam photographed her attacker and sent the picture directly to the police.

2. Caroline is a keen ornithologist and her MeCam soon homed in on a flock of exotic birds. Ruth was on her way to the gym when her MeCam posted something to a site beginning with M, unlike the MeCam of the woman heading for the business meeting.

3. Lindsey's MeCam sent its output to MeTube. The woman looking forward to visiting the café, who was next in the alphabetical list to the one whose MeCam snapped a fine display of flowers, was later able to view her picture on SnapMe.

Woman	Destination

	Business meeting	Café	Dog walk	Gym	Work	Birds	Dog	Flowers	Herself	Mugger	MeBook	MeTube	MyFace	Police	SnapMe
Brenda															
Caroline															
Clara															
Lindsey															
Ruth															
MeBook															
MeTube															
MyFace															
Police															
SnapMe															
Birds															
Dog															
Flowers															
Herself															
Mugger															

Photograph	Website

Annie Get Your Gun

Most people know that to go with the many gunmen, famed and fabled, of the Wild West, there were a number of equally skilled women, including that most famous sharpshooter who traveled with Buffalo Bill's Wild West Show. Here we meet five others who also used their dead-shot skills in smaller, much less well-known theatrical extravaganzas. Can you work out the state in which each Annie was born and bred and the occupation she followed there before joining whose Wild West Show?

Clues

1. Annie Maplcy, the former stagecoach robber, wasn't the markswoman who joined Longhorn Luke's Wild West Show; Longhorn Luke didn't find his sharpshooter in Arizona.

2. One of the sharpshooters was earning her living as a bounty hunter in Santa Fe, New Mexico, before being lured away by one of the showmen.

3. Annie Laurely, from Colorado, was neither a cattle rustler nor a deputy sheriff.

4. The sharpshooting lady who joined Grizzly Gus' Wild West Show, wasn't Annie Limey and wasn't the former rustler or stagecoach robber.

5. One of the crack shots joined Bison Ben's Wild West Show when it traveled though her home state of Utah; Annie Alderly gave up her previous occupation to become part of Coyote Clem's Wild West Show.

6. The woman who worked as a barmaid and bouncer at the Six-Shooter Saloon joined the Wild West Show run by Moose Matt who, despite the much-heard theory, wasn't the inspiration for a computer accessory.

7. The gunwoman from Texas, who wasn't a sheriff or a bounty hunter, was neither Annie Eldery nor her fellow sharpshooter who teamed up with showman Longhorn Luke.

Name	Location

	Arizona	Colorado	New Mexico	Texas	Utah	Bounty hunter	Deputy sheriff	Rustler	Saloon worker	Stagecoach robber	Bison Ben	Coyote Clem	Grizzly Gus	Longhorn Luke	Moose Matt
Annie Alderly															
Annie Eldery															
Annie Laurely															
Annie Limey															
Annie Mapley															
Bison Ben															
Coyote Clem															
Grizzly Gus															
Longhorn Luke															
Moose Matt															
Bounty hunter															
Deputy sheriff															
Rustler															
Saloon worker															
Stagecoach robber															

Occupation	Wild West Showman

Civil Service

Not all the soldiers who fought in the American Civil War were Americans—there were, for instance, regiments of Irish troops on both sides. The men we're concerned with here were all British but joined American units. Can you work out each man's name, where he came from, which regiment he served in, and what rank he eventually attained?

Clues

1. George Holt, who joined the Texas Light Cavalry when he arrived in America in 1861, wasn't the man from Edinburgh; neither George nor the Edinburg native ended the Civil War as a Lieutenant.

2. The man from Aberdeen who joined the Louisiana Tigers, a Zouave Regiment who wore uniforms copied from those of France's celebrated Algerian troops, wasn't Alf Browder.

3. The man who joined the 2nd Mississippi Rifles didn't achieve the rank of lieutenant or major.

4. Cedric Dunn came originally from Preston, though he had traveled to many parts of the world as a British soldier before emigrating to America.

5. Isaac Jones didn't come from Scotland; Edgar Fitch never rose above the rank of Private.

6. The man from Ipswich ended his Civil War service as a sergeant, while the one who joined the 17th Georgia Infantry finished as a corporal.

Name	Hometown

	Aberdeen (Scotland)	Bedford	Edinburgh (Scotland)	Ipswich	Preston	1st Tennessee Artillery	2nd Mississippi Rifles	17th Georgia Infantry	Louisiana Tigers	Texas Light Cavalry	*In ascending order* Private	Corporal	Sergeant	Lieutenant	Major
Alf Browder															
Cedric Dunn															
Edgar Fitch															
George Holt															
Isaac Jones															
Private															
Corporal															
Sergeant															
Lieutenant															
Major															
1st Tennessee Artillery															
2nd Mississippi Rifles															
17th Georgia Infantry															
Louisiana Tigers															
Texas Light Cavalry															

In ascending order (left vertical label for ranks rows)

AFTER YOU, SIR.

NO, I INSIST. YOU ADVANCE FIRST.

The American Civil War

Regiment	Final rank

Getting the Bird

The Georgetown Bird Sanctuary had some new arrivals in the breeding season earlier this year. With the mothers fervently defending their young who are nearly old enough to leave the nests, the keepers, who have to approach the sites to check on feeding and wellbeing, run the risk of antagonizing the parents. Can you work out the number of surviving offspring each type of bird has, the name given to the mother of the brood, and the name of the keeper who has to make the daily hazardous trip to the area where the family resides?

Clues

1. There are three surviving ducklings whose mother isn't named Ivy; Lily has more than four chicks to rear and defend.

2. After sneaking in food daily for the turkeys, Dominique often has trouble trying to outrun the mother, who is sometimes joined by the other adults; the mother isn't Daisy, who has five young.

3. The mother goose, who has a bigger brood than mummy swan, is named Iris; she and her young are not attended to by Beth who, much to her relief, doesn't go anywhere near the ostriches on her rounds.

4. Harvey tries to give food to Rose and her brood every day.

5. Ernie has to tackle the mother of six, when he checks on the chicks.

6. Roxy doesn't look after the mother who has four chicks or the mother who has seven chicks.

Bird	Number

	3 chicks	4 chicks	5 chicks	6 chicks	7 chicks	Daisy	Iris	Ivy	Lily	Rose	Beth	Dominique	Ernie	Harvey	Roxy
Duck															
Goose															
Ostrich															
Swan															
Turkey															
Beth															
Dominique															
Ernie															
Harvey															
Roxy															
Daisy															
Iris															
Ivy															
Lily															
Rose															

Mother's name	Keeper's name

Sign In

Each row and column is to contain the digits 1-6. The given signs tell you if a digit in a cell is plus 1 (+) or minus 1 (-) the digit next to it. Signs between consecutive digits always work from left to right or top to bottom.
Examples: $3 + 4$ or $\frac{2}{1}$
ALL occurrences of consecutive digits have been marked by a sign.

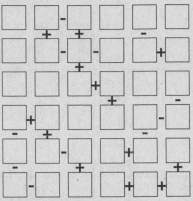

Killer Sudoku

The normal rules of Sudoku apply. In addition, the digits in each inner shape (marked by dots) must add up to the number in the top corner of that box.

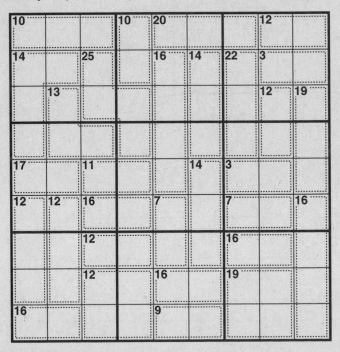

Logi-5

Each line, across and down, is to have each of the letters A, B, C, D, and E, appearing once. Also, every shape—shown by the thick lines—must also have each of the letters in it. Can you fill in the grid?

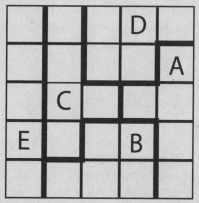

Sudoku

Complete this grid so that each column, each row, and each marked 3 X 3 square contains each of the numbers 1 to 9.

					2		9	
		5				1		
4		8	9				7	5
						6		
7	6	4	8		9	3	2	1
	8							
9	4				1	7		2
		3				4		
		1		2				

Not So Fast Food

At the Turn Turtle Eatery, six tortoises are standing in line. They have each ordered a cricket and mealworm pizza but are lining up to choose their favorite side salad. Can you name each tortoise and say on what leafy item his or her side dish will be based?

Clues

1. Shelbourne is waiting immediately behind Michelle and immediately ahead of the tortoise who will base their salad on lettuce leaves.

2. In the line, Shelley is waiting immediately between Shelford, who isn't first in the line, and the tortoise who prefers red chard for their side salad, who isn't last in line; Hershel is somewhere behind the tortoise who likes dandelion salad and somewhere ahead of the one who chooses kale salad.

3. The tortoise who will make their salad from baby spinach leaves is standing immediately ahead of Sheldon, and immediately behind the one who likes watercress salad with their pizza; Sheldon is somewhere behind Hershel.

Names: Hershel; Michelle; Shelbourne; Sheldon; Shelford; Shelley
Leaves: dandelion; kale; lettuce; red chard; spinach; watercress

1st   2nd   3rd

4th   5th   6th

Starting tip: Work out who is at the head of the line.

Domino Search

A standard set of dominoes has been laid out, using numbers instead of dots for clarity. Using a sharp pencil and a keen brain, can you draw in the lines to show where each domino has been placed? You may find the check grid useful—crossing off each domino as you find it.

0	1	0	5	1	1	3	0
2	3	6	2	1	3	2	4
5	4	4	6	3	4	2	6
6	6	1	4	5	0	2	3
2	0	2	0	0	5	4	5
4	5	5	2	5	1	3	1
1	4	6	6	0	3	3	6

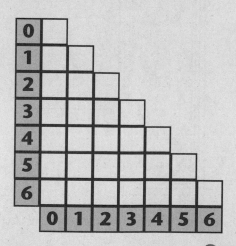

Lift Off

Five shoppers, one on each floor and each going to a different floor, have simultaneously pressed the buttons for the elevator in Fairview Mall and the elevator is hovering between floors while its software tries to make up its mind what to do. Can you find out which facility is on each floor, the name of the would-be passenger waiting there, and which floor they intend to go to if the elevator ever arrives? (NB: Ena and Sushila are women; the others are men.)

Clues

1. One man is headed for the basement parking garage. A woman is pressing the up button in search of the bathrooms.

2. Sushila is on the second floor. Zbigniew is hoping to visit the cafe, which is more than one floor above him.

3. Ena is on the floor above Ali, who is heading for the ground floor, and the floor below the movie theater.

Facilities: cafe; parking garage; movie theater; news stand; bathrooms
Passengers: Ali; Ena; Rennie; Sushila; Zbigniew
Destinations: basement; ground floor; first floor; second floor; third floor

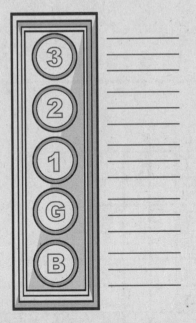

Starting tip: Pinpoint the passenger for the car park.

Audition

The Arlington Amateur Acting Association will be staging a performance of a new play, *An Afternoon Among an Artist, an Author, an Architect, and an Auctioneer,* and director Ava Angarde has four performers in mind for the title roles. She gathered them together and asked them to read the various roles, each person reading each role. Can you work out in which chair each auditioner sat and in what order each read the four roles? (Lefts and rights are from our point of view.)

Clues

1. The artist was the third part read by Alexis, who was next left to the person who read the role of the auctioneer first; the player in seat C read the role of the author next after Angel.

2. Ariel's first part, which was not the artist, was Angel's last and Ariel's second part was Angel's third.

3. The performer who read the role of the artist last was next left to Ashley; Ariel did not read the role of the author second.

4. The performer at D read the auctioneer's words later than they read those of the author but earlier than Alexis auditioned for the author.

Players: Alexis; Angel; Ariel; Ashley
Parts: Architect; Artist; Auctioneer; Author

Starting tip: Decide which part Alexis read last and then in what order they read the architect.

Use By

Patsy had just taken over a small convenience store in Chester and having had no previous retail experience, was finding it a little hard to remember all the things that needed doing, such as checking the use-by dates on perishable products. When these were brought to her attention by shoppers, she was both apologetic and generous in offering them something a little extra for their trouble. Can you work out which shopper discovered which item and how many days it was beyond its use-by date and the something extra that was offered?

Clues

1. Ms. Timms picked up a carton of cream which was more than four days past its use-by date.

2. Mr. Short was offered a fresh replacement for the product he wanted free of charge; he wasn't the shopper who wanted a pizza and found one that was six days past its use-by date at the back of one of the shelves.

3. Mr. Jennings, who didn't come away with a $3 credit coupon, came across an item, which wasn't the orange juice or veggie burger, that was eight days past its use-by date.

4. The shopper who noticed an item in their basket that was five days past its use-by date, was given a $2 credit coupon.

5. The customer who spotted a carton of orange juice on the shelf that was more than 2 days older than it should have been, who wasn't Ms. Hayward, was offered a fresh carton of orange juice at half price.

Shopper	Product

	Cream	Orange juice	Pizza	Salmon	Veggie burgers	2 days	4 days	5 days	6 days	8 days	Free other product	Replacement free	Reduced price	$2 credit coupon	$3 credit coupon
Ms. Hayward															
Mr. Jennings															
Ms. Matthews															
Mr. Short															
Ms. Timms															
Free other product															
Replacement free															
Reduced price															
$2 credit coupon															
$3 credit coupon															
2 days															
4 days															
5 days															
6 days															
8 days															

THEY'RE NO GOOD FOR US. WE HAVE TO WAIT UNTIL THEY'RE PAST THEIR SELL-BY DATE.

Days	Extra

Blooming Failures

Stuck at home this summer with a lingering chest infection, Keith has found himself agreeing to look after some plants belonging to his more globetrotting neighbors. Little did they know that Keith's fingers are not the greenest of the green and it wasn't too long before the blooms involved met an unfortunate demise despite, or maybe because of, his best attentions. Can you work out to which vacation destination each pair of his neighbors went, what type of plant they entrusted to Keith's care, and for how long it managed to survive?

Clues

1. Sadie and Tim had entrusted Keith with their prize aspidistra; they hadn't jetted off to Rio, which was the destination of the couple whose plant lasted half as long before expiring as did the one belonging to Martin and Paula.

2. The specimen belonging to the pair on a trip to Phuket in Thailand, who hadn't left a clematis in Keith's care, clung on to life for longer than that of the couple who were visiting Florida.

3. Deirdre and James were on the vacation of a lifetime cruising to Madeira.

4. Experts say that it's impossible to kill a spider plant. Keith managed it in just six days.

5. The horticultural pride and joy of Georgie and Mike resisted Keith's attentions for a whole 12 days; this wasn't the herb garden previously tended lovingly by the couple who had jetted off to Cape Town.

Neighbors	Destination

	Cape Town	Florida	Madeira	Phuket	Rio	Aspidistra	Clematis	Herb garden	Peace lily	Spider plant	5 days	6 days	8 days	10 days	12 days
Brian and Jackie															
Deirdre and James															
Georgie and Mike															
Martin and Paula															
Sadie and Tim															
5 days															
6 days															
8 days															
10 days															
12 days															
Aspidistra															
Clematis															
Herb garden															
Peace lily															
Spider plant															

FEED, ANYONE?

JUST CARBON DIOXIDE AND SUNLIGHT FOR ME. I'M ON A DIET.

Plant	Days

Household Gods

Recently, the chatter on our neighborhood internet forum turned to the subject of cats and we were surprised to discover that no fewer than five of the moggies in Olympus Street were named after luminaries of ancient Greek mythology. Can you work out which cat owner lives in each numbered house, the name of their pet, and its color? (Abel and Max are the only male owners and, as is usual in street numbering, No.22 is next door to No.24 and No.49 is next door to No.51.)

Clues

1. Apollo was named after the sun god because his coat is so ginger it's almost gold.

2. Leila, who lives next door to the owner of the white cat, has named her cat Hecate, so when she calls it people think she is saying, "Hey, kitty," and not invoking the spirit of witchcraft, oh no.

3. Mnemosyne at No.51 has recently produced a large litter of kittens, which her lady owner describes as the Nine Mewses; Heather lives at 24 Olympus Street.

4. The tabby lives at a lower number than the black cat and Max's pet lives at a higher number than Phoebe. Abel's gray cat exhibits no signs of wisdom, so it is not the cat amed Athena, who lives at a lower number.

House	Owner

	Abel	Heather	Leila	Lindsey	Max	Apollo	Athena	Hecate	Mnemosyne	Phoebe	Black	Ginger	Gray	Tabby	White
No.22															
No.24															
No.33															
No.49															
No.51															
Black															
Ginger															
Gray															
Tabby															
White															
Apollo															
Athena															
Hecate															
Mnemosyne															
Phoebe															

NOT AGAIN! COULDN'T WE JUST ONCE HAVE A BURGER AND A BEER?

MT. OLYMPUS CAFE

TODAY'S Special Ambrosia & Nectar

Cat name	Color

Phylum Feast

February 12 is Darwin Day and Evolution Revolution, one of Charles Darwin's many fan clubs, is celebrating in a traditional manner with a meal containing foods sourced from as many animal and vegetable families as possible. After the first course of Primordial Soup, served with bread made from wheat (*Streptophyta*) and yeast (*Saccharomycetales*), a selection of foods is laid out. Can you work out which food is in each numbered dish and how each was cooked? (NB: dish 1 is opposite dish 5, dish 2 opposite dish 6 and so on.)

Clues

1. The plain yogurt was served in a dish opposite the stewed food and numbered twice that of the scallops, which were not fried.

2. Dish 4 contained chicken but dish 8 was not composed of tuna. Dish 5 was boiled.

3. The prawns were next clockwise of the steamed dish and next anticlockwise of the pork which was opposite the snails.

4. The mushrooms were in a dish numbered half that of the baked food and one higher than the roast.

Cooking methods: baked; boiled; broiled; fried; plain; roast; steamed; stewed

Dishes: chicken (*Aves*); mushrooms (*Fungi*); pork (*Mammalia*); prawns (*Malacostraca*); scallops (*Bivalvia*); snails (*Gastropoda*); tuna (*Teleostomi*); yogurt (*Bacteria*)

Starting tip: Find the food in dish 8.

Logi-5

Each line, across and down, is to have each of the letters A, B, C, D, and E, appearing once. Also, every shape—shown by the thick lines—must also have each of the letters in it. Can you fill in the grid?

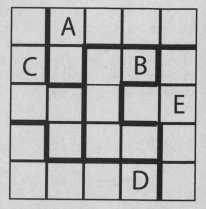

Killer Sudoku

The normal rules of Sudoku apply. In addition, the digits in each inner shape (marked by dots) must add up to the number in the top corner of that box.

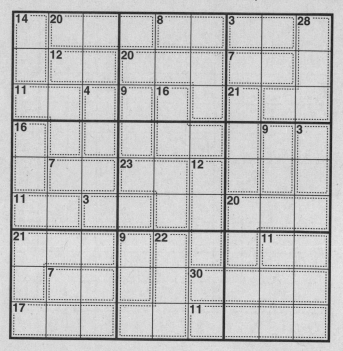

Battleships

Do you remember the old game of battleships? These puzzles are based on that idea. Your task is to find the vessels in the diagram. Some parts of boats or sea squares have already been filled in, and a number next to a row or column refers to the number of occupied squares in that row or column. The boats may be positioned horizontally or vertically, but no two boats or parts of boats are in adjacent squares—horizontally, vertically, or diagonally.

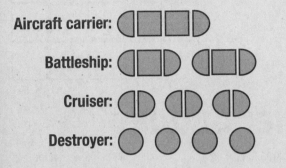

Aircraft carrier:

Battleship:

Cruiser:

Destroyer:

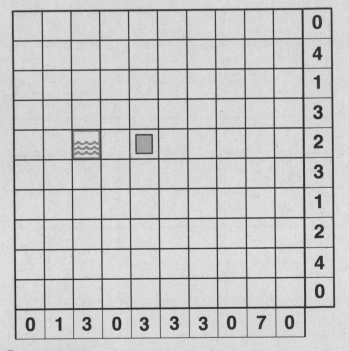

										0
										4
										1
										3
		≈		▪						2
										3
										1
										2
										4
										0
0	1	3	0	3	3	3	0	7	0	

USA TODAY

Pulling Strings

One of the attractions at the Greenville Spring Fair is the stand at which people pay their money to pull a string, which may or may not have a prize attached. At present there are six prizes attached to nine strings (the person running the stand regularly changes everything). Can you work out which prize is attached to each string?

Clues

1. One string in each row does not lead to a prize.

2. The string leading to the bottle of wine is immediately right of the one attached to the pen and is numbered three times that which ends in the charming floral scarf.

3. One of the unattached strings is directly below the one leading to the bottle of perfume and directly above the one attached to the packet of candies and another is immediately right of the one tied to the jar of coffee.

Prizes: coffee; pen; perfume; scarf; candies; wine

Starting tip: Find the strings attached to the candies and perfume.

Unboxing Days

Young Hugh Tube is an internet hit unpacking toys in front of a video camera, for which he gets gifted with a constant stream of free toys from companies keen to cash in on his unflagging enthusiasm. Last month, Hugh opened five surprise packages. Can you unpack the name of the toy in each box, its nature, and Hugh's comment?

Clues

1. "Wow wow wow!" said Hugh when he unwrapped his parcel in front of the camera on the 27th. The thing inside was not the squishy blob which elicited the comment, "Ha ha ha!"

2. Polly is a plastic parrot with movable wings and a set of small accessories including a tiny model pirate to attach to its shoulder. Hugh unpacked it the day before he opened the box containing Molly and the day after he unpacked the tiny cuddly cow.

3. "I love it!" Hugh said to camera the day after he opened the parcel containing Dolly and the day before the bouncing rubber baby, which was not in the last parcel to be unwrapped, was the star of the show.

4. On the 31st, Hugh unpacked Jolly. This was not the fairy doll whose box unfolded into a sparkly castle, which arrived the day before the package whose contents Hugh described as, "Super cute!"

Names: Dolly; Jolly; Lolly; Molly; Polly
Toys: baby; cow; fairy; parrot; squishy blob
Comments: Adorable!; Ha ha ha!; I love it!; Super cute!; Wow wow wow!

| 27th | 28th | 29th | 30th | 31st |

Starting tip: Work out the nature of Jolly.

InnFluencers

These four erstwhile bar workers have capitalized on their experience by setting up internet sites that have been so successful at attracting interest and advertising revenue that they have been able to buy their own drinking establishment. Can you work out the name of their website, the area in which they specialize, and the name of their bar?

Clues

1. BeerGoggles is the site that furnishes disquisitions on the arcane and often obscene semiology of the symbols on bottle caps. Its owner is separated in the illustration from the proprietor of the Top Hat, who isn't Millie, by the person who specializes in organizing drinking parties in breweries. The brewery party organizer isn't the owner of the Nightcrawler, who runs a site called BarBarian but does not carry out wine tastings by knocking back an entire bottle.

2. Billie's pub is called the Horse and Bucket. Jilly's site is called PubLicity. Lily's modus operandi does not involve mixing random cocktails from whatever is at hand.

Sites: BarBarian; BeerGoggles; InnOvations; PubLicity
USPs: bottle caps; cocktails; parties in breweries; wine tasting
Bar: Green Monkey; Horse and Bucket; Nightcrawler; Top Hat

Billie	Jilly	Lily	Millie

Starting tip: Work out BarBarian's stock in trade.

Battleships

Do you remember the old game of battleships? These puzzles are based on that idea. Your task is to find the vessels in the diagram. Some parts of boats or sea squares have already been filled in, and a number next to a row or column refers to the number of occupied squares in that row or column. The boats may be positioned horizontally or vertically, but no two boats or parts of boats are in adjacent squares—horizontally, vertically, or diagonally.

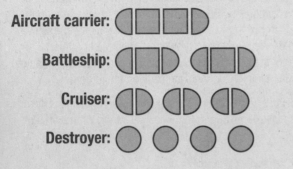

Aircraft carrier:

Battleship:

Cruiser:

Destroyer:

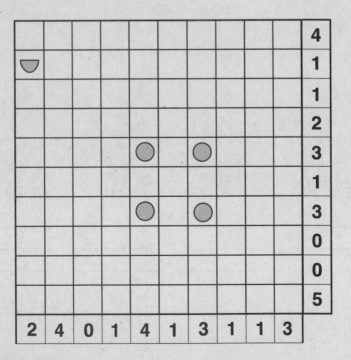

Domino Search

A standard set of dominoes has been laid out, using numbers instead of dots for clarity. Using a sharp pencil and a keen brain, can you draw in the lines to show where each domino has been placed? You may find the check grid useful—crossing off each domino as you find it.

4	6	5	6	4	0	1	1
1	5	5	5	4	6	2	0
3	1	2	0	5	1	2	3
2	1	4	6	6	0	0	4
0	3	5	3	4	1	6	1
4	5	2	2	4	3	3	5
3	6	0	3	0	2	6	2

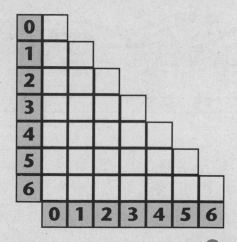

Festival Bands

Sue Perfan is a devotee of music in all genres and likes nothing better than spending a wet weekend in a leaky tent to appreciate it to the fullest. She attended eight festivals last year and has a fine collection of wristbands to prove it. Can you work out which style of music she enjoyed in each month and the color of the wristband which commemorates it?

Clues

1. Sue's band from the reggae festival was acquired the month after she spent a weekend grooving to rock music and the month before she obtained the purple band.

2. In August Sue enjoyed a weekend of heavy rain and light opera but did not wear a red band. The blues festival wristband was appropriately blue.

3. The jazz festival was some time after the world music festival and some time before Sue acquired the black band. All three were in the first half of the year.

4. The pop festival was two months after the event commemorated by the black wristband and two months before the folk festival. The September band was white and the yellow band was acquired a month after the pink one.

Music: blues; folk; jazz; opera; pop; reggae; rock; world
Colors: black; blue; gold; pink; purple; red; white; yellow

MAR   APR   MAY   JUN   JUL   AUG   SEP   OCT

___ ___ ___ ___ ___ ___ ___ ___
___ ___ ___ ___ ___ ___ ___ ___

Starting tip: Work out in which month Sue acquired the black band.

USA TODAY

Logi-5

Each line, across and down, is to have each of the letters A, B, C, D, and E, appearing once. Also, every shape—shown by the thick lines—must also have each of the letters in it. Can you fill in the grid?

A				
	C		E	
		B	D

Sudoku

Complete this grid so that each column, each row, and each marked 3 X 3 square contains each of the numbers 1 to 9.

				9			5
					8	7	
	6		5	7	2	3	
3	5	9			4			2
8			6			9	3	1
		7	2	9	3		8	
	4	3					
9			7				

Domino Search

A standard set of dominoes has been laid out, using numbers instead of dots for clarity. Using a sharp pencil and a keen brain, can you draw in the lines to show where each domino has been placed? You may find the check grid useful—crossing off each domino as you find it.

3	1	4	1	3	6	1	3
5	1	4	0	4	2	2	5
6	6	5	5	1	1	2	5
6	3	4	6	0	6	0	3
0	6	4	5	0	2	3	0
1	0	3	3	0	5	4	1
2	4	2	5	2	6	4	2

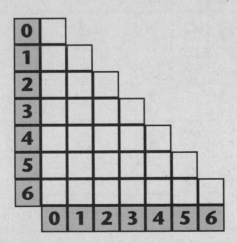

Answers

Battleships, p. 1

When in Rome, p. 2

Junius Marinus from Camulodunum isn't the senior centurion or the junior centurion (clue 1), the wine merchant, who is Decimus Arbanus (clue 5), or the administrator, who lives in Glevum (clue 6), so must be the servant dealer. Decimus Arbanus' companion is male (clue 4). He isn't the gladiator, who's traveling with Servius Valusius (clue 4), or the son of the man from Segedunum, who is a centurion (clue 2), so must be Decimus Arbanus' brother. Decimus Arbanus is not from Mamucium (clue 5), so must be from Londinium. Flavius Emilius isn't traveling with his daughter or his mother (clue 4), so must be traveling with his son and therefore comes from Segedunum. We know he is either the senior centurion or the junior centurion, but from clue 3 he's not the junior, so he must be the senior centurion. The administrator from

Glevum has a female companion (clue 6), so Servius Valusius, who's traveling with the gladiator (defined as male in clue 4), must be from Mamucium, and he must be the junior centurion. Junius Marinus, the servant dealer from Camulodunum, isn't traveling with his daughter (clue 1), so his companion must be his mother, and the man traveling with his daughter must be Publius Scaevolus, the administrator from Glevum.

Decimus Arbanus, wine merchant, Londinium, brother.
Flavius Emilius, senior centurion, Segedunum, son.
Junius Marinus, servant dealer, Camulodunum, mother.
Publius Scaevolus, administrator, Glevum, daughter.
Servius Valusius, junior centurion, Mamucium, gladiator.

Unwanted Job, p. 4

The person who stayed for 3 weeks had an encounter with Mrs. Kay (clue 1), and Miss Harringay upset Fay (clue 2), so Dan, who persevered for 5 weeks but who didn't deal with Mr. Stevens or Mr. Wilkes (clue 3), must have crossed swords with Mr. Miles, and so must have been offered extra holidays (clue 5). Bev was offered shopping vouchers (clue 1), so the bonus pay, which was promised to the person who stayed in the role for only two weeks who wasn't Hal or Joy (clue 4), must have been Fay. The employee who tried the job for three weeks wasn't Bev (clue

1) or Joy (clue 4), and so must have been Hal. The person who stayed for four weeks wasn't incentivized with a gym membership or medical insurance, so must have been Bev with her offer of vouchers, leaving Joy lasting six weeks in the job. So she wasn't incentivized with medical insurance (clue 6) and must have had the free gym membership, leaving Hal with the medical insurance. Finally, from clue 6, Joy didn't have a particularly unpleasant conversation with Mr. Wilkes and must have left after six weeks following an encounter with Mr. Stevens, leaving the last straw for Bev as a conversation with Mr. Wilkes.

Bev, shopping vouchers, four weeks, Mr. Wilkes.

Dan, extra holidays, five weeks, Mr. Miles.

Fay, bonus pay, two weeks, Miss Harringay.

Hal, medical insurance, three weeks, Mrs. Kay.

Joy, gym membership, six weeks, Mr. Stevens.

The Specialists, p. 6

The pediatric specialist from Seoul must have been at Harmony House (HH) for 2 years or 4 years (clue 1), but the doctor who's been there for 2 years was born in Madrid (clue 4), so the one from Seoul must have been there for 4 years and, from clue 1, Dr. Taverner must have been at HH for 2 years and was therefore born in Madrid, and Dr. Jackson, the sports medicine specialist (clue 2), must have been at HH for 1 year. He wasn't born in Madrid, Seoul, Singapore, which is the home of a doctor who had been at HH longer than the one from Port Antonio (clue 3), or Port Antonio itself, which is Dr. Drake's home (clue 5), so he must come from Omagh. The doctor from Singapore has been at HH longer than Dr. Drake from Port Antonio (clue 3), so the former must have been there for 5 years and

the latter for 3 years. The pediatrics specialist isn't Dr. Lee (clue 1), so must be Dr. Park, and Dr. Lee must have been born in Singapore. The alternative medicine specialist isn't from Madrid or Singapore (clue 4), so must be Dr. Drake from Port Antonio, The diabetes specialist has been at HH longer than the geriatrics specialist (clue 6), the former must be Dr. Lee, with 5 years' service, and the latter Dr. Taverner, with 2 years.

Dr. Drake, Port Antonio, alternative medicine, 3 years.

Dr. Jackson, Omagh, sports medicine, 1 year.

Dr. Lee, Singapore, diabetes, 5 years.

Dr. Park, Seoul, pediatrics, 4 years.

Dr. Taverner, Madrid, geriatrics, 2 years.

Room Service, p. 8

Lurimeg has been assigned cabin 5 (clue 7), so, from clue 1, the methane atmosphere can't be needed for cabin 1, 4, or 5. Cabin 3 has the water vapor removed (clue 5), so the methane atmosphere must be for cabin 2. So, from clue 1, Bodi-Nadi must have cabin 3 with no water vapor and cabin 1 must be the Pimtrian's. Sinuwei hasn't been assigned cabins 1 or 4 (clue 3), so must have cabin 2, with the methane atmosphere. So, from clue 3, cabin 1, the Pimtrian's, has the sub-zero temperature. The Pimtrian isn't Y'Alidan (clue 4), so must be Hravpak, leaving Y'Alidan with cabin 4. That cabin isn't being provided with low gravity (clue 4), so must require total darkness, and Y'Alidan is Gunitrian (clue 2). By elimination, cabin 5, Lurimeg's, has low gravity. From his cabin number, Lurimeg can't be Ordolase or Dravian, so he must be Jirrizic. Clue 6 now tells us the Ordolase is Sinuwei in cabin 2, and Bodi-Nadi in cabin 3 is Dravian.

Cabin 1, Hravpak, Pimtrian, sub-zero temperature.

Cabin 2, Sinuwei, Ordolase, methane atmosphere.

Cabin 3, Bodi-Nadi, Dravian, no water vapor.

Cabin 4, Y'Alidan, Gunitrian, total darkness.

Cabin 5, Lurimeg, Jirrizic, low gravity.

Playing for Courage, p. 10

Sir Spyneless engaged the Tuesday minstrel (clue 4) and the viol was played on Saturday evenings (clue 3). Clue 6 rules out Monday or Thursday as the evening the harp was played for Sir Coward, so that must have been on Friday night and, from clue 6, Madoc must have been the Thursday performer. We now know Blodwen did not play her dulcimer (clue 1) on Thursday, Friday, or Saturday, and clue 1 also rules out Monday, so she must have performed for Sir Spyneless on Tuesday. So, from clue 1, Sir Poltroon's music night must have been on Monday. We have now matched four evenings with a knight or a minstrel, so Idris, who was hired by Sir Sorely (clue 5), must have played on Saturday, and so played the viol. Madoc's Thursday instrument was not the lute (clue 2), so it must have been the lyre, and he must have played for Sir Timid. By elimination, the lute must have been played for Sir Poltroon on Monday. Aled did not play for Sir Coward on Friday (clue 2), so he must have played the lute for Sir Poltroon on Monday, leaving the Friday harpist as Myfanwy.

Sir Coward de Custarde, Myfanwy, Friday, harp.

Sir Poltroon à Ghaste, Aled, Monday, lute.

Sir Sorely à Frayde, Idris, Saturday, viol.

Sir Spyneless de Feete, Blodwen, Tuesday, dulcimer.

Sir Timid de Shayke, Madoc, Thursday, lyre.

Barbies and Kens, p. 12

The Ken who bought an Everage's "Deep Char" barbie lives in an even-numbered house (clue 5), but not at no. 2, where the Self-Basting model was bought (clue 6), or 8, whose Ken bought the Foster's machine (clue 3), so he must live at no.4. The Ken at no.8 didn't get the Acu-Timer (clue 1) or the Solar Flare machine at an odd-numbered house (clue 3), so he must have bought the Foster's Auto-Turn BBQ and is therefore Ken Singh-Tungor (clue 2). Since the Ken at no.2 bought the Self- Baster, Ken de la Bras can't live at no.4 and must have an odd-numbered house (clue 1 and intro). So, from clue 1, the Dundee's model must have been the choice of the resident at no.2. Ken Tuckey chose the Swagman's machine (clue 4), so must also live at an odd-number and so the Ken living at no. 2, who isn't Ken Airey (clue 6), must be Ken Aloney, leaving the last remaining even-numbered resident as Ken Airey at no. 4. Ken de la Bras didn't buy the Acu-Timer (clue 1), so must have bought the Solar Flare made by Kelly's. So the Acu-Timer must have been Ken Tuckey's purchase from Swagman's and, from clue 1, we can tell finally that Ken Tuckey lives at no.5, with Ken de la Bras in the next house higher at number 7.

Ken Airey, No.4, Everage's, Deep Char.

Ken Aloney, No.2, Dundee's, Self-Basting.

Ken de la Bras, No.7, Kelly's, Solar Flare.

Ken Singh-Tungor, No.8, Foster's, Auto-Turn.

Ken Tuckey, No.5, Swagman's, Acu-Timer.

Logi-5, p. 14

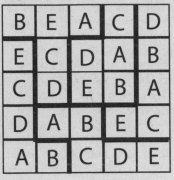

B	E	A	C	D
E	C	D	A	B
C	D	E	B	A
D	A	B	E	C
A	B	C	D	E

Battleships, p. 15

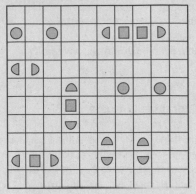

Killer Sudoku, p. 14

4	8	2	7	9	3	1	6	5
5	7	1	4	6	2	9	3	8
9	3	6	1	5	8	7	2	4
3	4	5	8	1	9	2	7	6
7	6	8	2	3	5	4	1	9
2	1	9	6	4	7	8	5	3
6	2	4	3	8	1	5	9	7
8	5	7	9	2	6	3	4	1
1	9	3	5	7	4	6	8	2

Forum Fashion, p. 16

Cluelus' shopper only spent 100 sesterces (clue 1) and Gormlus was following Cailia (clue 2), so the servant trying to keep up with Cimmia as she spent 300 sesterces, who wasn't Hopelus (clue 4) or Branelus (clue 3), must have been Euselus. Cimmia didn't buy the sandals that Hopelus' shopper snapped up (clue 4) or the 250 sesterces dress (clue 2). Nor was it the handbag, or the belt bought by Cloia (clue 5), so Cimmia must have fancied a fur coat (from the new Fendae range). The 250 sesterces dress wasn't the choice of the lady with Gormlus (clue 2), so the dress must have been bought by the lady with Branelus. This wasn't Cortnia (clue 3) or Cloia, who bought the belt (clue 5), so it must have been Cennia. Cailia, with Gormlus in tow, didn't buy the belt or the sandals, so her purchase was the handbag, leaving the 100 sesterces spent by the girl with Cluelus as the price of the belt bought by Cloia and Cortnia as the purchaser of the sandals with Hopelus. These didn't cost her 200 sesterces (clue 3), so she must have paid 150, leaving Gormlus looking embarrassed carrying the 200 sesterces handbag for Cailia.

**Branelus, Cennia, dress, 250 sesterces.
Cluelus, Cloia, belt, 100 sesterces.**

Euselus, Cimmia, fur jacket, 300
  sesterces.
Gormlus, Cailia, handbag, 200 sesterces.
Hopelus, Cortnia, sandals, 150 sesterces.

Animal Magnetism, p. 18

Crabtree Farm was visited on Monday (clue
1) and the sheep was treated on Wednesday
(clue 6), so clue 4 rules out Monday, Tuesday,
Wednesday, and Friday for the visit to treat
the sheepdog, which must have fallen ill on
Thursday. So, from clue 4, the sick sheep
must have been at Angleton Farm, and the
visit to Mirfield must have been on Friday. We
have now matched three days with a farm or
a patient, so the pig at Rockerby Farm, which
did not receive the Tuesday visit (clue 5),
must have been Jane's Friday patient, and so
belongs to Farmer Mirfield. Farmer Olroyd's
carthorse was not treated on Monday (clue 2),
so it must have been the Tuesday patient. So,
from clue 2, the cow was treated at Crabtree
Farm on Monday. Farmer Olroyd's farm,
visited on Tuesday, is not Willoughby (clue
2), so it must be Melrose, leaving Willoughby
Farm as the one visited on Thursday. From
clue 3, Farmer Carrick's farm must have
been visited on Wednesday and Farmer
Burtenshaw's on Thursday, leaving the owner
of Crabtree Farm, visited on Monday, as
Farmer Hirst.
Monday, Crabtree Farm, Hirst, cow.
Tuesday, Melrose Farm, Olroyd, carthorse.
Wednesday, Angleton Farm, Carrick,
  sheep.
Thursday, Willoughby Farm, Burtenshaw,
  sheepdog.
Friday, Rockerby Farm, Mirfield, pig.

Friends of Friends, p. 20

Norma patronized the Friends of Kirkdale
Market (clue 2) and Mandy bought a potted
plant (clue 3), so the person who bought a
book from the Friends of St. Bernard's Home
for Lost Dogs, who was not Liam (clue 1) or
Oliver (clue 4), must have been Paul. Norma
didn't buy the painting or the jam (clue 2), so
must have bought the mug. The friend who
bought the jam also won the chocolates (clue
2), so Liam, who won the haircut (clue 1),
must have bought the painting, leaving Oliver
as the buyer of the jam and the winner of the
chocolates. Liam didn't buy the painting from
Friends of Willow Park (clue 1) or Friends of
St. Barnabas Church (clue 2), so must have
patronized Friends of Fernwick Forest. Nor did
Mandy buy from Friends of Willow Park (clue
3), so Oliver must have bought the jam there,
leaving Mandy buying her plant from Friends
of St. Barnabas Church. The wine was not
won by the patrons of either of the "saints"
(clue 4), so must have been Norma's prize.
Finally, Mandy didn't win the teddy bear (clue
3), so must have won the perfume, leaving
Paul winning the teddy.
Liam, Friends of Fernwick Forest,
  painting, haircut.
Mandy, Friends of St. Barnabas Church,
  plant, perfume.
Norma, Friends of Kirkdale Market, mug,
  wine.
Oliver, Friends of Willow Park, jam,
  chocolates.
Paul, Friends of St. Bernard's Home for
  Lost Dogs, book, teddy.

Extra Time, p. 22

John Green is going to Stage 1 (clue 4), Peter
Smith is in *Judgment* (clue 2), and clues 1
and 6 confirm Linda and Susan as female,
so the man who's appearing in *Sparks*
in medieval costume on a sound stage
numbered two higher than the one where

Susan West's going (clue 6) must be Alan Brown. *Sparks* isn't being made on Stage 5, where *Close Friends* is shooting (clue 3), so, from clue 6, it must be on either Stage 3 or Stage 4. We know Susan West is not going to Stage 1, so *Sparks* must be shooting on Stage 4 and Susan West must be going to Stage 2. We now know that the extra who's to be in *Close Friends* on Stage 5 isn't Alan Brown, John Green, Peter Smith, or Susan West, so she must be Linda Jones, who'll be wearing motorcycle leathers (clue 1), and Peter Smith must be going to Stage 3. We know which movies for three of the extras, so John Green, who's not going to be in *Like a King* (clue 4), is going to be in *I Confess* and Susan West will be in *Like a King* on Stage 2. She won't be wearing overalls (clue 4) or Regency costume (clue 5), so must be dressed for the beach. Also from clue 5, John Green's movie is not the Regency drama, so Peter Smith must be in the Regency costume, leaving John Green in overalls.

Alan Brown, doublet and hose, Stage 4, *Sparks*.

John Green, overalls, Stage 1, *I Confess*.

Linda Jones, motorcycle leathers, Stage 5, *Close Friends*.

Peter Smith, Regency costume, Stage 3, *Judgment*.

Susan West, beach clothes, Stage 2, *Like a King*.

Early Profits, p. 24

The time between the purchase of the shares in Albion Group and BBF was 10 minutes (clue 4), so the first was not made at 9:00 and, since the Euro-Amalgamated shares were acquired at 9:30 (clue 1), it was not 9:20. So the Albion shares must have been bought at 9:50 for $11 each (clue 5) and the BBF shares at 10:00. From clue 3, Gordon must have bought 600 BBF shares. We know that the AD&G shares were not purchased

at 9:30, 9:50, or 10:00, nor was it 9:00 (clue 2), so it must have been 9:20 and they cost $12.60 each (clue 2), leaving the Imperial Holdings bought at 9:00. The 400 shares cost $7.30 per share (clue 6), so the even number of hundreds of AD&G shares bought at $12.60 (clue 2) must have been 200. The 600 shares purchased at 10:00 were not priced at $4 (clue 3), so they must have been $14.20. The Imperial Holdings shares were more expensive than those in Euro-Amalgamated (clue 1), so the former must have been the 400 at $7.30, leaving those in Euro Amalgamated priced at $4 each. From clue 1, Gordon must have bought 500 of them (clue 1). By elimination, the number of Albion shares bought at $11 must have been 300.

9:00, Imperial Holdings, $7.30, 400 shares.
9:20, AD&G, $12.60, 200 shares.
9:30, Euro-Amalgamated, $4, 500 shares.
9:50, Albion Group, $11, 300 shares.
10:00, BBF, $14.20, 600 shares.

Flower Rearrangement, p. 26

The boss was sent the message "Love from Flopsy Bunny" (clue 2) and Chris Anthemum sent something to his girlfriend (clue 1), so the message "You're passed it" from Rhoda Dendran, which wasn't received by a fellow worker (clue 3) or her aunt (clue 4), must have gone to her brother. So the message didn't accompany the wedding bouquet (clue 6). The cheese-plant came with the "Made me think of you" card (clue 1), Daisy Cheyne's recipient got the red rose (clue 5), and the memorial wreath went to the aunt (clue 4); so Rhoda's brother must have received the Bonsai tree. The aunt's wreath wasn't from William Sweet (clue 4), so must have been from busy Lizzie Potts. Its accompanying message wasn't "Deepest sympathy" (clue 4), so must have read "Saying it with flowers." The "Made me think of you" message and the cheese-plant didn't go to Chris' girlfriend (clue 1), so must have been the fellow worker's gift which, by elimination, must have come from William Sweet, leaving Daisy's red rose going to her boss with the "Love from Flopsy Bunny" card and Chris Anthemum's girlfriend receiving a wedding bouquet and the message "Deepest sympathy."

Chris Anthemum, girlfriend, wedding bouquet, Deepest sympathy.

Daisy Cheyne, boss, single rose, Love from Flopsy Bunny.

Lizzie Potts, maiden aunt, memorial wreath, Saying it with flowers.

Rhoda Dendran, brother, Bonsai tree, You're passed it.

William Sweet, fellow worker, cheese-plant, Made me think of you.

Getting Lost, p. 28

The parcel was left on the 8:42 train (clue 3) and the umbrella was left on the Ceefield train (clue 1), so the 8:05 from Beaford (clue 2) was not the train on which the shopping bag was left (clue 5) or the gloves (clue 2) so it must have been where the suitcase was left by Miss Knighton (clue 1). Mr. Cox traveled on the 8:23 (clue 4), so Mrs. Hughes must have left Aywood (clue 5) at 8:40 at the earliest and the shopping bag must have been on a later train than that. It wasn't the 8:42 (clue 3), so it must have been the 8:51. This train wasn't from Deeleigh (clue 4), so it must have started at Eamouth. Mr. Cox caught the 8:23, but not from Deeleigh (clue 4), so it must have been Ceefield, and he must have lost the umbrella. By elimination, the gloves must have been left on the 8:40. Mr. Farrell doesn't travel from Deeleigh (clue 4), so he must have been on the 8:51 from Eamouth. Finally, Mr. Nichols, who didn't catch the 8:40 (clue 6), must have left his parcel on the 8:42, which, by elimination, must be the train from Deeleigh. This leaves Mrs. Hughes as the passenger who left her gloves on the 8:42.

Mr. Cox, umbrella, 8:23 from Ceefield.

Mr. Farrell, shopping bag, 8:51 from Eamouth.

Mrs. Hughes, gloves, 8:40 from Aywood.

Miss Knighton, suitcase, 8:05 from Beaford.

Mr. Nichols, parcel, 8:42, from Deeleigh.

Bastille Day, p. 30

From clue 1, the Q must be in C2 and there cannot be a U in any of squares B2, B3, D2, or D3. So the one below an I (clue 3) cannot be in columns B, D, or E, or in column C (clue 1) and must be in column A. A1 contains a consonant (clue 4), so the I must be in A2 and the U in A3. Now, the word JET, which reads diagonally downwards (clue 3), cannot start in B1 going right, C1 going left, or D1 going left. Clue 4 rules out A1 going right, and the letter in E1 is repeated (clue 2), so it cannot be J, ruling out E1 going left. So, from clue 3, J must be in C1, E in D2, and T in E3. From clue 2, the second E must be in B3. The repeated letter in E1 (clue 2) cannot be the second T (clue 2) or the second U (clue 3) and we know it is not an E, so it must be an L. The only places now available for the U and Z referred to in clue 3 are E2 and D3 respectively. So it cannot be the T in E3 which is referred to in clue 4, the only possible place for which is now B2 with the O in B1. The consonant in A1 (clue 3) cannot be the second L (clue 2), so it must be the R, and, from clue 3, the second L must be in C3, leaving the letter in D1 as the A.

R	O	J	A	L
I	T	Q	E	U
U	E	L	Z	T

Battleships, p. 31

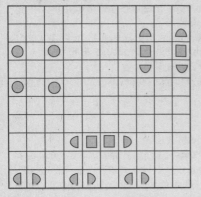

Easy Electro-rider, p. 32

Dennis rode along Gere Avenue on Friday (clue 3) and Cheyne Rise required power level 4 (clue 1), so the venue for Thursday's ride with no power assistance, which wasn't Spowke Lane (clue 2) and was too late in the week to have been Peddle Street (clue 5), must have been Saddell Road. Tuesday's Green testing wasn't Cheyne Rise (clue 1) and the run along Spowke Lane was with the Distance setting (clue 2), so Tuesday's Green trial must have been along Peddle Street. So, from clue 5, Dennis must have tested power level 1 on Wednesday and used the Travel setting on Thursday—a somewhat euphemistic term for "off" (clue 2). Power level 2 is called Boost (clue 4), so the Green setting used on Tuesday's run along Peddle Street must be level 3, leaving level 2, Boost, as Friday's Gere Avenue setting. By elimination, the level 4 climb up Cheyne Rise must have been on Monday with the power setting at Cruise, and Wednesday's run on level 1 must have been along Spowke Lane with the power knob turned to Distance.
Monday, 4, Cheyne Rise, Cruise.
Tuesday, 3, Peddle Street, Green.
Wednesday, 1, Spowke Lane, Distance.
Thursday, off, Saddell Road, Travel.
Friday, 2, Gere Avenue, Boost.

Going Dutch, p. 34

Jan Hertzog from Hilversum was not the engineer who knew Miss Raffles as Rosa Van Dyck (clue 3), and neither was Frans Drees (clue 2). Dirk Cort thought Miss Raffles was Else de Geer (clue 5) and Willem Wolf was a burglar (clue 7), so the engineer must have been Pieter Swart. The diamond cutter from Haarlem can't have been Frans Drees (clue 1), so, from clue 2, Frans Drees must have been a diamond dealer. We have now matched four names with a profession or a town, so the diamond cutter from Haarlem must have been Dirk Cort, leaving Jan Hertzog from Hilversum as the forger. Frans Drees didn't know Miss Raffles as Marie LaBonne (clue 2) or Kitty O'Riley (clue 4), so he must have thought she was Lili Kruger and so Frans Drees lived in Rotterdam (clue 6). Willem Wolf can't have lived in Nijmegen (clue 1), so that must have been Pieter Swart's home and Willem Wolf must have lived in Amsterdam. So he didn't know Miss Raffles as Marie LaBonne (clue 2), and must have thought she was Kitty O'Riley, leaving Marie LaBonne as the alias used when contacting Jan Hertzog the forger in Hilversum.
Dirk Cort, diamond cutter, Haarlem, Else de Geer.
Frans Drees, diamond dealer, Rotterdam, Lili Kruger.
Jan Hertzog, forger, Hilversum, Marie LaBonne.
Pieter Swart, engineer, Nijmegen, Rosa Van Dyck.
Willem Wolf, burglar, Amsterdam, Kitty O'Riley.

Dog Days, p. 36

The dog in the sailor hat, directly above the model in a month beginning with J (clue 2), must either be in March or April. But the dog in March is either wearing a fleece or a sweater (clue 1), so the sailor hat must be

April's apparel. So, from clue 2, the April dog must be the Jack Russell and August's mutt must be modelling a swimsuit. The Dalmatian, right of the Labrador and left of the tutu wearer, now cannot be seen in February, May, or November, so must be the swim-suited August pin-up, with the Labrador in July, the tutu-clad tyke in September and May's model wearing aut (clue 3). Now, from clue 2, the boxer must be June's icon. The Labrador is below the Jack Russell so, from the same clue, the borzoi must be November's model. From clue 4, the chihuahua three months after the dog in the tank top and three months before the Pekinese, must now be in September, with June's boxer in a tank top and December's picture as a Pekinese in a Santa hat. Now, from clue 2, the collie must be in the bottom row in October and July's Labrador must be wearing a panama hat. We have found the boxer and the panama hat so January's St. Bernard must be wearing the high-vis jacket. From clue 1, the red setter in a sweater must be the March model and the collie must be wearing a fleece. We have named two dogs in the top row so the Yorkshire terrier must be the February model, leaving May's picture as an Alsatian in boots. Finally, the chihuahua appears earlier than the dog in the hoodie, so that must be the garment worn by the borzoi in November, leaving the Yorkshire terrier in a bow tie in February.

January, St. Bernard, high-vis jacket; February, Yorkshire terrier, bow tie; March, red setter, sweater.

April, Jack Russell, sailor hat; May, Alsatian, boots; June, boxer, tank top.

July, Labrador, panama hat; August, Dalmatian, swimsuit; September, chihuahua, tutu.

October, collie, fleece; November, borzoi, hoodie; December, Pekinese, Santa hat.

Spending Spree, p. 38

Shopper C bought the bedspread and shopper D had popped out for a sandwich (clue 2), so the woman who had nipped out for a newspaper and came back with a picnic hamper, who wasn't A or E (clue 1), must have been shopper B, Alison (clue 2). So, from clue 1, shopper A must be Rowan and shopper C must have bought the shoes. Now, the person who braved the weather for a coffee, who is more than two places left of the woman who wanted a chocolate bar (clue 3) must have been Rowan in position A with the chocolate and the handbag being the purchases of the woman in position E, leaving the shopper in position C popping out for a sandwich, and being Charlotte (clue 2), and coming back with a pair of shoes and a bedspread. The chocolate wanter in position E wasn't Tina (clue 3), so must have been Margaret, leaving Tina needing the phone top-up in D. She didn't buy the pants or the dress (clue 3), so must have bought the jacket. We now know at least one of the sale items for four shoppers, so the person who bought pants and the dinner plates (clue 2) must have been Rowan in position A when she popped out for a coffee. Nor did Tina buy the dress (clue 3), so she must have bought the jacket, leaving Alison in position B going to buy a newspaper but returning with a dress and a picnic hamper. Finally, Margaret didn't buy a set of wine glasses to go with her chocolate bar and handbag (clue 3), so must have bought the curtains, leaving Tina buying the jacket and wine glasses while topping up her phone.

A, Rowan, coffee, pants, plates.

B, Alison, newspaper, dress, picnic basket.

C, Charlotte, sandwich, shoes, bedspread.

D, Tina, phone top-up, jacket, wine glasses.

E, Margaret, chocolate bar, handbag, curtains.

Curses, p. 40

Circe was told to mix the smelly potion and the girl cursed with the headache tested it (clue 4) and the girl punished for running in the corridors had to feed the mascot (clue 2), so Hazel, punished for drawing (clue 2), was not tasked with cleaning cages (clue 2), so must have been ordered to collect poisonous toadstools in the Weird Woods. She was not cursed with a headache or stomachache (clue 2). The girl punished for cursing was herself cursed with boils (clue 1) and Cassandra suffered cramp (clue 5), so Hazel must have been punished with ten minutes of itching. We now know the crime or the chore for three curses, so Cassandra, inflicted with cramp but who didn't feed the mascot (clue 5), must have cleaned the familiars' cages. The pupil afflicted with a headache and who tested the potion wasn't Hecate (clue 5) so must have been Zelda, leaving Hecate being charged with feeding the mascot and so had been caught running in the corridor (clue 3). By elimination, she must have been afflicted with a temporary stomachache, leaving Circe cursed with boils for cursing (clue 1). Finally, Zelda was not punished for fighting (clue 5) so must have been punished for answering back, leaving Cassandra cursed for fighting with cramps and cage cleaning.

Cassandra, fighting, cramp, cleaning familiars' cages.
Circe, cursing, boils, mixing potion.
Hazel, drawing on desk, itching, collecting toadstools.
Hecate, running in corridor, stomachache, feeding mascot.
Zelda, answering back, headache, testing potion.

The Meal Deal, p. 42

Thursday's meal was at a restaurant on 6th Street with a multi-word name (clue 3) and the lamb was eaten on 10th Street (clue 6), so Goldberg's, where Sam ate beef, which is also on a street with a number (clue 4), must be on 24th Street. The Monday dinner of sole wasn't eaten on Union Street (clue 1) or 6th Street, where we know Sam had dinner on Thursday, so Monday's restaurant must have been on Temple Street. The Imperial, where Sam dined on Tuesday, isn't on 24th Street, so, from clue 2, Sam didn't have chicken on Thursday, and so didn't eat it on 6th Street, so he must have had it on Union Street. Sam didn't eat there on Monday or Tuesday (clue 2), nor, since he ate on Temple Street on Monday, on Wednesday (clue 2), so the chicken dinner must have been on Friday, and the beef dinner at Goldberg's on 24th Street must have been on Wednesday, leaving the Tuesday dinner at the Imperial as the lamb eaten on 10th Street. By elimination, the pork must have been eaten on 6th Street on Thursday and, since the restaurant there has a multi-word name but was not Chez Maurice (clue 5), it must have been Ma Tante Adele. The Tower wasn't where Sam had sole on Monday (clue 1), so that must have been at Chez Maurice and the Tower must have been the Union Street restaurant where he had chicken on Friday.

Monday, sole, Chez Maurice, Temple Street.
Tuesday, lamb, Imperial, 10th Street.
Wednesday, beef, Goldberg's, 24th Street.
Thursday, pork, Ma Tante Adele, 6th Street.
Friday, chicken, Tower, Union Street.

Soap Opera, p. 44

Callum was third to shower (clue 1). The second person to shower wasn't Jenny or Nathan (clue 4), or Lucy, who found the empty bottle of shower gel (clue 3) that had been successfully used by the person who was going to the theater (clue 5), so the second person must have been Kelvin, who was planning on going to the wine bar (clue 2). The person who ran out of hot water was first to shower (clue 4) and the person who was going to the theater didn't have any shampoo to use (clue 5), so Kelvin, who didn't find the damp towel (clue 2), must have found the empty bottle of hair conditioner. Nathan wasn't going to the movie theater or pub (clue 4), or the theater (clue 5), so he must have been going to the Italian restaurant and was the fourth one to use the shower (clue 6). So he didn't have the problem with the hot water or the empty shampoo and must have discovered all the dry towels had gone, leaving Callum as the student who first discovered the empty shampoo bottle. This leaves Jenny as the first one in the shower and Lucy fifth. She wasn't going to the movie theater (clue 7), so must have been going to the pub leaving Jenny having a partly cold shower before going to see a movie.

First, Jenny, hot water, movie theater.
Second, Kelvin, hair conditioner, wine bar.
Third, Callum, shampoo, theater.
Fourth, Nathan, clean, dry towel, Italian restaurant.
Fifth, Lucy, shower gel, pub.

Bard Chart, p. 46

From verse 1 lines 2 and 3, Craig must have either 25 or 50 lines. But it's not 25 lines (verse 1 lines 1 and 2), so he must have 50 lines and so makes his entrance in scene 4 (verse 3 lines 1 and 2), with Orlando speaking 100 lines after his scene 1 entrance (verse 1 line 3) and John delivering 25 lines as Duke Pedro (verse 1 line 1). Ben makes his entrance in scene 3 (verse 2, line 3), so Orlando, who isn't played by Ralph (verse 2 line 1), must be played by Peter. Ben doesn't have 125 lines in his opening scene (verse 2 lines 2 and 3), so he must have 75 and the scene 2 entrant, who has more (verse 2 and 3), must have 125 lines, leaving John with 25 lines as Duke Pedro in scene 5. Also by elimination, Ralph's entrance must be in

scene 2 in which he has 125 lines. So he's not playing Edmund (verse 3 lines 3 and 4) or Godwin (verse 2 line 4), so he must be playing Lorenzo. Nor does Godwin first appear in scene 4 (verse 3 line 1), so he must be played by Ben in scene 3 with 75 lines, leaving Craig playing Edmund and making his entrance in scene 4 with 50 lines.

Ben, Godwin, Scene 3, 75 lines.
Craig, Edmund, Scene 4, 50 lines.
John, Duke Pedro, Scene 5, 25 lines.
Peter, Orlando, Scene 1, 100 lines.
Ralph, Lorenzo, Scene 2, 125 lines.

Wild Wilde Life, p. 48

Hector is having one week's vacation (clue 5) and Alexander is not heading for a European destination (clue 1), so the brother spending two weeks in Austria (clue 3), who is not Sebastian or Ranulph, the pony-trekker (clue 3), must be Ferdinand. He won't be pony-trekking or cycling, which is the five-week vacation (clue 5), nor will he be diving, which is the Seychelles vacation (clue 6) and the climbing vacation is not in Europe (clue 1), so the Austrian vacation must be hiking. The five-week cycling vacation is not being taken by Alexander (clue 1), so it must be Sebastian. So the Mexican vacation must be Hector's one-week activity (clue 5), which must be climbing, leaving the diving vacation as Alexander's. Now, from clue 2, Ranulph must be going to the Pyrenees and Sebastian to Brazil. Alexander's vacation is shorter than the one being taken in the Pyrenees (clue 1), so it must be three weeks, and Ranulph must be spending four weeks pony-trekking in the Pyrenees.

Alexander, Seychelles, diving, 3 weeks.
Ferdinand, Austria, hiking, 2 weeks.
Hector, Mexico, climbing, 1 week.
Ranulph, Pyrenees, pony-trekking, 4 weeks.
Sebastian, Brazil, cycling, 5 weeks.

Head to the Hills, p. 50

Win hasn't forgotten her gloves (clue 2), airbed (clue 3), or sleeping bag or toothbrush (clue 4) and so must have forgotten her woolly hat and spare socks. The knapsack in the back row which should have an airbed but doesn't isn't Sue's (clue 1) and must be Tom's. He hasn't forgotten his socks (clue 1), so the man who has forgotten both his airbed and socks, who isn't Rob (clue 3), must be Vic. So the gloves missing from the left end of one of the rows (clue 1) must be missing from Sue's bag and Rob must also have forgotten his gloves. Now Tom's second forgotten item to go with his airbed isn't his woolly hat, socks, or gloves (clue 1), or his toothbrush (clue 4), so must be his sleeping bag. So, from clue 1, Sue must have forgotten her toothbrush. Neither Rob nor Vic has forgotten his woolly hat (clue 3), so Una must have done so. Since Sue has forgotten her toothbrush and gloves, from clue 1, Rob hasn't also forgotten his toothbrush and must have forgotten his sleeping bag, leaving Una forgetting her woolly hat and toothbrush.

Tom, airbed and sleeping bag; Win, woolly hat and spare socks; Sue, toothbrush and gloves.

Rob, gloves and sleeping bag; Una, woolly hat and toothbrush; Vic, spare socks and airbed.

Sign In, p. 51

Sudoku, p. 51

1	7	2	4	9	6	5	8	3
3	5	9	7	8	1	2	4	6
4	8	6	5	2	3	7	1	9
2	9	4	6	7	8	1	3	5
8	1	3	2	4	5	9	6	7
7	6	5	3	1	9	8	2	4
9	3	8	1	5	4	6	7	2
6	2	1	9	3	7	4	5	8
5	4	7	8	6	2	3	9	1

Domino Search, p. 52

0	3	4	4	2	4	6	4
1	6	5	6	3	1	3	0
1	6	2	4	5	1	0	6
0	3	6	0	0	2	4	6
6	3	2	5	1	5	3	5
1	2	0	5	5	3	2	2
1	4	2	1	3	4	5	0

Barbershop Bassmen, p. 53

Bassman D isn't a librarian (clue 1), a banker (clue 2), or a nurse (clue 3) and so must be Leo the painter (clue 3) and, from clue 3, the nurse must be bassman C. He is separated from Kit by another bassman (clue 3), so Kit must be bassman A. He doesn't sing baritone (clue 1) or bass (clue 2) and Mac sings the lead (clue 2), so Kit must sing tenor. So he's not the librarian (clue 1) and must be the banker, leaving bassman B as the librarian. So, from clue 1, Jed must be bassman C and bassman D, Leo the painter, must be the baritone. Now, Mac the lead singer must be the librarian in position B, leaving bassman C, Jed the nurse, as the bass singing bassman.

A, Kit, tenor, banker.
B, Mac, lead, librarian.
C, Jed, bass, nurse.
D, Leo, baritone, house painter.

Soames and Wearson, p. 54

The Kentish Town case was presented on Thursday by a woman (clue 2) and the murder had taken place in Stepney (clue 6), so the disappearance reported by Edward Nicholson, which had not taken place in either Camberwell or Paddington (clue 4), must have happened in Peckham. The robbery was reported on Monday (clue 1), so it had not taken place in either Stepney or Peckham, nor was it Paddington (clue 1). Soames and Wearson heard of the Kentish Town case on Thursday, so Monday's must have been the Camberwell case. Sir Caleb Dewar called on Tuesday (clue 2), but not to describe the Peckham case (clue 3), so the kidnapping had not happened on Thursday (clue 2). So it had not taken place in Kentish Town and must have been Paddington. From clue 3, it cannot have been brought to Candlestickmaker Street on Monday or Tuesday and, as Monday's crime had taken place in Camberwell, it was not on Wednesday, so the

kidnapping must have been Friday's case. So Edward Nicholson must have told Soames and Wearson about the disappearance in Peckham on Wednesday (clue 3), leaving the Stepney murder as Tuesday's case. So the person who reported this must have been Sir Caleb Dewar. By elimination, the blackmail case must have been located in Kentish Town. So it was a woman who asked for help but it was not Lady Grant (clue 5), so must have been Miss Campbell. Silas Hodgson did not ask for help with a robbery (clue 1), so that must have been the case brought to him on Monday by Lady Grant, leaving Silas Hodgson as the visitor asking for assistance with the Paddington kidnapping.

Monday, Lady Grant, robbery at Camberwell.
Tuesday, Sir Caleb Dewar, murder at Stepney.
Wednesday, Edward Nicholson, disappearance at Peckham.
Thursday, Miss Campbell, blackmail at Kentish Town.
Friday, Silas Hodgson, kidnapping at Paddington.

Click and Collect, p. 56

Polly's box is either 1, 5, or 6 (clue 1). It is right of something else (clue 1) so it cannot be no.1 and, since she does not share an initial with another shopper, it cannot be no.5 (clue 3), so must be no.6 with the bedspread in box 5 and Mark's purchase in box 9. The saucepan must have an even number (clue 4). It was ordered by a man, so it cannot be Mary's purchase at 2 or Polly's at 6 and, since it is numbered twice Mike's purchase, it cannot be at 4 and must be at 8, leaving Mike's order at 4. From clue 3, the buyer of the bedspread in box 5 must also have a name beginning with M. We have placed Mark, Mike, and Mary, so he must be Malcolm. Bernard bought his daughter a toy truck (clue 2), so the man who bought the saucepan (clue 4) must be Bryan. Now the only place for Lisa's purchase, which isn't on the top shelf (clue 5) is in box 7. From the same clue, the shoes cannot be in boxes 1, 3, or 4 and must be Mary's purchase in box 2, with the dress at 3. Now from clue 4, the perfume cannot be in box 6 and must be Mark's order in box 9, leaving Susan as the buyer of the dress at 3 and Lisa's purchase as the DVDs (clue 3). By elimination, Bernard's toy must be in box 1. Polly didn't purchase a coat (clue 1), so must have bought a jacket, leaving the coat as Mike's order at no.4.

1, Bernard, toy; 2, Mary, shoes; 3, Susan, dress.

4, Mike, coat; 5, Malcolm, bedspread; 6, Polly, jacket.

7, Lisa, DVDs; 8, Bryan, saucepan; 9, Mark, perfume.

Behind Bars, p. 58

The 1883 saloon was the Rancher's Rest (clue 4) and the 1886 town was Tombstone (clue 7), so Phineas' time at the North Star saloon in Tucson, which wasn't his in the 1870s (clue 1), must have been in 1869. His famous visitor there wasn't Jesse James (clue 1) or Buffalo Bill (clue 2), Calamity Jane visited the saloon in Phoenix (clue 3) and Wyatt Earp drank at the Golden Horseshoe (clue 5), so the visitor in Tucson must have been Mark Twain. So, from clue 6, Phineas must have been running the Liberty Bell in 1872. So he wasn't at the Queen of Spades in 1876 (clue 6) and must have been there in 1886 in Tombstone (clue 7). This leaves the Golden Horseshoe, visited by Wyatt Earp, as the 1876 saloon. So, from clue 1, Jesse James must have visited the Liberty Bell in 1872. The Queen of Spades was in Tombstone, so it wasn't visited by Calamity Jane and it must have been Buffalo Bill, who Phineas met

there, and the saloon Calamity Jane visited in Phoenix must have been the Rancher's Rest in 1883. The Golden Horseshoe, the 1876 saloon, wasn't in Flagstaff (clue 5), so must have been in Yuma, leaving the saloon in Flagstaff as the Liberty Bell.

1869, North Star, Tucson, Mark Twain.

1872, Liberty Bell, Flagstaff, Jesse James.

1876, Golden Horseshoe, Yuma, Wyatt Earp.

1883, Rancher's Rest, Phoenix, Calamity Jane.

1886, Queen of Spades, Tombstone, Buffalo Bill.

Original Features, p. 60

The range is in the kitchen (clue 1) and photo 5 shows the stained-glass window (clue 4), so the living room in photograph 1, which does not have the fireplace (clue 3) or the patterned tiles (clue 4), must have the original paneling concealing the household robots (clue 2). The fireplace is not in the kitchen (clue 1), bathroom, or nursery (clue 3), so must be in the bedroom. The ionic heater is not in the kitchen (clue 1) or in the bedroom with its fireplace (clue 1), and the bathroom has the ultrasonic shower (clue 3), so it must be warming the nursery. We now know the rooms for three original features, so the bathroom, which cannot be the room in picture 5 with the stained-glass window (clue 3), must be floored with patterned tiles, leaving photograph 5 as the nursery with the stained-glass window. Now, from clue 3, picture 3 must show the bathroom with its old tiles and new shower, and picture 4 must be of the bedroom with the fireplace, leaving picture 2 showcasing the kitchen. Also from clue 3, the kitchen must have house battery, leaving the holographic TV in the bedroom.

Photograph 1, living room, paneling, robots.

Photograph 2, kitchen, range, house battery.

Photograph 3, bathroom, patterned tiles, ultrasonic shower.
Photograph 4, bedroom, fireplace, holographic television.
Photograph 5, nursery, stained-glass window, ionic heating.

Regal Regalia, p. 62

The piece named after St. Sylvester dates from the 19th century (clue 6), so the 15th-century sapphire-adorned item (clue 3), which is not dedicated to King Julius or King Humbert (clue 3) or St. Ludwig (clue 5), must be the Cross of Alpenburg (clue 1). Now from clue 5 the diamond-encrusted piece must be from either the 16th or 17th century (clue 5), but as the St. Sylvester item is 19th-century, the treasure named after St. Ludwig must be 18th-century and the one with the diamonds 16th-century (clue 5). The latter does not carry the name of King Julius (clue 3), so it must be King Humbert, leaving the 17th-century sceptre (clue 1) as the Sceptre of King Julius. It is not decorated with emeralds (clue 4) or the ruby, which is the ring (clue 2), so it must be the pearls. The orb is not named after King Humbert (clue 2), it is not from the 16th century and, as it is older than the ring (clue 2), it cannot be 19th-century, so it must be 18th-century and must be the Orb of St. Ludwig. Therefore the ring must date from the 19th century (clue 2) and be known as the Ring of St. Sylvester. By elimination, the crown must be the Crown of King Humbert and the Orb of St. Ludwig must date from the 18th century and be decorated with emeralds.
Cross of Alpenburg, 15th century, sapphires.
Crown of King Humbert, 16th century, diamonds.
Orb of St. Ludwig, 18th century, emeralds.
Ring of St. Sylvester, 19th century, ruby.
Sceptre of King Julius, 17th century, pearls.

I Scream, p. 64

The November release was *Fires of Hell* (clue 5), so the killer in that movie can't have been the vampire, who appeared in *Claw of the Demon* (clue 2). Clue 1 rules out the November release for the gorilla and clue 3 rules out the alien, while the zombies were in the October release (clue 6), so Mandy must have been killed by a giant spider in *Fires of Hell* and was playing a student (clue 3). That clue now rules out the March release for the alien killer. In the August release Mandy played a maid (clue 4), so the alien wasn't in the June release and must have done Mandy in in the August release, when she played a maid. So, from clue 3, the October release with the zombies must have featured Mandy as a policewoman. She can't have played the journalist in the March release (clue 1), so must have done so in the June release, leaving her role in the March release as that of a nurse. From clue 1, it must have been the gorilla that killed the nurse, and the March release was *Night of Terror* (clue 7), leaving the vampire killing the journalist in the June release, which was therefore *Claw of the Demon*. Finally, from clue 6, *The Curse* wasn't the October release in which Mandy played the policewoman, so that must have been *Devil's Dawn*, leaving *The Curse* as the August release in which she played the maid.
March, *Night of Terror*, nurse, gorilla.
June, *Claw of the Demon*, journalist, vampire.
August, *The Curse*, maid, alien.
October, *Devil's Dawn*, policewoman, zombies.
November, *Fires of Hell*, student, giant spider.

Hand-me-down Sports, p. 66

Vicky played baseball for a while (clue 3) and Harvey's 15-year-old sister gave him the roller skates (clue 4), so Lewis, his 13-year-

old brother (intro) who didn't take up fencing or horse riding (clue 1), must have had the kendo outfit that he handed down after 9 months (clue 5). Hayley's activity lasted for 10 months (clue 2), so the 18-year-old, who tried an activity for 5 months (clue 6) but who wasn't Jessica (clue 2) or Alfie (clue 6), must have been Vicky the baseballer. Harvey's brother Alfie (intro) never had roller skates (clue 4) and didn't have a go at fencing (clue 6), so he must have been a horse rider for three months (clue 7). So he isn't 12 (clue 7) and must be 17, leaving the 12-year-old as the one-time fencer. Finally, from clue 2, Hayley is older than Jessica, so must be the 15-year-old ex-roller skater who gave up after 10 months, leaving Jessica as the 12-year-old who gave up fencing after 6 months.

Alfie, 17, horse riding, 3 months.
Hayley, 15, roller skating, 10 months.
Jessica, 12, fencing, 6 months.
Lewis, 13, kendo, 9 months.
Vicky, 18, baseball, 5 months.

Red Handed, p. 68

Basher dressed as a nun (clue 1) and the man dressed as a laborer turned up at 1:30 (clue 4), so Prof, who arrived at 2:00 but who wasn't the chef and who can't have been the businessman who arrived 30 minutes after the laborer (clue 4), must have been the motorcyclist and was therefore gang leader Prof Hopkins (clue 6). Also from clue 6, Jelly must be Jelly McLaren turning up at 2:30 (clue 2). Tarzan is Acroyd (clue 5), so Basher, who isn't Briggs (clue 1), must be Basher Riley. So he didn't arrive at 3:00 and his nun disguise rules out 1:30, so he must have turned up at 1:00. By elimination, Fingers must be Fingers Briggs. The gang member disguised as a businessman didn't arrive at 3:00 (clue 5), so must have been Jelly McLaren arriving at 2:30. So from clue 5, Tarzan Acroyd must have arrived at 3:00 and

he must have dressed as the chef, leaving Fingers Briggs arriving at 1:30 as a laborer.

Basher Riley, 1:00 p.m., nun.
Fingers Briggs, 1:30 p.m., laborer.
Jelly McLaren, 2:30 p.m., businessman.
Prof Hopkins, 2:00 p.m., motorcyclist.
Tarzan' Acroyd, 3:00 p.m., chef.

Guest List, p. 70

Tommy went to the party in June (clue 1) and Richie is a canvasser (clue 3), so the person who lost their cat, who attended a party in July (clue 2) but wasn't Jackie or Simone (clue 2), must have been Annette. Jackie went to a party with Will (clue 2) and the courier went to a party with Brandon (clue 4), so the canvasser, Richie, who wasn't accompanied by Aron or Sally (clue 3), must have been accompanied by Maddie to the April party (clue 5). Simone didn't attend the March party (clue 6), so must have been invited to the May party, leaving Jackie and Will going to the party in March. We now know either the reason for calling or the guest to go with three party dates, so Brandon, who didn't attend the May party (clue 4), must have accompanied Tommy to the June do. Simone's guest wasn't Sally (clue 6), so must have been Aron, leaving Sally accompanying Annette, who had lost her cat, in July. Finally, the May attendee, Simone, wasn't the gardener (clue 4), so she must be the pizza delivery driver, leaving the gardener as Jackie who attended the March party with Will.

March, Jackie, garden maintenance, Will.
April, Richie, canvasser, Maddie.
May, Simone, pizza delivery driver, Aron.
June, Tommy, courier, Brandon.
July, Annette, lost cat enquiry, Sally.

Clubland, p. 72

The club Inspector Mullen is to raid isn't the Equator or Foxx's (clue 2), the Chicago, which is to be raided by Inspector Carter (clue 6), or the Aztec, which is to be raided by a sergeant (clue 1), so must be Mr. Hyde in Forsyth Street (clue 3). He won't be looking for forged credit cards (clue 2), stolen cash (clue 3), drugs, which Sergeant Pomeroy's squad will be searching for (clue 4), or stolen goods, which will be searched for in the club in Walpole Lane (clue 1), so he must be going to look for guns. The club Inspector Harvey will be raiding isn't in Walpole Lane or Lincoln Street (clue 1), Sergeant Lyndon will be raiding the club in Erskine Street (clue 5), so Inspector Harvey must be going to raid the club in Buckland Street. Now, the club in Walpole Lane, where stolen goods will be sought (clue 1), must be the Chicago, to be searched by Inspector Carter. By elimination, the club in Lincoln Street must be going to be searched by Sergeant Pomeroy, seeking drugs. This club isn't the Aztec (clue 1), so that must be the club in Erskine Street to be raided by Sergeant Lyndon. The Equator isn't in Lincoln Street either (clue 2), so must be in Buckland Street and due for a raid by Inspector Harvey, and, as he won't be looking for forged credit cards (clue 2), he'll be seeking stolen cash. By elimination, the club in Lincoln Street searched for drugs by Sergeant Pomeroy must be Foxx's, and Sergeant Lyndon will be searching the Aztec for forged credit cards.

Aztec, Erskine Street, Sergeant Lyndon, forged credit cards.

Chicago, Walpole Lane, Inspector Carter, stolen goods.

Equator, Buckland Street, Inspector Harvey, stolen cash.

Foxx's, Lincoln Street, Sergeant Pomeroy, drugs.

Mr. Hyde, Forsyth Street, Inspector Mullen, guns.

Dolphin Speak, p. 74

Dolphin 3 is named after a tuna (clue 1), so dolphin 1, who isn't Eel (clue 3), Shrimp or Coral (clue 4), Shark (clue 5), or Salmon (clue 6), must be Squid. Squid isn't either Dignified or Peaceful (clue 5, so Shark can't be 2 (clue 5). Dolphin 8 is Wise something (clue 2), so Shark isn't dolphin 7 (clue 5) and must be dolphin 6 with Dignified and Peaceful each either dolphin 5 or 7. Now, from clue 4, Shrimp, on the back row directly behind Coral, can't be dolphin 2 and must be dolphin 4, with dolphin 3 being Cultured Tuna and dolphin 8 being Wise Coral. So Fearless Eel (clue 3), who we know can't be dolphins 5 or 7, must be dolphin 2. Tranquil is directly behind Salmon (clue 6) and so must be dolphin 1, Tranquil Squid, and dolphin 5 must be Salmon, leaving dolphin 7 as Whale. Thoughtful isn't dolphin 4 (clue 2), so must be Thoughtful Shark, dolphin 6, leaving dolphin 4 as Wandering Shrimp. So dolphin 5 isn't Peaceful (clue 5), and must be Dignified Salmon, leaving dolphin 7 as Peaceful Whale.

1 Tranquil Squid; 2 Fearless Eel; 3 Cultured Tuna; 4 Wandering Shrimp; 5 Dignified Salmon; 6 Thoughtful Shark; 7 Peaceful Whale; 8 Wise Coral.

Passage to San Guillermo, p. 76

Paul's cabin is between Brett's and the gangster (clue 1). It's not number 3 (clue 1), so must be either number 2 or number 4 and either Brett or the gangster is in either cabins 1 and 5 with the other in cabin 3. Brett isn't in cabin 3 (clue 4), so the gangster must be there. Kevin McPhee isn't the mercenary (clue 3), the prospector (clue 5) or the jewel thief, who is Gary (clue 6). Kevin McPhee's cabin is next door but one to the prospector's, which isn't cabin 4 (clue 5), so he can't be the novelist in cabin 2 (clue 2), and must be the gangster in cabin 3. The mercenary is next door (clue 3) but not in cabin 2 (clue 2), so must be in cabin 4. So Gary the jewel thief and the prospector must each be in either cabin 1 or cabin 5, so Tom, like Paul, must be in either cabin 2 or cabin 4. Stone is in cabin 1 (clue 2), so cabin 5, which can't be Jovanic's (clue 5) or Valdez's, which is next to Gary the jewel thief's (clue 6), which we know isn't cabin 4, must be Walden's. He isn't Brett (clue 4), so he must be Gary Walden the jewel thief. So Valdez must be the mercenary in cabin 4, and Jovanic must be in cabin 2 and is the novelist. We know that Brett's not in cabin 5, so he must be Brett Stone in cabin 1, and he must be the prospector. So, from clue 1, Paul must be Jovanic the novelist in cabin 2, and Tom must be Valdez the soldier of fortune in cabin 4.

1, Brett Stone, prospector.
2, Paul Jovanic, novelist.
3, Kevin McPhee, gangster.
4, Tom Valdez, mercenary.
5, Gary Walden, jewel thief.

Battleships, p. 77

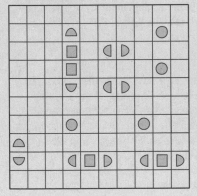

In the Year 2525, p. 78

Michael is Burroughs (clue 5), so the man with the last name Rocklynne, who isn't Donald (clue 1), must be Stephen Rocklynne.

Joanne wrote *The Horsemen* (clue 3), so she can't be Wells, who wrote *Judgment* (clue 5), nor is she Leinster (clue 3), so she must be Joanne Smith and her story is about an alien invasion (clue 2). *Dog Days*, about toxic pollution, isn't by Stephen Rocklynne (clue 4), nor is his story called *Endgame* (clue 1), so it must be *Red Sky*. It can't feature the famine, which is in Abigail's story (clue 2), nor the plague (clue 6), so the problem it deals with must be nuclear war. Michael Burroughs' story doesn't feature the plague (clue 6), so must feature toxic pollution and is therefore *Dog Days* (clue 4). Donald's story isn't *Endgame* (clue 1), so must be *Judgment* and he is Donald Wells. By elimination, it must feature the plague, leaving Abigail as Abigail Leinster and her famine story must be *Endgame*.

Abigail Leinster, *Endgame*, famine.
Donald Wells, *Judgment*, plague.
Joanne Smith, *The Horsemen*, alien invasion.
Michael Burroughs, *Dog Days*, toxic pollution.
Stephen Rocklynne, *Red Sky*, nuclear war.

Knights Out, p. 80

Knight C ate junket (clue 3), so can't have been Sir Sorely à Frayde or Sir Spyneless de Feete (clue 2). From clue 2, knight D must have been Sir Sorely or Sir Spyneless and must have eaten either marchpane or suckets. Knight B ate either comfits or honeycakes, so knight C can't have been Sir Poltroon à Ghaste (clue 2). Since knight D can't have eaten comfits (clue 2), knight C can't have been Sir Coward de Custarde (clue 1), so must have been Sir Timid de Shayke. From clue 3, knight E, like knight D, must have been either Sir Sorely or Sir Spyneless. Knight B can't have been Sir Coward (clue 1), so must have been Sir Poltroon and Sir Coward must have been knight A. So knight B ate comfits (clue 1), leaving knight E with the honeycakes. Neither of the knights adjacent to Sir Poltroon ate comfits or honeycakes (clue 2), so knight A, like knight D, must have eaten either marchpane or suckets. Knight B wasn't Sir Sorely, so knight A can't have eaten suckets and must have eaten marchpane (clue 5), leaving knight D as the one who ate suckets. From clue 5, knight E must have been Sir Sorely, so knight D must have been Sir Spyneless whose game dish was grouse (clue 3), leaving Sir Timid's bird-based game dish (clue 1) as pigeon pie. Now, from clue 4, the hippocras wine must have been drunk by knight E, while from clue 5, the mead must have been drunk by knight A and the ale by knight C. The knight who ate venison didn't drink hippocras or Lyonesse wine (clue 4), so must have been knight A, Sir Coward and, from clue 4, knight B must have eaten the roast boar, leaving the jugged hare as the game eaten by knight E, Sir Sorely. Finally, from clue 1, the Lyonesse wine must have been drunk by knight B, Sir Poltroon, and the cider must have been drunk Sir Spyneless' tipple in seat D.

A, Sir Coward de Custarde, venison, marchpane, mead.

B, Sir Poltroon à Ghaste, roast boar, comfits, Lyonesse wine.

C, Sir Timid de Shayke, pigeon pie, junket, ale.

D, Sir Spyneless de Feete, grouse, suckets, cider.

E, Sir Sorely à Frayde, jugged hare, honeycakes, hippocras.

Under Wraps, p. 82

Chloe's present was the dog basket (clue 1) and Molly's was wrapped in green paper (clue 3), so the silver paper, which was used to wrap the boomerang (clue 2), but wasn't for Ivan or Eddie (clue 2), must have been for Fern. The present with the kangaroo gift tag was for Ivan (clue 2) and the tag with the dingo design was attached to the wrapped tankard (clue 5), so Chloe's dog basket, which didn't have a koala or Tasmanian devil tag (clue 1), must have had a tag with a picture of a platypus and was wrapped in black paper (clue 4). We now know the gift or tag for three recipients, so the tankard with the dingo tag, which wasn't for Eddie (clue 5), must have been Molly's gift wrapped in green. The hoodie wasn't for Ivan (clue 6), so must have been for Eddie, leaving the Aboriginal clapsticks intended for Ivan. Eddie's hoodie wasn't wrapped in blue paper, so must have been in white. So it didn't have a Tasmanian devil tag and must have had a koala tag, leaving Fern's silver-wrapped boomerang with the Tasmanian devil tag and Ivan's clapsticks in blue paper with the kangaroo tag.

Chloe, dog basket, black, platypus.
Eddie, hoodie, white, koala.
Fern, boomerang, silver, Tasmanian devil.
Ivan, Aboriginal clapsticks, blue, kangaroo.
Molly, tankard, green, dingo.

Yummy Gummy, p. 84

Hill was making baby pandas (clue 5), Kevin was on the tiger production line (clue 6), and one worker ate 5 fox Gummy Cubs (clue 1), so Moira Stevens who didn't eat the least or the bear Gummy Cubs, must have been making and eating lion Gummy Cubs. Lawson ate 18 Gummy Cubs (clue 4), so wasn't making foxes or bears (clue 2) and must have been Kevin Lawson tucking into 18 tiger cub Gummy Cubs. Reeves wasn't making bear cubs (clue 2), so must have been on the fox cub production line, leaving Bowman making bear cubs. Shirley helped herself to 12 Gummy Cubs but not pandas (clue 5), so she isn't Reeves, who has only 5, or Hill (clue 5) and must be Shirley Bowman making bears and eating 12. So, from clue 2, Moira Stevens must have tested 14 lion cub Gummy Cubs. Finally, Onslow didn't eat 8 Gummy Cubs (clue 3), so he must be Onslow Reeves who tried only 5 fox cub candies, leaving Anita as Anita Hill who tested 8 panda cub Gummy Cubs during her shift.

Anita Hill, panda, 8 Gummy Cubs.
Kevin Lawson, tiger, 18 Gummy Cubs.
Moira Stevens, lion, 14 Gummy Cubs.
Onslow Reeves, fox, 5 Gummy Cubs.
Shirley Bowman, bear, 12 Gummy Cubs.

Close Encounters, p. 86

Mr. Featon-Ground made his claim in 2017, but he is not the real estate agent (clue 2). Nor is he the librarian (clue 3) or the doctor, whose claim was made in 2001 (clue 3). Mr. Sayne is the teacher (clue 6), so Mr. Featon-Ground must be the bus driver, and it was he who claimed that his children are aliens (clue 1). The claim of having been abducted by aliens was made eight years before Miss Clerehead publicized her story (clue 3), so it was not 2009. That was also not the year that someone claimed to have seen alien spacecraft (clue 4). The claim that someone had originally come from another planet was made in 2013 (clue 5), so 2009's claim must have been the body taken over by aliens by Mrs. Sobers (clue 1). So, from clue 3, the 2001 claim was not made by Miss Clerehead or, from his occupation, Mr. Sayne, so it must have been Mr. Normhall. Miss Clerehead could not have made her claim in 2005 (clue 3), so she must have claimed in 1993 that she was originally from another planet, leaving the 2005 story as Mr. Sayne's. From clue 3, Mrs. Sobers, whose claim was made in 2009, must be the librarian (clue 3), and Mr. Sayne must have claimed that he had been abducted by aliens. By elimination, Mr. Normhall must have claimed in 2001 that he had seen alien spacecraft, and Miss Clerehead must be the real estate agent.

2001, Mr. Normhall, doctor, saw spacecraft.
2005, Mr. Sayne, teacher, abducted by aliens.
2009, Mrs. Sobers, librarian, body taken over.
2013, Miss Clerehead, real estate agent, from another planet.
2017, Mr. Featon-Ground, bus driver, children are aliens.

Sign In, p. 88

5	3	2	4	6	1
4	5	1	3	2	6
3	1	6	2	4	5
6	2	3	5	1	4
1	4	5	6	3	2
2	6	4	1	5	3

Killer Sudoku, p. 88

1	5	8	6	2	4	7	9	3
3	2	6	9	5	7	4	1	8
4	7	9	3	8	1	5	2	6
9	6	4	8	3	2	1	7	5
7	8	1	5	4	6	9	3	2
2	3	5	7	1	9	8	6	4
8	9	2	4	7	3	6	5	1
6	4	3	1	9	5	2	8	7
5	1	7	2	6	8	3	4	9

Model Members, p. 89
The resident of 23 Railway Road isn't Harold Sleeper (clue 1) or Imogen Poynts or Kenneth Halt (clue 3), so must be Jemima Syding. Her layout doesn't have 45m of track (clue 2), 55m (clue 1), or 60m, (clue 2) so must have 50m. So, from clue 3, Imogen's track must be 55m long and the track in the shed must be 60m long. Neither the 55m nor the 60m track can be at No.16 (clues 1 and 2), so that address must have the 45m track. Jemima's house is on the same side of the road as the layout in the attic (clue 2), so that must be at No.7, so the shed with the 60m layout must be at No.12. By elimination, Imogen's 55m track must be in her attic at No.7. Kenneth doesn't have a shed (clue 3), so it must be Harold's 60m layout in the shed at No.12, leaving Kenneth at No.16. Finally, Jemima's 50m layout isn't in the guest bedroom (clue 2), so must be in the garage at No.23, leaving Kenneth's layout as the 45m track in the guest bedroom.
No.7, Imogen Poynts, attic, 55m.
No.12, Harold Sleeper, shed, 60m.
No.16, Kenneth Halt, guest bedroom, 45m.
No.23, Jemima Syding, garage, 50m.

Read and Rejected, p. 90
The telephone appears in chapter 5 (clue 3), so the wireless, noted by Prof. Ayne, which wasn't in chapter 8 (clue 2), must have been in chapter 2, leaving the light bulb in chapter 8. Prof. Hound worried about the use of metaphor (clue 1), so Prof. Ayne, whose chapter 2 item rules out the grammar query (clue 3), must have found fault with the punctuation, leaving Prof. Legate noting the poor grammar. So he didn't note the light bulb and must have pointed to the telephone in chapter 5, leaving Prof. Hound noticing the light bulb in chapter 8.
Prof. Ayne, punctuation, wireless, chapter 2.

Prof. Hound, metaphor, light bulb, chapter 8.
Prof. Legate, grammar, telephone, chapter 5.

Locker Fit, p. 91
The bank manager is using locker 4, so Gareth's locker, in diagonal alignment with that of the lecturer can't be locker 1. Nor is the user of locker 1 Melvin (clue 1) or Denzil (clue 2), and so he must be Kieron. So, from clue 5, the attorney must have locker 2 and the chef, whose locker is immediately above Melvin's (clue 1) must be Kieron with locker 1 and Melvin must have locker 3. By elimination, he must be the lecturer and, from clue 4, Gareth must have locker 2, leaving Denzil's clothes in locker 4. So Fettle must be Melvin Fettle (clue 2). Finally, from clue 6, Spry can't have locker 4 or 2 and must be chef Kieron Spry with locker 1 and locker 2 must be attorney Gareth Hardy's, leaving locker 4 being used by bank manager Denzil Fitt.
1 Kieron Spry, chef; 2 Gareth Hardy, attorney.
3 Melvin Fettle, lecturer; 4 Denzil Fitt, bank manager.

Rose of Honor, p. 92
The rose named Tessa came onto the market in April (clue 2) and the rose on sale from June is named after the athlete (clue 4), so the rose created for Wesley in recognition of years of charity work, which didn't come onto the market in March or July (clue 3), must have been on sale first in May. The lilac rose was released in March (clue 5), so the yellow rose in honor of the police dog (clue 2), which wasn't first on sale in April (clue 2), must have been first available in July. We now know either the name or color of the roses for four months, so Bonny, the orange rose, must

be the one named for the athlete released in June. The lilac rose released in March wasn't created in honor of the swim coach (clue 5), so must have been for the retired politician, leaving the swim coach being honored by the rose released in April, Tessa. The lilac rose isn't named Winston (clue 5), so must be Sandy, leaving Winston as the yellow rose named after the police dog. Finally, Wesley, released in May, isn't red (clue 6), so must be white, leaving Tessa being a red rose named after a swim coach and released in April.

Bonny, orange, games athlete, June.
Sandy, lilac, retired politician, March.
Tessa, red, swim coach, April.
Wesley, white, charity work, May.
Winston, yellow, police dog, July.

The Drifters, p. 94

The Carneys traveled by tractor (clue 2) and there are five members of the Franklin family (clue 4), so the family with three members, who were pulled on dog sleds (clue 3) but who aren't the Dempsters or the Greens (clue 3), must have been the Evanses who took 35 mins to reach the restaurant (clue 1). The Carney family doesn't number seven (clue 2) and its mode of transport rules out five (clue 5), so there must be six Carneys who clung on to the tractor. The family of four arrived at the restaurant in 65 mins (clue 5), so the family that walked for 46 minutes with snow shoes, who weren't the five-strong Franklins (clue 4), must number seven. The Carneys didn't take 84 minutes (clue 2) and either their number or transport rules out 35, 46, and 65 minutes, so they must have taken 42 minutes on their tractor, leaving the five Franklins taking 84 minutes. The family of four didn't travel in the 4x4 truck (clue 5), so they must have traveled on skis, leaving the five Franklins struggling through the snow for 84 minutes in their 4x4 truck. Finally, from clue 6, the Dempsters didn't travel on skis, so

they must be the seven who walked for 46 minutes on snow shoes, leaving the Greens as the four diners who skied for 65 minutes.

Carney, six, tractor, 42 minutes.
Dempster, seven, snow shoes, 46 minutes.
Evans, three, dog sled, 35 minutes.
Franklin, five, 4x4 truck, 84 minutes.
Green, four, skis, 65 minutes.

Haven't a Clue, p. 96

Faith didn't complete 12 across in the *Daily News* (clue 1) and wasn't able to do 15 down for the crossword that should have been submitted by June 23 (clue 5), so the missing answer in *Cross Swords* (clue 2) for which the deadline was June 14, which wasn't 9 across or 21 across (clue 2), must have been 2 down and the prize was the pen set (clue 3). *Prize Puzzles'* prize was a dictionary (clue 5), so the *Daily Rag's* prize, which wasn't a DVD (clue 6), or, from its non-June deadline (clue 6), the book token prize of the June 7 deadline (clue 4), so must have been the thesaurus. 15 down wasn't the missing answer for *Prize Puzzles* (clue 5) or, from its June deadline, the *Daily Rag* (clue 6), so it must have been left blank in *Monthly Teasers*. We know the prize or deadline for four publications, so the book token prize and the June 7 deadline must have been in the *Daily News*, leaving the DVD as the prize in *Monthly Teasers*. The July 1 deadline puzzle didn't have 9 across missing, so must have lacked an answer for 21 across, leaving the 9 across clue missing from the crossword with the May 30 deadline. Finally, from clue 7, the missing 9 across wasn't in the puzzle with the thesaurus prize, so must have been in the one with the dictionary to be won, leaving the crossword with 21 across missing offering the thesaurus.

Cross Swords, 2 down, pen set, June 14.
Daily News, 12 across, book token, June 7.
Daily Rag, 21 across, thesaurus, July 1.

Nice Ice, p. 98

Hopelus named his mixture Muri (clue 2) and Euselus' mixture was based on sheep's milk (clue 3), so the water-based Sorbum, which wasn't invented by Branelus or Gormlus (clue 5), must have been Cluelus' creation. It wasn't flavored with lemons (clue 4), Branelus was carrying the peaches (clue 5), the Magnum contained cherries (clue 1) and the honey was mixed with asses' milk (clue 2), so it must have been Strawberry Sorbum. The honey and asses' milk weren't frozen together by Hopelus (clue 2), so this was Gormlus' discovery. He didn't call his iced offering a Cornettum (clue 3) and must have decided to call the threads of honey running through his frozen asses' milk Undulum, thanks to its pleasing ripple effect. By elimination, the cherry Magnum, must have been Euselus' invention using frozen sheep's milk leaving the lemons plastered over the walls by Hopelus. He wasn't carrying goat's milk (clue 4), so the lemon Muri must be made with cow's milk, leaving Branelus' invention as a frozen peach and goat's milk arrangement called a Cornettum.

Branelus, peach, goat, Cornettum.
Cluelus, strawberry, water, Sorbum.
Euselus, cherry, sheep, Magnum.
Gormlus, honey, ass, Undulum.
Hopelus, lemon, cow, Muri.

Pony Express, p. 100

Molly's surname is Algar (clue 7). Helen, whose team was the Round Up, wasn't Samantha's rider, Miss Mowis (clue 6), nor can her surname be Hugby (clue 1). Miss Eppie was riding for CDPC-A (clue 4), so Helen must be Helen Jowle. Muffin's rider, Edwin (clue 3), can't be Eppie (clue 1) and we already know he's not Algar, Jowle, or Mowis, so he must be Edwin Hugby. This rules out two teams and he didn't ride for the Greenflyers (clue 3). Bonnie and her rider represented St. Ursula's (clue 2), so Edwin Hugby must have ridden for Team Pegasus. We know that Helen Jowle didn't ride Samantha or Muffin, and her team rules out Bonnie. Nor was her mount Midnight (clue 5), so it must have been Lucky. Since Bonnie's rider was from St. Ursula's, that rules out three surnames, and we know it isn't Mowis, so she must be Molly Algar. Now Midnight's rider must have been Eppie, and Samantha's rider must have represented the Greenflyers. Finally, from clue 5, Midnight's rider, surnamed Eppie, wasn't Joshua, so she must have been Amanda Eppie, leaving Joshua as Joshua Mowis who rode Samantha.

Bonnie, Molly Algar, St. Ursula's.
Lucky, Helen Jowle, Round Up.
Midnight, Amanda Eppie, CDPC-A.
Muffin, Edwin Hugby, Team Pegasus.
Samantha, Joshua Mowis, Greenflyers.

Private Hire, p. 102

Miss Benson's automobile is parked at No.14 (clue 2) and the Garrets live at No.11 (clue 5), so the Ericsons, who rent their driveway to Mr. Child (clue 3) but don't live at Nos.6 or 9 (clue 3), must live at No.2. The Gastral 1.6 is parked daily at number 9 (clue 3), so Mrs. Dawson's Anda 1.4, which isn't parked at No. 11 (clue 1), must be parked at number 6. We now know either the resident family or the make of automobile for four house numbers, so the Stone family's driveway, which hosts a Matrix Saloon by day (clue 4), must be outside 14 Station Road and Miss Benson must own the Matrix Saloon. Mrs. Dawson's Anda isn't parked in the Peters' driveway (clue 1), so must be parked in the Brown's driveway, leaving the Peters at No.9.The Garrets' driveway isn't a daytime home to the Solstice XS (clue 5), so it must be a Vocus Estate, leaving the Solstice XS as Mr. Child's automobile on the Ericson's driveway at No.2. Finally, Mr. Andrews doesn't own the Vocus Wagon (clue 6), so he must own the Gastral on the Peters' drive, leaving Mr. Edison parking his Vocus Wagon at No.11 while the Garrets are out for the day.

No.2, Ericson, Mr. Child, Solstice XS.
No.6, Brown, Mrs. Dawson, Anda 1.4.
No.9, Peters, Mr. Andrews, Gastral 1.6.
No.11, Garret, Mr. Edison, Vocus Wagon.
No.14, Stone, Miss Benson, Matrix Saloon.

Tsarina Ballerina, p. 104

The girl who was 2 minutes late had been playing on the swings (clue 4), so Evangelina, who was 4 minutes late (clue 3), can't be wearing Ugg boots, as that girl was twice as many minutes late as the one who had been playing on her bike (clue 5). Emmalina Ballerina is in her rubber boots (clue 1), so Evangelina's boots (clue 3) must be the walking boots. So, she hasn't been picking mushrooms (clue 6), playing on her bicycle (clue 5) or playing in the sandpit (clue 5). Angelina had been walking the dog (clue 3) and we know the girl who was 2 minutes late was on the swings, so Evangelina must have been gardening. So, from clue 4, the girl who was 2 minutes late after playing on the swings must have been Wilhelmina. She isn't wearing sneakers (clue 1) or loafers (clue 4). The girl in flip-flops had been kicking through leaves (clue 2) and the girl in sandals was 5 minutes late (clue 6), so Wilhelmina must be wearing Ugg boots. So, from clue 5, the girl who had been cycling must have been 1 minute late. So, this isn't what Emmalina was doing (clue 1). Nor, from her footwear, was she kicking piles of leaves or playing in the sandpit, so Emmalina must have been picking

mushrooms and, from clue 6, Philippina must have arrived 5 minutes late and Thomasina must be dancing in her sandals. Philippina wasn't kicking leaves (clue 2) or playing on her bike (clue 5), so must have been playing in the sandpit. Now, the girl who was kicking leaves and is now in her flip-flops must be Katarina, leaving Thomasina playing on her bicycle in her sandals and being 1 minute late. The girl in loafers arrived before both of her immediate neighbors (clue 4), so she can't be Philippina and must be Angelina, leaving Philippina in her sneakers. So, from clue 1, Emmalina must have been 6 minutes late. Finally, from clue 4, Angelina wasn't 7 minutes late and must have been 3 minutes late after walking Nureyev in her loafers, and Katarina must have been 7 minutes late after changing into her flip-flops following a morning's leaf kicking.

Thomasina, 1 minute, playing on bicycle, sandals.
Philippina, 5 minutes, sandpit in park, sneakers.
Emmalina, 6 minutes, picking mushrooms, rubber boots.
Angelina, 3 minutes, walking dog, loafers.
Katarina, 7 minutes, kicking leaves, flip-flops.
Evangelina, 4 minutes, gardening, walking boots.
Wilhelmina, 2 minutes, swings in park, Ugg boots.

Animal Magic, p. 106

The fourth spell produced the yellow wagtail (clue 4). The fifth cannot have resulted in Sir Sorely becoming a chicken (clue 2) or have produced a rabbit (clue 5), and clue 7 rules out the marmalade cat, so it must have been the knight tended by Thomas when he became a little white bull (clue 1). The first spell cannot have been cast on Sir Coward (clue 5), nor was its victim Sir Spyneless, looked after by Frederick (clue 6), and clue 7 rules out Sir Poltroon, while Sir Timid was involved in the second spell (clue 5), so Sir Sorely must have been transformed first. So, from clue 2, Elton was put in charge of Sir Timid, the subject of the second spell. Since the first spell produced the chicken, clue 7 rules out Sir Poltroon for the third spell and, since Clifford looked after this knight (clue 3), he cannot have been Sir Spyneless. We know he was not Sorely or Timid, so he must have been Sir Coward. Nor can Sir Spyneless, looked after by Frederick, have been the fifth knight, so he must have been the fourth, leaving the fifth as Sir Poltroon. Clue 5 now tells us Sir Timid became a rabbit, and so Sir Coward himself became a marmalade cat, confirmed by clue 7. This leaves Aled, the minstrel, as the lad who looked after Sir Sorely while he remained a chicken.

First, Sir Sorely à Frayde, chicken, Aled.
Second, Sir Timid de Shayke, rabbit, Elton.
Third, Sir Coward de Custarde, marmalade cat, Clifford.
Fourth, Sir Spyneless de Feete, yellow wagtail, Frederick.
Fifth, Sir Poltroon à Ghaste, little white bull, Thomas.

Starlet Hopes, p. 108

The girl who would be Imogen Valentine arrived in Hollywood in 1930 (clue 4), the girl from Illinois became Sabrina Banks (clue 1), and Simone Lamont arrived later than the girl from Missouri (clue 3), so the girl from Ohio who moved west in 1929 and who didn't become Meryl Day (clue 2), must have been Grace Horne, born Grace Waghorn (clue 6). So the year that the girl from Louisiana arrived in Hollywood, which was the year after Audrey Mullett (clue 3), cannot have been 1930 or 1932. Hyacinth Mudge arrived in 1932 (clue 5), so the aspiring actress from Louisiana who also didn't arrive in 1933, must have

done so in 1934. So, Audrey Mullett must have traveled to Tinseltown in 1933 (clue 3). As Eunice Wigg was from New York (clue 1), she didn't travel west in 1932 or 1933, so it must have been 1930 and she must have become Imogen Valentine. Simone Lamont wasn't from Missouri (clue 3), so she must have moved from Louisiana in 1934, and the girl from Missouri must have become Meryl Day. So, she must have arrived in Hollywood in 1932 and been born Hyacinth Mudge (clue 5), and Audrey Mullett, arriving in 1933, must have been the Illinois girl who became Sabrina Banks, leaving Janice Allibone as the Louisiana girl who went to Hollywood in 1934 and found fame as actress Simone Lamont.

1929, Ohio, Grace Waghorn, Grace Horne.
1930, New York, Eunice Wigg, Imogen Valentine.
1932, Missouri, Hyacinth Mudge, Meryl Day.
1933, Illinois, Audrey Mullett, Sabrina Banks.
1934, Louisiana, Janice Allibone, Simone Lamont.

Cheaper Chips, p. 110

Luke Sterne holds the jack of hearts (clue 3) and Donna Flinch a club (clue 1), so the jack of spades, which has not been dealt to Norah Clewes (clue 2) or Ted Pann (clue 3), must have been dealt to undertaker Woody Le Blanc (clue 6). He has not brought $60 to the table (clue 2), $100 (clue 6), $120, which is the player holding the king of clubs (clue 5), or $50, which is the chef (clue 1), so Woody must have $75. The player dealt the king of diamonds is neither the chef nor the grocer (clue 1), nor is it the car mechanic with the queen of clubs (clue 4), so it must be the plumber. The player with the king of clubs is gambling with $120, so the chef with $50 must be Luke Sterne, holding the jack of hearts, leaving the king of clubs in the grocer's hand. This is not Donna Flinch (clue 1), so she must have the queen of clubs and must be the car mechanic. Norah Clewes is not the grocer (clue 2), so she must be the plumber who has been dealt the king of diamonds. She is not carrying $60, so it must be $100. This leaves the grocer as Ted Pann and Donna Flinch holding the queen of clubs and ready to bet some of her $60 on the first hand.

Donna Flinch, car mechanic, queen of clubs, $60.

Luke Sterne, short-order chef, jack of hearts, $50.

Norah Clewes, plumbing contractor, king of diamonds, $100.

Ted Pann, grocer, king of clubs, $120.

Woody Le Blanc, undertaker, jack of spades, $75.

districts, so he must be the Brooklyn boss, leaving "Diamonds" as the Little Italy boss. Vito DeLinqui is in seat 4 (clue 2), so Jo Villani, who is sitting immediately counterclockwise of Tommy Racketti (clue 4), can't be in seat 3. Nor, since he must be directly opposite Al "Shark" Feloni (clue 5), can he be in seat 2, so he must have seat 1, with Tommy Racketti in seat 2. So, from clue 4, Al "Shark" Feloni must have seat 3. So he is the mobster who doesn't survive the opening scene (clue 2). Finally, from clue 1, Tommy Racketti must be "Diamonds" from Little Italy, leaving Vito DeLinqui in seat 4 as "Uncle," boss of Greenwich Village.

1, Jo Villani, Boots, Brooklyn.

2, Tommy Racketti, Diamonds, Little Italy.

3, Al Feloni, Shark, Queens.

4, Vito DeLinqui, Uncle, Greenwich Village.

Battleships, p. 112

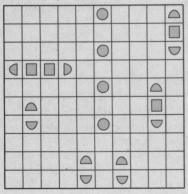

The Movie Mob, p. 113

"Uncle" ran Greenwich Village and one mobster was Jo "Boots" Villani (clue 3), so Al Feloni, the boss of Queens (clue 1) who isn't "Diamonds" (clue 1), must be Al "Shark" Feloni. Jo "Boots" Villani isn't from Little Italy (clue 3) and his nickname rules out two other

There Were Ten in a Bed . . . , p. 114

The first to fall out was not Ray, Kay, or Fay (clue 1), or Meg, Tom, Sue, Lee, or Dan (clue 2). Sue can't have been second as then both Tom and Pam would be first, so Pam can't have been first. So the first out must have been Bob, with Meg second and Tom third. Now from clue 2, Sue must be sixth and Pam must be fifth. Ray, Kay, and Fay did not fall out in succession (clue 1), so Ray cannot be any of the last four and must have fallen out fourth. The last one left in bed was not Lee (clue 2), Kay, or Fay (clue 1), so must have been Dan. Kay did not fall out immediately before Fay (clue 1), so she must have fallen out seventh and Fay ninth, leaving Lee as the eighth to leave the bed.

1, Bob; 2, Meg; 3, Tom; 4, Ray; 5, Pam; 6, Sue; 7, Kay; 8, Lee; 9, Fay; 10, Dan

Logi-5, p. 115

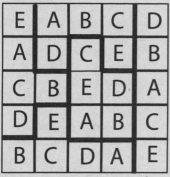

E	A	B	C	D
A	D	C	E	B
C	B	E	D	A
D	E	A	B	C
B	C	D	A	E

Sudoku, p. 115

5	2	7	8	1	9	3	4	6
8	9	6	5	3	4	7	1	2
3	4	1	2	7	6	8	5	9
2	5	3	9	8	7	1	6	4
6	8	4	1	5	3	9	2	7
7	1	9	6	4	2	5	8	3
1	6	2	3	9	5	4	7	8
4	3	8	7	2	1	6	9	5
9	7	5	4	6	8	2	3	1

golf club maker must be the 31-year-old. So Bernice, who isn't 25 and who isn't the male 26-year-old, must be the 28-year-old at Chippestuff and the 26-year-old must be the new MD at Chippesit. By elimination, 28-year-old Bernice, MD at Chippestuff must be the computer chips manufacturer who used be a photographer and the new MD at Chippetts making casino chips must be 25, leaving the 31-year-old as Daphne at Chippeworld (clue 2). Ariadne was the singer (clue 3), so Daphne, making the golf clubs, who wasn't the TV assistant (clue 4), must have been the aid worker and Eugene the former TV assistant. Finally, from clue 1, Bernice's 29-year-old sister at the French fries plant must be frustrated singer Ariadne, leaving Eugene as the 25-year-old who gave up being a TV assistant to become MD at Chippetts, making casino chips.

Ariadne, 29 years, singer, Chippeworx, French fries.

Bernice, 28 years, photographer, Chippestuff, computer chips.

Clinton, 26 years, clothes designer, Chippesit, chocolate chips.

Daphne, 31 years, aid worker Chippeworld, golf clubs.

Eugene, 25 years, TV assistant, Chippetts, casino chips.

Pass the Chippes, p. 116

The former photographer is now MD of the computer chips division (clue 3), so the 26-year-old former would-be clothes designer (clue 4) who can't be the French fries manufacturer (clue 1) or the golf club maker (clue 4) and who isn't in charge of Chippetts, the casino chip maker (clue 5), must be the new MD at the chocolate chip factory. He's male (clue 2) but not Eugene (clue 5), so must be Clinton. So the Chipworx MD, who is two years younger than the golf club maker (clue 4), must be the 29-year-old and the

All at Sea, p. 118

The ship that was washed up did not sail in 1785 or 1790 (clue 1) or, since the 1795 journey was to the Cape of Good Hope (clue 2) and not the Americas, 1805 (clue 1). The 1800 expedition was taken aback (clue 2), so the ship that was washed up must have been the 1795 launch bound for the Cape of Good Hope (clue 1). Now, from clue 1, *Sisyphus* must have sailed in 1790 and been holed below the waterline, and the 1785 voyage must have been to the Americas. *Orpheus*, which sailed in 1805 (clue 3), was not bound for the Indies so must have set sail for the Antipodes. The ship that keeled over set sail some time before 1800 (clue 2), so *Orpheus* must have been left high and dry, leaving the 1785 sailing to the Americas as the vessel that keeled over and, from clue 2, *Tantalus* setting out for the Cape of Good Hope in 1795 (clue 2) only to leave its crew washed up. The ship that sailed for the East Indies did not depart in 1800 (clue 2), so that must have been *Sisyphus'* destination in 1790 and the 1800 voyage must have been bound for the West Indies. It was not *Icarus*, so must have been *Nemesis*, and *Icarus* must have been the ship that set sail for the Americas in 1785 but unfortunately keeled over.

Icarus, 1785, keeled over, Americas.
Nemesis, 1800, taken aback, West Indies.
Orpheus, 1805, left high and dry, Antipodes.
Sisyphus, 1790, holed below waterline, East Indies.
Tantalus, 1795, washed up, Cape of Good Hope.

Chubby Felines, p. 120

Richie Guy was paid $10 million (clue 4), so the Financial Director, whose bonus was $6 million and was not Phil Banks or Robin Staff (clue 2) or Saul Meine (clue 1), must have been Isaiah Payde, who works for Dunn Pawley (clue 5). Richie Guy received a bonus of $10 million, so, from clue 1, Saul Meine must have been paid $9 million and the President $7 million. The latter was not Phil Banks (clue 2), so must be Robin Staff, leaving the $8 million paid to the Detzer-Reisin executive as Phil Banks' bonus. He is not the company's Chief Executive (clue 2) or Managing Director, who worked for Pryce, Lowe, and Fawling (clue 3), so Phil Banks must be Chairman. The Weir-Fayling executive is not Robin Staff (clue 3), so he wasn't paid $7 million. He was paid less than the Pryce, Lowe, and Fayling executive

(clue 3), so it wasn't $10 million and must have been $9 million and the executive concerned must be Saul Meine. So the Pryce, Lowe, and Fawling Chief Executive who was paid $10 million must have been Richie Guy (clue 4), leaving Robin Staff working for Stocksdown, and Saul Meine as the Chief Executive of Weir-Fayling, who was paid $9 million this year.

Detzer-Reisin, Phil Banks, $8m, Chairman.
Dunn Pawley, Isaiah Payde, $6m, Financial Director.
Pryce, Lowe, and Fawling, Richie Guy, $10m, Managing Director.
Stocksdown, Robin Staff, $7m, President.
Weir-Fayling, Saul Meine, $9m, Chief Executive.

Jack-o'-lanterns, p. 122

Daisy's frowning pumpkin was either D or E (clue 1) but pumpkin D was created by a boy (clue 2), so Daisy must have carved pumpkin E. Dylan's Jack-o'-lantern, with a boy's work on its left and a girl's on its right (clue 4) cannot be A or F, C, which was the work of a girl (clue 2), or D, which has a girl's work with its star-shaped eyes (clue 2) on the left, so must be pumpkin B. Now pumpkin A must be the work of a boy but not Frankie (clue 3) so must have been carved by Jackson. Now the smiling pumpkin C must be Miranda's and Jack-o'-lantern D with its circular eyes must be by Frankie, leaving pumpkin F as the creation of Poppy.

A Jackson; B Dylan; C Miranda; D Frankie; E Daisy; F Poppy

Well Pressed, p. 123

John's surname is Horton (clue 2) and Markham was a pieman (clue 3), so Matthew, who was a groom but who isn't Bacon (clue 4), must be Matthew Jones. Markham the

ex-pieman isn't Samuel (clue 3), so he must
be Henry Markham and Samuel must be
Samuel Bacon, figure C (clue 4). So, from clue
3, Henry Markham the ex-pieman must be
figure B. Now, from clue 1, the ex-cobbler is
figure 3, Samuel Bacon, leaving John Horton
as a former dairyman. He isn't figure A (clue
2), so he must be figure D, leaving figure A as
Matthew Jones who used to be a groom.

A, Matthew Jones, groom.
B, Henry Markham, pieman.
C, Samuel Bacon, cobbler.
D. John Horton, dairyman.

Prints Charming, p. 124

The peony fabric is not being worn by Fiona or
Shania (clue 1), Layla, who is in front of Olivia
wearing pants, or Olivia, who is behind Layla
wearing red (clue 2), so it must be on Paula's
choice of outfit and, from clue 1, Olivia must
be wearing purple pants and Shania must be
wearing a dress. The peacocks on a yellow
background are not being worn by Fiona
or Layla (clue 3), Olivia in purple, or Paula
wearing peonies, so must be the pattern on
Shania's dress. Fiona is not wearing green
(clue 5) so she must be in orange, leaving
Paula's peony outfit on a background of
green. So, Olivia's purple pants don't show
poppies (clue 5) or pomegranates (clue 3) and
so must show passion flowers. From clue 4,
Layla must be wearing the jacket and Fiona's
outfit must have the poppies, leaving Layla's
jacket with the pomegranates. Finally Fiona's
garment isn't a coat (clue 4), so must be a
blouse, leaving Paula modeling a coat.

Fiona, blouse, poppies, orange.
Layla, jacket, pomegranates, red.
Olivia, pants, passion flowers, purple.
Paula, coat, peonies, green.
Shania, dress, peacocks, yellow.

Bridging the Gap, p. 126

The architect of the shortest span wasn't Baili
(clue 2), Archova (clue 4), Gettova (clue 5), or
Krosser (clue 6) and so must be Voltski. It
doesn't cross the Bolta or the Ghames (clue
4), or the Nole or the Rhane, and must span
the Taber. Now, from clue 4, the designer of
the bridge over the Ghames must be Krosser.
The longest bridge wasn't the work of Baili
(clue 2), Archov (clue 3), or Krosser (clue 6),
so must be the work of Gettova and, from
clue 3, the bridge in Balonia must span 120ft.
So the bridge designed by Baili isn't 115ft
long (clue 2) or the 120ft bridge in Balonia
(clue 1), so must be the 110ft bridge and the
bridge in Navonia must be 115ft long (clue 2).
Baili's 110ft bridge isn't in Cashenia (clue 3)
or Barania (clue 1), so must be in Greatovia.
So, from clue 6, Krosser's bridge over the
Ghames must be the 115ft example in
Navonia and the 120ft bridge in Balonia must
span the river Nole. The 125ft bridge isn't
over the Rhane (clue 5), so must be over the
Bolta, leaving Baili's 110ft bridge in Greatovia
as the one over the Rhane. By elimination, the
120ft Nole bridge must have been designed
by Archov. Finally, the 105ft Taber bridge by
Voltski isn't in Cashenia (clue 3), so must be
in Barania, leaving Cashenia as the location of
Gettova's 125ft bridge over the Bolta.

Balonia, Nole, Archov, 120 feet.
Barania, Taber, Voltski, 105 feet.
Cashenia, Bolta, Gettova, 125 feet.
Greatovia, Rhane, Baili, 110 feet.
Navonia, Ghames, Krosser, 115 feet.

Tree Surgery, p. 128

A tree at No.15 was being crown-lifted (clue
5) and the dangerous branch was removed
by Trimms (clue 2), so Jack Lumber & Son
working at no. 11, who weren't treating an
infestation or removing a fallen tree (clue
3), must have been cutting down a dead
specimen. It wasn't a beech (clue 1) or a

horse chestnut (clue 3). Dr. Tree was dealing with a maple (clue 1) and the sycamore job was at no. 17 (clue 4), so the Lumbers must have been cutting down the dead evergreen oak. The sycamore was at No.17, so, from clue 1, the beech must have been at No.15 being crown-lifted (clue 5). Also from clue 1, Dr. Tree was working on the maple at No.21. Its problem wasn't the dangerous branch or the infestation which plagued the horse chestnut (clue 3), so it must have fallen and needed to be removed. The sycamore job didn't involve Choppitt & Co. or A Cut Above (clue 4), so this must have been the tree with the dangerous branch dealt with by Trimms. Also from clue 4, Choppitt & Co. must have been working at No.9 and A Cut Above at No.15, crown-lifting the beech, leaving Choppitt & Co. treating the horse chestnut for its infestation at No.9.

A Cut Above, 15, beech, crown-lift.
Choppitt & Co., 9, horse chestnut, treat infestation.
Dr. Tree, 21, maple, remove fallen tree.
Jack Lumber & Son, 11, evergreen oak, cut down dead tree.
Trimms Ltd., 17, sycamore, dangerous branch.

One-hit Backers, p. 130

Johnny Day made the charts in 1956 (clue 1) and Gene Goldman had his hit after 1957 (clue 2), so the 1955 hit, which was not sung by Frankie Lewis (clue 4) or Phil Nash (clue 5), must have been by Bill Bounty and the Mutineers (clue 1). The title wasn't *Just One Kiss* (clue 4), *You're My Baby* (clue 1), *Don't Say Goodbye*, or *Susie Do* (clue 3), so it must have been *River of Tears*. The 1957 hit did not feature the Melodaires or the Songbirds (clue 3), nor was it the Mutineers, who had the 1955 hit, or the Highnotes, in the charts in 1958 (clue 6), so the backing vocals must have been provided by the Heartbeats. *Don't Say*

Goodbye was the 1959 hit (cue 2), so *Susie Do*, featuring the Melodaires (clue 3), must have been Johnny Day's 1956 hit, leaving the 1959 release featuring the Songbirds. The singer was not Gene Goldman (clue 2), so he must have had the 1958 hit with the Highnotes. Frankie Lewis was not backed by the Songbirds (clue 4), so he must have been backed by the Heartbeats on the 1957 song. It was not *Just One Kiss* (clue 4), so it must have been *You're My Baby*. By elimination, the Songbirds must have been Phil Nash's backing group on *Don't Say Goodbye,* and Gene Goldman and the Highnotes must have had the 1958 hit *Just One Kiss.*

Bill Bounty and the Mutineers, 1955, *River of Tears*.
Johnny Day and the Melodaires, 1956, *Susie Do*.
Gene Goldman and the Highnotes, 1958, *Just One Kiss*.
Frankie Lewis and the Heartbeats, 1957, *You're My Baby*.
Phil Nash and the Songbirds, 1959, *Don't Say Goodbye*.

Running Men, p. 132

Bob is after the suit (clue 2) and Matt has his eye on an item of furniture (clue 1), so the shoes, which are not the sale item sought by Keith (clue 3) or Ryan (clue 2), must be the target of Scott, and the shoes must be on offer at Barber and Groves (clue 1). The saving is not 70% (clue 3), 50% (clue 1), 80%, which is the leather couch (clue 6), or 45%, which is the offer on the item at Mitchells (clue 4), so the shoes must be priced at 60% off. The golf clubs are not in the sale at Mitchells or at Lawton and Son (clue 4), nor is it Oakworld, where the desk is on sale (clue 5), so it must be S and L. The leather couch is 80% off (clue 6), so the Mitchells item at 45% off must be the suit that Bob wants, leaving the leather couch in Lawton and Son's sale. It is not Matt's chosen buy (clue 1), so he must want the desk. Keith will not be hurrying to Lawton and Son's sale (clue 3), so it must be S and L, and he must be after the golf clubs. They are not in the sale at 70% off (clue 3), so the reduction must be 50%. By elimination, Lawton and Son must be offering the item wanted by Ryan, and Matt must want a new desk at 70% off.

Bob, Mitchells, suit, 45%.
Keith, S and L, golf clubs, 50%.
Matt, Oakworld, desk, 70%.
Ryan, Lawton and Son, leather couch, 80%.
Scott, Barber and Groves, shoes, 60%.

Weekend Working, p. 134

Kirkby's is a sports store (clue 4), Noble's is in North Street (clue 3), and the bakery is in East Street (clue 6), so Kirkby's, which is the only store with a seven-letter name and so can't be either the one in King Street where Ann works or the one on Market Hill (clue 5), must be in Friars Street. From clue 5, the stores in King Street and Market Hill must each have an eight-letter name and Marsh's, where Shane works (clue 2), must be the bakery in East Street. The pupil who works at Kirkby's isn't Rachel, who works at the newsdealers (clue 3), or Dawn (clue 4), and can't be Ann or Shane, so must be Matt. Rachel doesn't work for Noble's (clue 3), so that must be where Dawn works and Rachel's employer, the newsdealer, must be on Market Hill. The shoe store has a longer name than Kirkby's, where Matt works (clue 1), so it must be either Jackson's or Lubbock's. It's not Jackson's (clue 1), so it must be Lubbock's. From its business, Rachel can't work there, so Ann must do so and Rachel must work for Jackson's, leaving Dawn's employers, Noble's of North Street, as the grocer.

Ann, Lubbock's, shoe store, King Street.
Dawn, Noble's, grocer, North Street.
Matt, Kirkby's, sports store, Friars Street.
Rachel, Jackson's, newsdealer, Market Hill.
Shane, Marsh's, bakery, East Street.

Pulling Rank, p. 136

Tim Shaw's driving cab number 2 (clue 4). Cab 6 is drawn by Old King (clue 2), so clue 1 rules out George Ford as the driver of cab 7, nor can that be Daniel Crick's cab (clue 5) or Robert Quayne's (clues 2 and 7). Clue 7 also rules out Harry Gable's cab, drawn by Zed, as cab 7 and, from clue 3, Wilfred Vine's cab must have an even number, so cab 7 must be Percy Ogden's. His horse can't be Bert (clue 1), Noddy (clue 2), or Venus (clue 3). Cab 4 can't be Harry Gable's, drawn by Zed (clue 6), so cab 6 can't be driven by Robert Quayne (clue 7), so, from that clue, Lincoln can't be pulling cab 7, so cab 7's horse must be Molly. Cab 5 can't be drawn by Zed (clue 7), Venus (clue 3), or Noddy (clue 2). We know Robert Quayne isn't driving any of cabs 2, 6, or 7, nor, since Tim Shaw is driving cab 2, can he be driving cab 4 (clue 7). Clue 7 also rules out cab 1, so Robert Quayne must be driving either cab 3 or cab 5. In either case, cab 5 can't be drawn by Lincoln (clue 7), so, cab 5's horse must be Bert. Clue 1 now tells us that George Ford is the driver of cab 6, drawn by Old King. So the even-numbered cab drawn by Venus (clue 3) can't be cab 4 and must be cab 2 and cab 4 must be driven by Wilfred Vine (clue 3). Neither Daniel Crick (clue 5) nor Robert Quayne (clue 7) can be the driver of cab 1, so that must be Harry Gable's cab, drawn by Zed. This places Robert Quayne as driver of cab 3 (clue 7), leaving Daniel Crick as driver of cab 5. From clue 7, Wilfred Vine's horse must be Lincoln, leaving Robert Quayne's horse as Noddy.

1, Harry Gable, Zed.
2, Tim Shaw, Venus.
3, Robert Quayne, Noddy.
4, Wilfred Vine, Lincoln.

5, Daniel Crick, Bert.
6, George Ford, Old King.
7, Percy Ogden, Molly.

Domino Search, p. 137

0	4	4	6	3	4	2	3
1	5	3	3	3	3	1	6
1	2	1	6	5	5	1	0
6	4	0	0	4	2	5	0
3	4	6	2	0	2	1	6
6	1	0	5	5	0	5	6
2	5	3	2	4	2	1	4

Star Hunting, p. 138

The heptathlete has a pronounced New York accent (clue 2), so the movie stuntwoman, who isn't pregnant or clumsy and is 5 feet 11 inches tall (clue 6), can't be the 5 feet 2 inches tall woman who is too short (clue 4), and must have a squeaky voice. The woman who is too short, who is experienced in children's theater (clue 4), isn't the swimmer (clue 4), and the model's acting experience was in a school play (clue 5), so the diminutive woman must be the circus acrobat. Patsy Quinn is clumsy but isn't the model who was in a school play (clue 5), so she must be the swimmer, leaving the model as the woman who has recently become pregnant. We now know either the name or the acting experience to go with three occupations, so Kim La Veigh, who has no acting experience at all but isn't the heptathlete (clue 1), must be the movie stuntwoman with the squeaky voice. The heptathlete wasn't in the off-broadway play (clue 2), so she must have played herself in

TV ads and it must have been Patsy Quinn, the clumsy swimmer, who had the one non-speaking part. The heptathlete who played herself in TV ads isn't Georgia Hart (clue 2) or Tracey Urban (clue 3), so she must be Andrea Berry. Finally, Tracey Urban isn't the pregnant model (clue 3), so she must be the circus acrobat who has some experience of children's theatre and is too short, leaving Georgia Hart as the model who was in her school play and is now pregnant.

Andrea Berry, heptathlete, played self in TV ads, New York accent.

Georgia Hart, model, school play, pregnant.

Kim La Veigh, movie stuntwoman, none at all, squeaky voice.

Patsy Quinn, swimmer, one non-speaking part, clumsy.

Tracey Urban, circus acrobat, children's theater, too short.

Pass the Parcel, p. 140

Mr. Jarvis' parcel was taken by Miss Isaacs (clue 3) and Mr. Kirby kept his neighbor's parcel in his cloakroom (clue 5), so Mr. Norris' parcel, which was placed in a conservatory (clue 2) but not by Miss Flannagan (clue 2) or Miss Nichols (clue 3), must have been accepted by Mr. Granger and Mr. Norris must live at No.11 (clue 4). The parcel for No.3 was put in the shed (clue 6), so the parcel for Mrs. Kennedy at No.9 (clue 1), which wasn't accepted by Mr. Kirby and so wasn't put in a bathroom (clues 3 and 5) and wasn't put in a garage (clue 1), must have been placed in the summerhouse. It wasn't placed there by Miss Nichols (clue 7), so must have been accepted by Miss Flannagan. Neither Mr. Fletcher nor Miss Holt live at number 3, so this must be Mr. Jarvis's address and Miss Isaacs put his parcel in her shed. Mr. Kirby didn't take the parcel for No.12 (clue 5), so must have accepted a parcel for No.8. This isn't where Miss Holt lives (clue 6, so it must be Mr.

Fletcher's home, leaving the parcel for Miss Holt at No.12 being taken by Miss Nichols and placed in her garage.

Mr. Fletcher, No.8, Mr. Kirby, bathroom.
Miss Holt, No.12, Miss Nichols, garage.
Mr. Jarvis, No.3, Miss Isaacs, shed.
Mrs. Kennedy, No.9, Miss Flannagan, summerhouse.
Mr. Norris, No.11, Mr. Granger, conservatory.

Tennis Aces, p. 142

Each player played three full sets (clue 1), so the three players who lost their first set (clue 4) must have won their second, and similarly the remaining two who won their first set must have lost their second. Also from clue 4, U. Kannat must have lost by the 1-6 score. E. Sagrunta won two sets (clue 5), so he must have won in set 3. From the same clue A. Stitagen, who also won his first set, must have lost the other two. Since only E. Sagrunta was not involved in a tie break at some point (clue 7), the lost tie-break in set 2 must have been recorded by A. Stitagen, who then went on to lose the third set 2-6 (clue 6) and E. Sagrunta must have had the set 2 losing score of 2-6. C. Dedbotham played the same number of games in sets 1 and 2 (clue 3), and we know he lost set 1, but not by 1-6 and neither included a tie break (clue 3), so he must have lost set 1 by 2-6, and therefore won set 2 by 6-2 and, from clue 7, he must have won his third set tie break. Now the only tie-break that U. Kannat could have been involved in is the win in set 2. B. Cereas who lost in set 1 must have done so in the tie break and he must have won the second set 6-4. Now, from clue 1, the only player who could have won set 1 by 6-4 and also won set 3 is E. Sagrunta, leaving A. Stitagen winning the first set 6-3. We know B. Cereas had a 6-4 win in set 2, so from clue 2 his final set must have lasted for nine games and he was the player who lost 3-6. Finally, from clue 7, E. Sagrunta must have won set 3 by 6-1, and U. Kannat won his by 6-4.

A. Stitagen, won 6-3, lost tie-break, lost 2-6.
B. Cereas, lost tie-break, won 6-4, lost 3-6.
C. Dedbotham, lost 2-6, won 6-2, won tie-break.
E. Sagrunta, won 6-4, lost 2-6, won 6-1.
U. Kannat, lost 1-6, won tie-break, won 6-4.

Ant Hill Mob, p. 144

The ant at the back of the line, number 9, can't be Adam or Sybil (clue 1), Gall ant, Dorm ant, or Flip ant (clue 2), or Fez ant or Boy ant (clue 3). Since Gall ant can't be number 7 (clue 1), Fond ant can't be number 9 (clue 2), so Seal ant must be in position 9 with, from clue 3, Fez ant in position 8. So ant 7 can't be Adam ant, Gall ant, Dorm ant, or Flip ant (clue 2), or Boy ant or Sybil ant (clue 3), and so must be Fond ant. So, from clue 2 Adam ant must be ant 6 and Gall ant 5. So Sybil ant's odd-numbered position, which isn't 1 (clue 3), must be 3. Boy ant isn't in position 2 (clue 1) or position 4 (clue 3), so must be at the head of the line. Finally, from clue 2, Dorm ant must be ant 4, and Flip ant must be ant 2.

9 Seal; 8 Fez; 7 Fond; 6 Adam; 5 Gall; 4 Dorm; 3 Sybil; 2 Flip; 1 Boy

4	6	3	5	2	1
6	3	2	4	1	5
2	4	1	3	5	6
5	1	4	2	6	3
1	2	5	6	3	4
3	5	6	1	4	2

Sudoku, p. 145

1	7	3	6	4	9	2	8	5
4	5	8	7	1	2	6	9	3
9	2	6	8	3	5	1	7	4
8	6	4	9	2	7	3	5	1
5	1	2	3	6	8	9	4	7
7	3	9	4	5	1	8	6	2
2	4	7	1	8	6	5	3	9
6	9	5	2	7	3	4	1	8
3	8	1	5	9	4	7	2	6

Before the Pen, p. 146

Jessica's surname is Del Rey (clue 3) and Wallace writes war novels (clue 1), so Brenda, who isn't Wallace or Gordon (clue 1), or McIlwain, whose first name is listed alphabetically after that of the fantasy writer (clue 2), must be Brenda Tiptree, the former flight attendant (clue 5). So she doesn't write humorous novels, which is the genre of the former ferry boat captain (clue 3). Nor is the comedy writer Penny, who writes whodunnits (clue 2), Dave, who was a teacher (clue 6), or Mike (clue 3), so must be Jessica Del Rey.

Penny, the whodunnit writer, isn't McIlwain (clue 2), so she must be Penny Gordon. McIlwain isn't the fantasy writer (clue 2), so must write science fiction, leaving Brenda Tiptree as the fantasy writer. McIlwain the science fiction writer isn't Mike (clue 4), so must be Dave McIlwain, the former teacher, leaving Mike as Mike Wallace, who writes war novels. He's not the former forensic scientist (clue 1), so must have been an undertaker, leaving the forensic scientist as Penny Gordon, who now writes whodunnits.

Brenda Tiptree, fantasy, flight attendant.
Dave McIlwain, science fiction, teacher.
Jessica Del Rey, humorous novels, ferry boat captain.
Mike Wallace, war novels, undertaker.
Penny Gordon, whodunnits, forensic scientist.

Mosaic Mischief, p. 148

Euselus was working in the caldarium (clue 3) and Branelus used the BF signature (clue 5), so the spearing fisherman figure in the natatio, who wasn't representing Cluelus or Hopelus (clue 2), must have been the avatar of Gormlus. The sea nymphs, signed with a heart, weren't being depicted in the apodyterium or the caldarium (clue 3), and Neptune was starring in the tepidarium (clue 1), so they must have been cavorting in the palaestra (exercise room). The romantically inclined servant with the heart signature wasn't Euselus (clue 3) or Hopelus, who was perfecting Medusa (clue 2), so their artist must have been Cluelus. Hopelus wasn't at work in the tepidarium (clue 1), so he must have been in the apodyterium, leaving Branelus adding his BF signature to Neptune in the tepidarium. Gormlus wasn't responsible for the octopus mosaic (clue 4), so he must have been creating dolphins, and the octopus was the work of Euselus. So Euselus didn't identify himself with a shell motif (clue 4) and must have chosen a ship, leaving Hopelus signing his Medusa mosaic with a shell.

Branelus, tepidarium, Neptune, BF.
Cluelus, palaestra, sea nymphs, heart.
Euselus, caldarium, octopus, ship.
Gormlus, natatio, dolphins, fisherman.
Hopelus, apodyterium, Medusa, shell.

Straight and Narrow, p. 150

Sam was placed fifth (clue 5). Aaron received an odd-numbered placing (clue 3), but cannot have been third, ahead of Goliath's partner (clue 7), so must have been the winner. The man on strip B finished sixth (clue 4), so Aaron, who plowed alongside Punch's partner, who also finished in an odd-numbered position (clue 3), cannot have plowed either strip A or strip B. Similarly, since strip E was plowed by Brownie, who did not partner the winner (clue 2), Aaron cannot have been allocated strip E or strip F. Strip D was Billy's (clue 6), so Aaron must have plowed his winning furrows on strip C. So, from clue 3, Punch, who cannot have been part of the team placed sixth on strip B, must have been Billy's horse and their odd-numbered place must have been third. Now, from clue 1, the pairing which gained sixth place on strip B must have been George and Judy. We have matched four men to their finishing positions, so Tom, who was not second (clue 5), must have been Goliath's fourth-placed partner, leaving Harry in second place. Harry's horse was not Brownie (clue 2) or Hector (clue 5), so must have been Caesar. Goliath did not work on strip F (clue 7), so he and Tom must have earned their fourth position on strip A, leaving Harry and Caesar plowing strip F, Brownie's owner as Sam, and Aaron's horse as Hector.

Strip A, Tom, Goliath, fourth.
Strip B, George, Judy, sixth.
Strip C, Aaron, Hector, first.
Strip D, Billy, Punch, third.

Strip E, Sam, Brownie, fifth.
Strip F, Harry, Caesar, second.

Paradisus Lost, p. 152

Yves complained about the view (clue 1) and room 318 has a dysfunctional air conditioner (clue 3), so Zack in room 412, who wasn't complaining about the balcony without any railings (clue 4), must have been in the noisy room with Bridget (clue 2). So Claudia and Xavier, on the floor above Abigail (clue 5), must have been in room 318 with the non-conditioning air conditioner and Abigail must have been in room 216. Yves' partner isn't Deborah (clue 1), so must be Abigail and they must be in room 216 with a view of the water treatment plant, leaving Deborah and Will in room 514 with the decidedly scary "infinity" balcony.

Abigail and Yves, room 216, no view.
Bridget and Zack, room 412, noisy.
Claudia and Xavier, room 318, air con. broken.
Deborah and Will, room 514, balcony unfenced.

Carnival Fun, p. 154

Daisy, who splashed her cash on the cotton candy, didn't end up with $0.50 (clue 1), $1 (clue 2), -$0.64 (clue 3) or a teddy (clue 4), so must have ended the day with nothing. The child who played the slot machine and ended up $0.64 in the red was not Jackson or Frankie (clue 4) so must have been Dylan. Now, from clue 4, Jackson must have ended the day with $0.50 and Frankie must have held onto his dollar after his queasy ride. Daisy didn't ride on the Ferris wheel (clue 1), rollercoaster (clue 2), or Rotor (clue 5), and Jackson rode the ghost train (clue 4), so Daisy must have had a go on the carousel. Miranda spent all her cash so didn't ride on the Rotor either and must have taken a spin on the Ferris wheel, leaving the Rotor as Frankie's dizzying ride. By elimination, Dylan must have ridden the rollercoaster before getting into debt on the slot machine. Jackson didn't have a go on the hook-a-duck (clue 4), so must have had a try on the rifle range, leaving Miranda spending her dollar on the hook-a-duck and winning a teddy bear.

Daisy, carousel, cotton candy, $0.00.
Dylan, rollercoaster, slot machine, -$0.64.
Frankie, Rotor, nothing, $1.
Jackson, ghost train, rifle range, $0.50.
Miranda, Ferris wheel, hook-a-duck, teddy bear.

Saving the Planet, p. 156

Blake has been charged with giving covering fire (clue 4) and the pair who are getting close under cover will be reporting the enemy's movements (clue 1), so Brett, climbing the hill on the left but not to create a diversion (clue 3) or to cut off the alien's retreat (clue 2), must have been told to take out the enemy. So Brett's partner isn't Hayden (clue 5) or Cassidy (clue 2). Regan was ordered to circle round (clue 2) and Ellis and Sean made up one pairing (clue 1), so Brett must have been teamed with Madison to take out the enemy from the hill on the left. We now know either the second partner or order for three first partners, so Cassidy, cutting off the alien retreat but not with Frankie (clue 2), must be partnered with Mason. Since they are cutting off the retreat, they aren't heading for the river (clue 6), so must be starting from the hill on the right. Regan isn't with Frankie (clue 2), so must be circling round with Blake and giving covering fire, leaving Frankie working with Hayden, They aren't going anywhere near the river (clue 2), so must be sneaking close and reporting movements, leaving Ellis and Sean following the river and creating a diversion.

Blake and Regan, circle round and give cover.
Brett and Madison, hill on left and take out enemy.
Ellis and Sean, river and create diversion.
Frankie and Hayden, get close and report movements.
Mason and Cassidy, hill on right and cut off retreat.

Hitting the Wrong Note, p. 158

Cluelus was hoping to join the local band (clue 4) and the hydraulis player wanted to play at Nero's temple (clue 5), so Gormlus, who wasn't out to impress anybody specific with his tibia (clue 1), must have been the servant arrested by Prefect Crassus whilst out playing for tips (clue 4). The servant whose instrument was stolen wasn't Branelus or Euselus (clue 2), and Hopelus managed to break his, so the theft victim was Cluelus. Also from clue 2, it wasn't Euselus who argued with his teacher, so that must have been Branelus, leaving Euselus as the servant who failed to get a note out of his new cornu (clue 3). He wasn't trying to impress his girlfriend (clue 3), so must have been hoping his boss would like his horn playing. The hydraulis aspirant wasn't Hopelus (clue 5), so must have been Branelus until he realized practicing was involved, leaving Hopelus hoping to impress his girlfriend. Cluelus wasn't taking up the cithara (clue 4), so this must have been Hopelus' scheme to impress the young lady, and Cluelus must have been hoping to join the Peperoncini as their new drummer on the tympanum.

Branelus, hydraulis, play in temple, row with teacher.
Cluelus, tympanum, join band, stolen.
Euselus, cornu, impress boss, failed to play.
Gormlus, tibia, playing for tips, arrested.

Hopelus cithara, impress girlfriend,
broke it.

Hello, Wee Ones!, p. 160

Child 4 has fewer candies than both child 3
and child 5 but more than Freddy (clue 4). So
Freddy must be either child 1 or 2, as must
Polly (clue 1). So Rosie, with her 11 candies
at one end of the line (clue 3), must be child
5 and from clue 3, child 1 must have the
bucket. Now, from clue 1, child 4 can't be the
astronaut and child 3 can't be the child with
12 candies, and so must have 10 candies,
with child 4 having 9 and Freddy, 8. The
astronaut collecting in his space helmet is
a boy but not Tommy (clue 1) or Freddy the
firefighter (clue 2), so must be Bobby. So he
isn't child 4 with the plastic bag (clue 1), who
we also know isn't Freddy or Polly (clue 1),
so child 4 must be Tommy with, from clue
1, child 3 as Bobby the astronaut and child 2
must have the 12 candies. We now know the
name, costume or number of candies for four
children, so Freddy the firefighter must have
collected his 8 candies in the bucket of child
1. Now, from clue 1, Polly must be child 2 and
carrying her mom's handbag (clue 2), and
Tommy, in position 4, must be the mermaid.
By elimination, Rosie must be carrying the
pumpkin. Finally, Polly isn't wearing a pirate
costume (clue 1), so must be disguised as
a witch, leaving Rosie dressed as a pirate
and carrying 11 candies in a hollowed-out
pumpkin.

1, Freddy, firefighter, bucket, 8 candies.
2, Polly, witch, handbag, 12 candies.
3, Bobby, astronaut, space helmet, 10
    candies.
4, Tommy, mermaid, plastic bag, 9 candies.
5, Rosie, pirate, pumpkin, 11 candies.

Battleships, p. 161

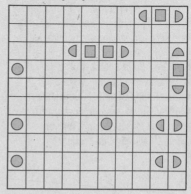

Land of Nod, p. 162

The Minister of Culture has seat 1 (clue 7), so
the man in seat 5 isn't the Minister of Foreign
Affairs (clue 7) or the Doctor who is Minister
of Home Affairs (clue 4). The Admiral has seat
4 (clue 5), so clue 2 rules out the Minister of
Justice for seat 5 and clue 3 rules out the
Minister of Trade, so, it must be the seat of
the Minister of Finance, Miguel Zorra (clue
1). So, from the same clue, the General has
seat 2. Brigadier Jacobo Rata can't have seat
6 (clue 2), nor can the Doctor (clue 4) or the
Professor (clue 3, and we know where the
Admiral and the General sit, so seat 6 must
be the Colonel's and so he is Colonel Felipe
Bicho (clue 6). Now, from clue 7, the Minister
of Foreign Affairs, who we know doesn't have
seat 5, must be the Admiral in seat 4. We
now know that the Doctor doesn't sit in seat
2 and his Ministry rules out seat 1, so, from
clue 4, he must have seat 3. We have now
matched five seats with a title or a name, so
Brigadier Jacobo Rata must sit in seat 1. So,
from clue 2, the General in seat 2 must be
the Minister of Justice, leaving Miguel Zorra
as the Professor and Colonel Felipe Bicho as
the Minister of Trade (clue 3). The Doctor's
name isn't Rafael Arafia (clue 4) or Tadeo
Gusano (clue 6), so he must be Doctor Emilio

Culebra. So, from clue 6, Tadeo Gusano isn't the General who is Minister of Justice, and must be Admiral Tadeo Gusano, the Minister of Foreign Affairs, leaving the General as General Rafael Arafia.

1, Brigadier Jacobo Rata, Culture.
2, General Rafael Arafia, Justice.
3, Doctor Emilio Culebra, Home Affairs.
4, Admiral Tadeo Gusano, Foreign Affairs.
5, Professor Miguel Zorra, Finance.
6, Colonel Felipe Bicho, Trade.

must be Lt. Trowell, and Hut F's tunnel must be under the control of Major Warren.

Hut A, under bed, Sqn. Ldr. Shovell, 341 yards.
Hut C, under stove, Lt. Trowell, 176 yards.
Hut D, back of cupboard, Capt. Burrows, 218 yards.
Hut F, beneath hut steps, Major Warren, 65 yards.
Hut K, in latrine, Sqn. Ldr. Digwell, 22 yards.

Digging Out, p. 164

Sqn. Ldr. Digwell's tunnel begins in Hut K (clue 2) and the one from Hut A is an odd number of yards long (clue 1), so Capt. Burrows' 218-yard tunnel, which doesn't start in Hut F or Hut C (clue 2), must originate in Hut D from the back of the cupboard (clue 4). The tunnel hidden in the latrine is not being supervised by Major Warren or Lt. Trowell (clue 3) or Sqn. Ldr. Shovell, whose tunnel begins beneath a bed (clue 6), so must be Sqn. Ldr. Digwell's excavation and so starts from Hut K. The 22-yard tunnel doesn't start in Hut C (clue 3) or Hut F (clue 2), nor is it Hut A (clue 1), so it must begin in Hut K. So the Hut A tunnel, which is an odd number of yards and longer than the one that starts under the stove (clue 1), must be 341 yards long. So it is not hidden beneath the hut steps (clue 5) or under the stove (clue 1) and must be Sqn. Ldr. Shovell's tunnel starting under the bed. The 65-yard tunnel does not start under the stove (clue 1), so it must be under the hut steps, leaving the 176-yard tunnel as the one starting under the stove. Hut C's tunnel is longer than the one from the latrine, and Major Warren's added together (clue 3), so it must be the one starting under the stove, and the one beneath the steps must be Hut F's. Finally, the Hut C tunnel is not being supervised by Major Warren (clue 3), so it

Jupiter's Feast, p. 166

Priest Suspex is in charge of the meal for Mars (clue 4), so Perspex, looking after a male god with Branelus, but not Vulcan (clue 2), must be preparing the meal for Mercury. Euselus' meal for Minerva wasn't spilt (clue 3) and, being female, she wasn't the deity who had supposedly turned vegan (clue 5). Cluelus' guest was allegedly on a diet (clue 1), and Vulcan apparently liked his meal burnt (clue 2), so Minerva must have developed a sudden allergy. Now Mercury, attended by Perspex, whose meal also wasn't spilt (clue 3), must have, according to Branelus, decided to turn vegan. The priest serving Vulcan with his burnt offering wasn't Suspex (clue 4) or Circumspex (clue 3) and Prospex was serving a goddess (clue 5), so Vulcan's priest was Inspex. Minerva also wasn't served by Circumspex (clue 3), so she must have been Prospex' guest, leaving Circumspex looking after Juno when the servant spilt her food, and Mars must have been the god on the diet attended by Suspex, aided and abetted by Cluelus. Finally, Hopelus was attending a male deity (clue 5), so he was the servant serving burnt food to Vulcan to the dismay of Inspex, leaving Circumspex watching aghast as Gormlus spilt Juno's food.

Branelus, Mercury, Perspex, vegan.
Cluelus, Mars, Suspex, on diet.
Euselus, Minerva, Prospex, allergic.

Gormlus, Juno, Circumspex, spilt.
Hopelus, Vulcan, Inspex, burnt.

Going Nuts, p. 168

Bushy has buried a nut by the rose bed (clue 3), so Chippy hasn't buried any nuts by the potting shed (clue 1), the middle of the lawn (clue 2), or the greenhouse (clue 3), so must have been digging by the pond. So, from clue 2, the squirrel who dug a hole in the middle of the lawn must be Rocky. Now, from clue 1, the hazelnut storer can't be Chippy, Rocky, or Skippy and must be Kernel. So Skippy must have buried nuts near the potting shed (clue 1), leaving Kernel burying hazelnuts by the greenhouse. So, from clue 3, Rocky must have buried pine nuts in the middle of the lawn and, from clue 1, Chippy must have buried a beechnut. Finally, Skippy doesn't like chestnuts (clue 2), so must have buried an acorn by the potting shed, leaving Bushy burying a chestnut by the rose bed.

Chippy, beechnut, pond; Rocky, pine nut, middle of lawn; Kernel, hazelnut, greenhouse; Skippy, acorn, potting shed; Bushy, chestnut, rose bed.

Domino Search, p. 169

0	2	4	6	2	3	4	0
1	4	3	3	5	6	5	1
2	4	1	0	0	2	4	6
2	6	3	5	2	1	1	1
3	5	5	2	3	6	5	1
4	6	0	2	0	6	4	3
3	5	5	0	4	1	0	6

Art Felt, p. 170

Nimbus is by Patience Thynne (clue 2) and *Northern Sky* comprises pebbles in liquid (clue 6), so Gerda Weld's iron rod sculpture, which is not called *Sands of Time* or *Silence* (clue 5), must be *Retribution*. *Silence* is October's sculpture (clue 4), so Ida Grant is not the sculptor of August's car tires (clue 3), which is also not by Connor Cheatham (clue 1), so it must be Adam Pyle and must be called *Sands of Time*. Patience Thynne's sculpture is not made from cinder blocks (clue 2), so it must be the chrome spirals, leaving the cinder blocks as the October piece, *Silence*. Now, from clue 3, the chrome spirals must be on display in November, with Ida Grant's piece in October and Gerda Weld's iron rods in December. So Ida Grant must have used the cinder blocks, and the pebbles in liquid, *Northern Sky*, must be Connor Cheatham's sculpture, on display in September.

August, Adam Pyle, *Sands of Time*, car tires.
September, Connor Cheatham, *Northern Sky*, pebbles in liquid.
October, Ida Grant, *Silence*, cinder blocks.
November, Patience Thynne, *Nimbus*, chrome spirals.
December, Gerda Weld, *Retribution*, iron rods.

Veg Revolt, p. 172

Amy left the veg with the salmon dish (clue 3), and brussels sprouts were in the prawn stir fry (clue 5), so the rutabaga left by Freddie (clue 2), which didn't accompany the breaded cod or veggie burger (clue 2), must have been with the macaroni and cheese served on Monday (clue 4). Lewis left a root veg (clue 1), so the child who left the brussels sprouts, who wasn't Neville (clue 5), must have been Daisy. Lewis left a portion of veg on Tuesday (clue 1), so the salmon dish, which wasn't had on Thursday (clue 3) or Friday (clue 6), must have been the Wednesday dinner. The veg left on this occasion wasn't parsnips (clue 3) and the fava beans were served on Friday (clue 6), so Wednesday's veg must have been beets, leaving Lewis' disliked root veg (clue 1) on Tuesday as parsnips, the prawn stir fry and brussels sprouts as Thursday's offering disliked by Daisy, and Neville leaving the fava beans on Friday. So this wasn't the cod meal (clue 6) and must have been the veggie burger, leaving Lewis leaving the parsnips when they had breaded cod.

Monday, Freddie, macaroni and cheese, rutabaga.
Tuesday, Lewis, breaded cod, parsnips.
Wednesday, Amy, salmon fillets, beets.
Thursday, Daisy, prawn stir fry, brussels sprouts.
Friday, Neville, veggie burgers, fava beans.

Counted Out, p. 174

Ellen instigated the gerbil hunt (clue 3) and Oscar had reached $37 when he was reminded to take the dog out for a walk (clue 5), so Michael, who interrupted him when he'd reached $15 but not to tell him of his favorite TV program or that his grandmother was on the phone (clue 1), must have offered him a cup of coffee, and so Michael was the second interrupter (clue 4). Marie was the fifth person to disturb him (clue 2), so the fourth person to interrupt him wasn't his mom Charlotte (clue 3), or Stanley (clue 6), but must have been Ellen, when he arrived at the sum of $56.40 (clue 6). So, when Marie interrupted for the fifth time and he hadn't counted to a whole number of dollars (clue 2), he must have counted to $53.50. $37 wasn't the running total at the third interruption (clue 5), so must have been first, leaving $48 as the third interruption total. Charlotte didn't make the third interruption, so must have been first, reminding Oscar to walk the

dog just as he got to $37, leaving Stanley interrupting third as the count reached $48. He wasn't telling Oscar about the TV program, so must have been handing over the phone, leaving Marie interrupting fifth and telling Oscar his program was about to start just as he'd reached $53.50

First, Charlotte, reminder to walk the dog, $37.
Second, Michael, coffee made, $15.
Third, Stanley, phone call from grandmother, $48.
Fourth, Ellen, hunt for gerbil, $56.40.
Fifth, Marie, favorite TV program, $53.50.

Snapping the Celebs, p. 176

The chef was due to arrive at 12:40 (clue 3), so the celebrity arriving at 11:40, who wasn't the tennis star (clue 2), the hotelier (clue 1), or the politician (clue 3), must have been the actress flying in from Italy (clue 1). The hotel magnate arrived at Gate 9 (clue 1), and the plane from Ireland arrived at Gate 12 (clue 2), so the actress from Italy, who didn't arrive at Gate 6 (clue 1) or, from her arrival time, Gate 10 (clue 4), must have landed at Gate 14. So, from clue 2, the tennis star must have arrived at Gate 10. The plane which landed at 14:10 hadn't come from Ireland (clue 2), Sweden (clue 3), or Cyprus (clue 4), so must have arrived from Slovakia. It didn't arrive at Gate 6, or, from its arrival time, Gate 9 (clue 1), so it must have landed at Gate 10 carrying the tennis star. So from clue 2 the plane from Ireland was due in at 13:40. The flight from Sweden wasn't bringing the chef or the politician (clue 3), so must have been carrying the hotelier. Arriving at 12:40, the chef couldn't have flown in from Ireland, so must have come from Cyprus, leaving the plane from Ireland carrying the politician due 13:40 at Gate 12, the chef's flight from Cyprus docking at Gate 6 and the hotelier from Sweden arriving at Gate 9 at 12:10.

Actress, Italy, Gate 14, 11:40.
Chef, Cyprus, Gate 6, 12:40.
Hotel magnate, Sweden, Gate 9, 12:10.
Politician, Ireland, Gate 12, 13:40.
Tennis star, Slovakia, Gate 10, 14:10.

What a Shower, p. 178

The peach essence is blended with watermelon (clue 1) and the gel with lime is colored orange (clue 3), so the red gel which contains lemon but not cranberry or orange (clue 4), must be a blend of lemon and mango. Blueburst is blue (clue 1), Fruitfool contains cranberry, and Summerset has essence of strawberry, so the red lemon and mango gel, which isn't Wellnow (clue 4), must be Cloudchaser. The blue Blueburst doesn't contain peach (clue 1), so must have orange as its first ingredient. By elimination, Summerset's strawberry essence must be blended with lime in the orange-colored gel, and the peach and watermelon gel must be Wellnow. It's not colored green (clue 1), so must be yellow and the cranberry Fruitfool must be green. So it doesn't contain banana (clue 5), and must be essence of cranberry and raspberry, leaving blue Blueburst with a combination of orange and banana.

Blueburst, blue, orange, and banana.
Cloudchaser, red, mango, and lemon.
Fruitfool, green, cranberry, and raspberry.
Summerset, orange, lime, and strawberry.
Wellnow, yellow, peach, and watermelon.

Battleships, p. 180

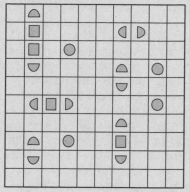

Americans Abroad, p. 181

The new member of the Mechanical Eng. Dept. arrived in January (clue 2), so Dr. Hancock of the Physics Dept., who arrived before Prof. Franklin (clue 2) must have arrived in February, Prof. Franklin must have turned up in March, and the January arrival at Mech. Eng. must be Dr. Bartlett. So, Prof. Franklin must have traveled to the History Dept. for some research for a book (clue 1). Dr. Bartlett is not on a teaching assignment (clue 3), so must have arrived in January to take part in some academic research, leaving Dr. Hancock joining the Physics Dept. in February on a teaching assignment.

Dr. Bartlett, Mechanical Eng., January, academic research.
Dr. Hancock, Physics, February, teaching.
Prof. Franklin, History, March, book research.

Gnomes and All, p. 182

The Wimseys cannot have two or six figures in their yard (clue 1), while the Stones have three (clue 4). Nor can the Wimseys live at No.9 (clue 1), where the yard boasts four ornaments (clue 6), so they must have five.

So, from clue 1, their higher-numbered neighbors must have six gnomes. Clue 1 now rules out No.1 for five or six figures and we know there are not four. Clues 1 and 4, taken together, rule out two, so there must be three figures in the yard at No.1, which must be the Stones' home. Clue 4 now tells us the Masons have four fairies in their yard, and so they must live at No.9. Clue 1 rules out the six gnomes for No.3 and clue 3 rules out only two ,so No.3 must have five and is where the Wimseys live. So, from clue 1, the six gnomes are at No.5, leaving No.7, home to the Lovetts (clue 5), with two figures in its yard and the owners of the six gnomes at No. 5 as the Deckhams. We have named the ornaments at No.5 and No.9, so clue 7 rules out both the cats and the rabbits for No.7, whose two figures must be dogs. Clue 7 now tells us the rabbits must be the three figures at No.1, and it must be the Wimseys at No.3 who have five cats on view.

No.1, Stone, 3 rabbits.
No.3, Wimsey, 5 cats.
No.5, Deckham, 6 gnomes.
No.7, Lovett, 2 dogs.
No.9, Mason, 4 fairies.

The Haunted *Oyster*, p. 184

Holly Jurado isn't the fund raiser (clue 2), the engineer who heard voices or the attorney (clue 4), or the police officer, who is Kent Larsen (clue 5), so must be the tour guide. She didn't see the lookout climbing the rigging (clue 2), nor did she see the ghostly parrot (clue 2). Velda Young saw the wounded pirate (clue 3), so Holly Jurado must have seen the pirate captain. So her experience wasn't on the poop deck (clue 3), nor on the fo'c'sle, where the attorney had his or her experience (clue 1), or by the ship's wheel, where Perry Riordan's experience took place (clue 1), so it must have been in the ship's hold. The attorney didn't see the pirates (clue

2), and since he or she had an encounter on the fo'c'sle, didn't spot the lookout in the rigging, so the attorney must have seen the wounded pirate and is Velda Young (clue 3). We now know the locations for three experiences, so the engineer, who heard voices but not at the ship's wheel (clue 1), must have done so on the poop deck, leaving Perry Riordan's experience at the ship's wheel as the spectre of a spectral parrot, leaving the engineer who heard voices on the poop deck as Boyce Cramer. Finally, Kent Larsen, the police officer, must have seen the lookout clambering through the rigging, leaving Perry Riordan, who saw the pirates at the ship's wheel, as the fund raiser.

Boyce Cramer, engineer, heard voices, poop deck.
Holly Jurado, tour guide, saw captain, ship's hold.
Kent Larsen, police officer, saw lookout, rigging.
Perry Riordan, fund raiser, saw parrot, ship's wheel.
Velda Young, attorney, saw wounded pirate, fo'c'sle.

Tricky Snaps, p. 186

Arnold sat on the deck (clue 1) and Deanna was the fourth person Jake tried to photograph (clue 4), so the second person targeted, who was by the vegetable plot but who wasn't Fiona or Nick (clue 5), must have been Petra. Nick wore the brimmed hat (clue 2), so the person who ducked out of the hammock (clue 4), who wasn't Deanna (clue 4), must have been Fiona. Nick wasn't by the apple tree (clue 2), so must have been by the pond, leaving Deanna by the apple tree. The third person snapped hid behind an umbrella (clue 3), so Petra, who didn't hide behind a book (clue 6), must have used her hands as a shield. By elimination, Deanna, fourth to be snapped, must have hid behind a book when snapped by the apple tree and it must have been Arnold who was Jake's third target and hid behind the golf umbrella by the deck. Finally Fiona, ducking out of the hammock, wasn't Jake's first attempted photo, so she must have been his last, leaving Nick's broad brimmed hat thwarting Jake's first picture by the pond.

First, Nick, brimmed hat, pond.
Second, Petra, hands, vegetable plot.
Third, Arnold, umbrella, deck.
Fourth, Deanna, book, apple tree.
Fifth, Fiona, ducked, hammock.

Models, p. 188

Dara's garment was woolen (clue 2), so Zara, who cannot have modeled Moochy's leather garment (clue 3) or the golden fleece or fake fur (clue 2), must be modeling mohair. Her garment isn't gold or silver (clue 2), or purple (clue 3), and Lara's outfit is pink (clue 1), so Zara's mohair garment must be black. Tara models for Moonshine (clue 1). Dara doesn't work for Marbles (clue 2) or Marshmallow (clue 3) and her woolen outfit rules out Moochy, so she must model for Mermaid, leaving Cara in the Moochy leather ensemble. It isn't purple (clue 3), pink, or gold (clue 1), so must be silver. By elimination, Dara is wearing purple wool and Tara is modeling the golden fleece, leaving Lara's pink costume as the fake fur creation. From clue 3, she is not modeling for Marshmallow, so must be working for Marbles, leaving Zara as the mannequin modeling for Marshmallow.

Cara, Moochy, silver leather.
Dara, Mermaid, purple wool.
Lara, Marbles, pink fake fur.
Tara, Moonshine, gold fleece.
Zara, Marshmallow, black mohair.

Going for a Paddle, p. 190

From clue 1, the Scottish kayaker is not 1st, 2nd, 3rd, or 6th. The Canadian is 4th (clue 6), so the Scot must be 5th and, from clue 1, Neville Langtry, who also cannot be numbered 1st, 2nd, 3rd, or 6th, must be the Canadian in 4th place in kayak 4. The English competitor is also not numbered 1st or 6th (clue 2), and we know he is not 4th or 5th. Collier is 2nd (clue 5), so the Englishman, Mr. Baldwin (clue 2), must be 3rd and is Jeff Baldwin (clue 7). So, from clue 2, the South African must be Mr. Collier in 2nd place. We now know the man in 6th place is not from Canada, England, Scotland, or South Africa, nor can he be the Australian, Craig (clue 4), so he must be from New Zealand, leaving the Australian leading the race. So, from clue 4, Rupert must be Rupert Collier in 2nd position. Craig, in the lead, cannot be Pearson or Scott (clue 3), so he must be Craig Gregson. Now, from clue 3, Pearson must be the Scot in 5th place and Scott the New Zealander in 6th. Mr. Scott is not Will (clue 3), so he must be Marlon Scott, leaving Will as Will Pearson.

1st, kayak 3, Craig Gregson, Australia.
2nd, kayak 1, Rupert Collier, South Africa.
3rd, kayak 6, Jeff Baldwin, England.
4th, kayak 4, Neville Langtry, Canada.
5th, kayak 2, Will Pearson, Scotland.
6th, kayak 5, Marlon Scott, New Zealand.

New Skills, p. 192

Prisoner 397 learned the art of pick pocketing (clue 1) and the arsonist learned forgery skills (clue 3), so Prisoner 124, who was in for burglary but who didn't learn to bake or speak Mandarin (clue 5), must have learned cabinet making. Prisoner 523 was sentenced to 6 months (clue 2), so the prisoner sentenced to 8 months for being disorderly (clue 4), who wasn't prisoner 418 or 649 (clue 6), must have been prisoner 397. The 12-month sentence wasn't handed down to

Prisoner 418 or Prisoner 649 (clue 6), so that must have been Prisoner 124's sentence for burglary, during which he trained as a cabinet maker. The prisoner who learned baking skills was given 15 months (clue 5), so the newly accomplished forger, who wasn't serving 18 months, must have been Prisoner 523 serving 6 months, leaving the new Mandarin speaker finishing an 18-month sentence. This wasn't Prisoner 418 (clue 6), so must have been Prisoner 649. So he wasn't convicted of vandalism and must have been sent down for dangerous driving, leaving Prisoner 418 learning to bake while serving a 15-month sentence for vandalism.

Prisoner 124, cabinet making, burglary, 12 months.

Prisoner 397, pick pocketing, disorderly conduct, 8 months.

Prisoner 418, baking, vandalism, 15 months.

Prisoner 523, forgery, arson, 6 months.

Prisoner 649, Mandarin, dangerous driving, 18 months.

If Not In . . . , p. 194

The second parcel is for King Row (clue 3) and the third can be left with a neighbor (clue 4), so the box for Sunny Lane that can be left in the shed, but which isn't fourth (clue 1), must be the first delivery, and, from clue 1, Mr. Hooper's box must be second, and so he lives in King Row. By elimination, Mrs. Angel's box, which can be left in the garage (clue 5), must be fourth to be delivered, and its street address, which isn't Middle Street (clue 5), must be Stable Hill. Now, by elimination, the third parcel might be left with a neighbor in Middle Street and the second delivery, to King Row, could be left in the greenhouse. Finally, from clue 2, the first delivery must be to Mr. Smith, leaving the third parcel addressed to Mrs. Frost.

First, Mr. Smith, Sunny Lane, shed.

Second, Mr. Hooper, King Row, greenhouse.

Third, Mrs. Frost, Middle Street, neighbor.

Fourth, Mrs. Angel, Stable Hill, garage.

Wardrobe Choice, p. 195

Suit 3 doesn't have green cloth (clue 2), red, or gray (clue 3) or yellow or blue (clue 4), and so must have white cloth. So the white fur, which, from clue 4, must be on suit 2 or 3, can't be on suit 3 (clue 1) and must be on suit 2. So, from clue 4, suit 5 must have yellow cloth and suit 4 must have red fur. Now, the green cloth, numbered twice the green fur (clue 2), isn't on suit 4 and isn't matched with the white fur on suit 2 (clue 2) and must be on suit 6 with the green fur accompanying the white cloth on suit 3. The blue fur isn't on suit 5 (clue 3) and can't be on suit 1 (clue 4), so must be on suit 6 with the green cloth. The yellow suit 5 doesn't have yellow fur (clue 1), so must have gray fur, leaving the yellow fur on suit 1. So this suit doesn't have red cloth (clue 3) and nor does the red-furred suit 4 (clue 1), so suit 2 must be red and white. Finally, the gray suit isn't suit 1 (clue 3) and must be suit 4 with red fur, leaving suit 1 as blue with yellow fur. Santa's chosen outfit for this year is not suit 3 or 6 (clue 2), suit 1 or 4 (clue 3), or suit 5 (clue 4), and so must be suit 2, the red and white—what were the odds?

1, blue cloth, yellow fur; 2, red cloth, white fur; 3, white cloth, green fur; 4, gray cloth, red fur; 5, yellow cloth, gray fur; 6, green cloth, blue fur.

McGann's Gun, p. 196

The gunrunner was arrested in June (clue 6), but not in the bath, where the bank-robber was arrested (clue 4), or at the card table, scene of the October arrest (clue 1). The gunrunner's arrest in June was the only one in that quarter of the year, so he can't have been either Buck Akins, who was arrested in bed, or the man arrested in the stable, as both were arrested in the same quarter (clue 5), so the gunrunner must have been arrested in the bar. The places of arrest of the two men mentioned in clue 5 tells us that neither of them was arrested in October (clue 1), so, both must have been arrested in the first quarter of the year—in February or March. So the bank robber caught in the bath must have been arrested in December and was Zeb Young (clue 2). The gunrunner arrested in June wasn't Deke Carroll (clue 6) or Rio Pike, who was a gunman (clue 1). We know where Buck Akins and Zeb Young were arrested, so the gunrunner arrested in the bar in June must have been Marty Lock. Rio Pike, the gunman, wasn't arrested in October (clue 1), so it must have been Deke Carroll who was arrested that month at the card table, leaving Rio Pike as the man arrested in the stable. The rustler was arrested earlier than Marty Lock, who we now know was arrested in June (clue 3), so he must have been arrested in the first quarter of the year. It wasn't in February (clue 3), so must have been in March and he must have been Buck Akins, who was arrested in bed. By elimination, Rio Pike the gunman must have been arrested in February and Deke Carroll, arrested at the card table in October, must have been the train robber.

Buck Akins, rustler, in bed, March.
Deke Carroll, train robber, at card table, October.
Marty Lock, gunrunner, in bar, June.
Rio Pike, gunman, in stable, February.
Zeb Young, bank robber, in bath, December.

Quest in Venice, p. 198

The form of transport to reach the first stop on the quest wasn't a vaporetto water-bus (clue 1), a gondola (clue 2), or by walking (clue 5), and the traghetto barge was third in the sequence (clue 4), so the first message was reached by a privately hired boat. It didn't take me to the Lido (clue 5), the Rialto Bridge, or St. Mark's Square (clue 3), and I walked to the Doge's Palace (clue 5), so it must have been when I found the Beware of the Doge envelope on Murano (clue 1). So from clue 1, I found the second envelope after a trip on a vaporetto. The final clue wasn't in an envelope inscribed Mariners Wanted (clue 2), Tadzio Was Here (clue 3), or My Other Attorney . . . (clue 5), so it must have been inscribed Iago Hearts Des. I didn't reach it after a trip by gondola (clue 2), so it must have contained the final clue discovered after walking to the Doge's Palace, leaving my gondola trip as fourth in the sequence. It didn't take me to St. Mark's Square (clue 3), or to the Lido, which, from clue 5, can't have been visited later than third, so the gondola must have taken me to Rialto Bridge. I didn't find the clue Tadzio Was Here at either the Rialto or St. Mark's Square (clue 3), so I must have found it at the Lido and, from clue 3, the visit to the Lido must have been second and St. Mark's Square, which wasn't the fourth location (clue 3), must have been third, reached by the traghetto ferry. From clue 2, the clue reached fourth at the Rialto Bridge by gondola wasn't Marco Polo's plea for a crew, and so must have concerned Portia the attorney, leaving the third envelope found after a trip on a traghetto to St. Mark's Square to discover the envelope inscribed Mariners Wanted.

First, Beware of the Doge, Murano, hired boat.
Second, Tadzio Was Here, Lido, vaporetto.
Third, Mariners Wanted, St. Mark's Square, traghetto.
Fourth, My Other Attorney, Rialto Bridge, gondola.
Fifth, Iago Hearts Des, Doge's Palace, walking.

Santa at Sea, p. 200

The *Santa Cristina* was sponsored by Denmark (clue 5) and the *Santa Almira* spent a few months in a "sea" (clue 2), so the *Santa Bonita*, which arrived back in December (clue 3) and so couldn't have been paid for by Holland (clue 3) or by Italy (clue 1) or Portugal (clue 5), must have been sponsored by France. So, from clue 4, the *Santa Cristina* must have arrived back in November and, from clue 6, the captain of the *Santa Dominga* must have claimed to have seen a hole in the seabed. The ship that arrived back in August wasn't the *Santa Almira* or the *Santa Eloisa* (clue 2) and so must have been the *Santa Domingo*. So the *Santa Eloisa* can't have returned in September (clue 2) and must have returned in October, leaving the *Santa Almira* as the ship sailing home in September. So, from clue 2, the *Santa Almira* must have discovered the West Pole. It wasn't sponsored by Italy (clue 1) or Portugal (clue 5), and so must have been paid for by Holland. So, from clue 3, the *Santa Eloisa* must have glimpsed the edge of the world. Captain Gander, who discovered the center of the world (clue 4), wasn't sponsored by France (clue 4), so must have been patronized by Denmark to sail the *Santa Cristina*, leaving the captain of the *Santa Bonita* claiming he had found a new continent. Now, from clue 1, the ship that hid in the Black Sea can only be the *Santa Cristina*, with the *Santa Bonita* being led by Captain Tourrite and the *Santa Dominga* being sponsored by Italy, leaving the *Santa Eloisa* sailing under the patronage of Portugal and, from clue 5, the *Santa Dominga* spending a few months in the South Atlantic. So, from clue 7, the *Santa Dominga* must have been under the command of Captain Brausch. The *Santa Almira* wasn't led by Pedlar, so must have been commanded by Captain Gonzales, leaving Captain Pedlar sailing the *Santa Eloisa* into the North Sea (clue 7). Finally, the "sea" in which the *Santa Almira* spent some time (clue 2) must have been the Mediterranean, leaving the *Santa Bonita* hiding in the North Atlantic.

Santa Almira, Capt. Gonzales, Holland, September, West Pole, Mediterranean Sea.

Santa Bonita, Capt. Tourrite, France, December, new continent, North Atlantic.

Santa Cristina, Capt. Gander, Denmark, November, center of the world, Black Sea.

Santa Dominga, Capt. Brausch, Italy, August, hole in the sea bed, South Atlantic.

Santa Eloisa, Capt. Pedlar, Portugal, October, edge of the world, North Sea.

Still Lifers, p. 202

Wax crayons were used for the picture of one student's husband (clue 2) and Delia d'Auber's offering was the pencil sketch (clue 1), so Tammy Tempera's fishbowl, which wasn't in oils or charcoal (clue 5), must have been a watercolor. The creditable oil painting wasn't of the husband or the vase (clue 5) or the unlucky missing dragonfly (clue 1), so must have been the boiled egg. Its painter wasn't Simone Smeare (clue 3) or Paula Pastell, whose work was unusual (clue 4), so it must have been Leona Lande-Scaype. Delia's pencil drawing wasn't of the twig/dragonfly (clue 1) or her husband (clue 2), so must have been of the vase. Pockson didn't say it needs refining (clue 3), so he must have thought it has potential. Nor did Simone's work need refining (clue 3), so hers must have been the unlucky choice of the elusive dragonfly and twig, leaving Tammy's fishbowl needing refining, the portrait of her husband in wax crayon being Paula's unusual subject choice and Simone sketching the twig in charcoal before the dragonfly flew off.

Delia d'Auber, vase, pencil, has potential.

Leona Lande-Scaype, boiled egg, oils, creditable effort.

Paula Pastell, husband, wax crayon, unusual.

Simone Smeare, dragonfly, charcoal, unlucky choice.
Tammy Tempera, fishbowl, watercolor, needs refining.

Cracking Up, p. 204

The Shellraiser cracks hazelnuts (clue 2), so the brazil-cracking gadget, which isn't the Kernelator or the Nutworker (clue 3), must be the Crackomatic. The cracker with added spannerism makes short work of almonds (clue 1), so the Kernelator with its vise device (clue 3) must handle walnuts, leaving the Nutworker as the cracker that uses spannerism to deal with almonds. The Shellraiser doesn't employ hammerology (clue 2), so must display pliersaction, leaving hammerology used by the Crackomatic to crack brazils. From clue 3, the Kernelator and the Crackomatic must each be either cracker A or D so, from clue 1, the Nutworker with its almond-crushing spannerism must be cracker C, and the pliersaction-employing Shellraiser must be cracker B. So the Crackomatic complete with hammerology must be cracker A (clue 2), leaving cracker D as the Kertnelator opening walnuts with its vise device.

A, Crackomatic, hammerology, brazils.
B, Shellraiser, pliersaction, hazelnuts.
C, Nutworker, spannerism, almonds.
D, Kernelator, vise device, walnuts.

Logi-5, p. 205

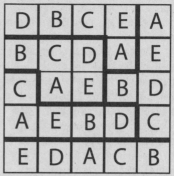

D	B	C	E	A
B	C	D	A	E
C	A	E	B	D
A	E	B	D	C
E	D	A	C	B

Killer Sudoku, p. 205

5	8	7	3	9	1	2	4	6
3	4	1	6	5	2	7	9	8
6	2	9	4	8	7	3	5	1
8	7	2	5	1	6	4	3	9
4	9	6	8	7	3	1	2	5
1	3	5	2	4	9	8	6	7
2	1	3	7	6	5	9	8	4
7	6	8	9	3	4	5	1	2
9	5	4	1	2	8	6	7	3

House Hunters, p. 206

Mr. and Mrs. Hall are interested in the Broadlands property (clue 6) and the Hawkeses have the midday appointment (clue 2), so the appointment at 1 o'clock in Grove Close, which is not with Mr. Jackson (clue 2) and cannot be with Mr. and Mrs. McDonald (clue 4), must be with Miss Cole who will be shown the extensive views (clue 5). From clue 4, the property with the large solid oak kitchen is not being viewed until midday at the earliest. The 1 o'clock viewer is Miss Cole, so, from clue 4, the kitchen isn't in the house being viewed at 2 o'clock so it must be the main selling feature of the property being seen at midday. So Southfields must be the property being viewed at 11 o'clock and Mr. and Mrs. McDonald must have the 10 o'clock appointment (clue 4), leaving the potential buyer of the Southfields house, being inspected at 11 o'clock, as Mr. Jackson and Broadlands as the 2 o'clock venue. The property with three en-suite bathrooms being viewed by the McDonalds at 10 isn't that in Bear Lane (clue 1), so it must be the Linden Drive one, leaving Mr. and Mrs. Hawkes as the couple looking at Bear Lane. Finally, the house with the original features is not in Southfields (clue 3), so it must be in Broadlands, leaving the property in Southfields as the one with the double garage.

10 a.m., Linden Drive, Mr. and Mrs. McDonald, en-suite bathrooms.
11 a.m., Southfields, Mr. Jackson, double garage.
12 noon, Bear Lane, Mr. and Mrs. Hawkes, oak kitchen.
1 p.m., Grove Close, Miss Cole, extensive views.
2 p.m., Broadlands, Mr. and Mrs. Hall, original features.

Five Children and IT, p. 208

Lolly is seven (clue 2), so Bill, who wants to make a flying carpet but isn't five or nine (clue 2) , must be six. Now Amber must be nine (clue 2) and in the care of Kez (clue 3) and the five-year-old twins must be Sunshine and Moondown (clue 1). From clue 3, Baz must now be helping six-year-old Bill with his flying carpet project and seven-year-old Lolly must be hoping to become invisible. Amber does not want to make a robot horse (clue 2) and Jez's charge is after a magic pencil (clue 1), so Amber must want to convert the remaining pencils into diamonds (clue 1). Caz isn't minding Moondown (clue 3) so she must

be looking after Sunshine, leaving Moondown as Jez's charge working on the magic pencil. By elimination, Sunshine must be trying to make a robot horse and Daz must be responsible for trying to make Lolly invisible.

Amber, 9 years, Kez, diamonds.
Bill, 6 years, Baz, flying carpet.
Lolly, 7 years, Daz, invisibility.
Moondown, 5 years, Jez, magic pencil.
Sunshine, 5 years, Caz, robot horse.

Monstrous, p. 210

One movie features a monster played by Glen Ogle and designed by Gus Hoch (clue 4), and the monster in *Heartquake* was designed by Eddie Gold (clue 5), so the director with both initials from the same half of the alphabet who designed Emily Donner's costume for *Shock After Shock* (clue 3) must have been Riley Palmer. The movie featuring Count Roden, directed by and with a monster designed by Josie Royce, wasn't *Anomaly* (clue 6), nor *The Pit*, which featured the Alien Angel (clue 1), so Count Roden must feature in *Monsteropolis*. Since the monster was created by director Josie Royce, Count Roden can't have been played by Glen Ogle or Emily Donner, nor by Dan Chaney (clue 2) or Jay Kingston, who played Croc Man (clue 5), so the star of *Monsteropolis* must be Tania Strange. The movie in which Jay Kingston plays Croc Man isn't *Heartquake*, for which director Eddie Gold created the monster (clue 5), and we know the directors to go with three other movies, so Croc Man must have been created by director Meg O'Brian, leaving the *Heartquake* monster played by Dan Chaney and *The Pit*'s Alien Angel must have been played by Glen Ogle and created by Gus Hoch. By elimination, *Anomaly* must feature Croc Man, played by Jay Kingston and created by Meg O'Brian. Finally, *Shock After Shock*, which didn't feature the Faceless Killer (clue 3), must have featured the Stalker and the Faceless Killer must have featured in *Heartquake*.

Anomaly, Croc Man, Jay Kingston, Meg O'Brian.

Heartquake, Faceless Killer, Dan Chaney, Eddie Gold.

Monsteropolis, Count Roden, Tania Strange, Josie Royce.

Shock After Shock, Stalker, Emily Donner, Riley Palmer.

The Pit, Alien Angel, Glen Ogle, Gus Hoch.

French Connection, p. 212

The Belgian volunteered because he wanted a change (clue 3) and the Swiss was in the Murder Squad (clue 2), so the Organized Crime expert who isn't French but who joined up to avoid investigation (clue 4) and therefore isn't Briton Chris Brookes (clue 1), must be the Canadian. He's not Jules Lebrun (clue 2), Etienne Delacroix, who joined up to get promoted (clue 5), or Armand Bonvin, who was in the Robbery Squad (clue 6), so he must be Olivier St. Michel. Chris Brookes from Britain didn't volunteer as an alternative to sacking or for promotion, so he must have been avoiding his ex-wife. His speciality wasn't Vice (clue 1), so it must have been Car Crime. The Belgian's speciality wasn't Robbery (clue 3), so it must have been Vice, and Armand Bonvin, the Robbery expert, must be French, leaving Etienne Delacroix, who volunteered to get promoted, as the Swiss ex-Murder Squad man, Jules Lebrun as the Belgian ex-Vice Squad man who joined for a change, and Armand Bonvin as the French ex-Robbery Squad man who volunteered as an alternative to being sacked.

Armand Bonvin, French, Robbery, avoid sacking.

Chris Brookes, British, Car Crime, avoiding ex-wife.

Etienne Delacroix, Swiss, Murder, wants promotion.

Jules Lebrun, Belgian, Vice, wanted a change.

Olivier St. Michel, Canadian, Organized Crime, avoid investigation.

PC Ballets, p. 214

Sleeping Person is by Klunka (clue 2) and Felicia Makeover is dancing the work by Teesonsky (clue 3), so Marcie Hussle in *Nutstacker*, which isn't a score by Beliebes or Nokofiev (clue 1), must be interpreting the ballet by Edith Eve. This isn't in Stoneville (clue 6) or Storbury (clue 1). *Romeo & Julian* is on in Madison (clue 5) and Hannah Vacherin is appearing in Chester (clue 2), so Marcie must be dancing at the Clinton Garden Bowl. Hannah in Chester isn't in the ballet by Klunka (clue 2) or Teesonsky and the Nokofiev work is in Storbury (clue 1), so Hannah must be in the work by Beliebes. The Nokofiev score isn't *Sleeping Person* (clue 2) or *The Differently Attractive Sisters* (clue 3), so must be *Duck Pond*. Its star isn't Felicia or Frasquita Cornward (clue 4), so must be Margery Cascayde, leaving the Klunka ballet featuring Frasquita in *Sleeping Person*. She's not delighting her fans in Madison (clue 5), so must be gracing the stage in Stoneville, leaving the diva appearing in Madison as Felicia, dancing in *Romeo & Julian,* and Hannah starring in *The Differently Attractive Sisters* by Beliebes in Chester.

Felicia Makeover, *Romeo & Julian*, Teesonsky, Madison Odeon.

Frasquita Cornward, *Sleeping Person*, Klunka, Stoneville Arena.

Hannah Vacherin, *The . . . Sisters*, Beliebes, Chester Arts Center.

Marcie Hussle, *The Nutstacker*, Eve, Clinton Garden Bowl.

Margery Cascayde, *Duck Pond*, Nokofiev, Storbury Opera House.

Cluney Tunes, p. 216

David Cluney, Simon's nephew, didn't play Sergeant Wood or Jean (clue 2), Ginger, who was played by John Cluney (clue 4), or Dr. Jones, who was played by his stepson (clue 1), so he must have played the Store Worker in episode 2 (clue 5). So, from clue 2, Sergeant Wood appeared in episode 3 and so was played by Simon's brother (clue 6). John Cluney, who played Ginger, isn't Simon's son (clue 4), so he must be his cousin, leaving his son as the one who played Jean. John Cluney didn't play Ginger in episode 1 or 5 (clue 4), so must have done so in episode 4. Clue 1 rules out episode 1 for Dr. Jones, so Simon's stepson must have played him in episode 5, leaving Jean, Simon's son's character, in episode 1. The stepson who played Dr. Jones in episode 5 wasn't Gary Jones (clue 1) and can't have been Larry Cluney (clue 3), so must have been Wayne Rovik. Larry Cluney didn't play Sergeant Wood in episode 3 (clue 6), so he must have played Jean in episode 1 and is therefore Simon's son, leaving Gary Jones as the one who appeared as Sergeant Wood in episode 3 and so is Simon's brother.

Episode 1, Jean, Larry Cluney, son.
Episode 2, Store Worker, David Cluney, nephew.
Episode 3, Sergeant Wood, Gary Jones, brother.
Episode 4, Ginger, John Cluney, cousin.
Episode 5, Dr. Jones, Wayne Rovik, stepson.

Witches' Brew?, p. 218

Florence helped to brew Gory Gizzards (clue 2) and the Blood Sucker wine was first to be drunk (clue 4), so the second wine that was tried, which Tamsin helped to brew (clue 1) but which wasn't Bony Finger or Witch's Warts (clue 1), must have been Toads and Tails, initially mixed by the six-year-old (clue 3). The Blood Sucker wine wasn't brewed by Grace or Jody, so must have been mixed

by Amy. Jody was seven years old (clue 4), so the nine-year-old whose brew was the last to be drunk (clue 5), but who isn't Grace, must be Florence, and Gory Gizzards was the last tipple to be drunk. Amy wasn't ten (clue 6), so must have been eight, leaving Grace as the ten-year-old. Her brew wasn't sampled fourth (clue 6), so must have been third. So it wasn't called Witch's Warts (clue 6) and must have been Bony Finger, leaving seven-year-old Jody mixing up the brew that was called Witch's Warts and tasted fourth.

Amy, eight, Blood Sucker, first.
Florence, nine, Gory Gizzards, fifth.
Grace, ten, Bony Finger, third.
Jody, seven, Witch's Warts, fourth.
Tamsin, six, Toads and Tails, second.

Animal Magnetism, p. 220

The boy with 16 goats got together with the lass with 29 sheep (clue 1) and Clarissa fell for the beaming smile of the boy with 10 goats (clue 4), so Francis, who fell in love with Mary and who had fewer than 20 goats (clue 2), must have had 18 goats. Lucy had 37 sheep (clue 5) and Seth hooked up with the shepherdess who had 30 sheep (6), so Mary, who didn't have the fewest sheep (clue 2), must have had 43. Seth had more goats than Thomas, so couldn't have been the object of Clarissa's affection (clue 4) and didn't get together with Dorinda (clue 6), so he and Phyllida must have become an item. We now know the shepherdess or the number of sheep for three numbers of goats, so Lucy's boyfriend, who didn't have 25 goats to go with her 37 sheep (clue 5), must have had 22 sheep, leaving Phyllida's lad Seth with 25 goats to go with her 30 sheep. By elimination, Dorinda must have been the shepherdess with 29 sheep who fell in love with the boy with 16 goats (clue 1) and Clarissa must have had 26 sheep in her flock. Now, from clue 3, Garth's goats can't have numbered 22 or 16, and so he must have had 10 and hooked up with Clarissa, and Ralph must have had 16 goats and fell in love with Dorinda with the 29 sheep, leaving Thomas and Lucy getting together with 22 goats and 37 sheep.

Francis, Mary, 18 goats, 43 sheep.
Garth, Clarissa, 10 goats, 26 sheep.
Ralph, Dorinda, 16 goats, 29 sheep.
Seth, Phyllida, 25 goats, 30 sheep.
Thomas, Lucy, 22 goats, 37 sheep.

Battleships, p. 222

Fireworking It Out, p. 223

The third firework is the $29 item (clue 4), so the $23 firework, which can't be first or second (clue 1), must be fourth. It's not the firework that produces a Roman candle display (clue 1) or the crackling sparkler or the shooting explosions (clue 3), and so must display shooting stars, and is therefore Comet's Revenge. The first firework isn't Screaming Angel (clue 1) or Saturn Starburst (clue 3), so it must be Earthquake. From clue 3, it's not priced at $27 or $29 (clue 3), so it must be the $25 firework and the $29 third item must create crackling sparklers and, by elimination, the second firework must have been bought for $27. The third firework, with

its crackling sparklers, isn't Saturn Starburst and must be Screaming Angel, leaving the second firework as the Saturn Starburst. So, from clue 3, Earthquake must create shooting explosions, leaving Saturn Starburst as the Roman candles.

1st, Earthquake, shooting explosions, $25.
2nd, Saturn Starburst, Roman candles, $27.
3rd, Screaming Angel, crackling sparklers, $29.
4th, Comet's Revenge, shooting stars, $23.

Classical Catalog, p. 224

The symphony was written in 2008 (clue 4) and the concerto is dedicated to Moscow (clue 1), so the piece written in 2018 and dedicated to Prague, which is not the sonata (clue 3) and can't be the étude (clue 2), must be the cantata. The London work, which isn't the étude (clue 2) or, from its 38-minute length, the sonata (clue 3), must be the symphony written in 2008. So, from clue 2, the étude was written in 2004. The longest work at 55 mins isn't the concerto (clue 1), the sonata (clue 3) or the cantata (clue 4), so must be the étude. We now know the shortest piece wasn't written in 2004 or 2008. Nor could it have been written in 2000 (clue 5) and the 2018 Prague cantata is too long (clue 3), so the 20-minute work was composed in 2013. Now from clue 4, the Prague cantata must last 30 minutes, with the sonata being the 2013 20-minute work (clue 3), leaving the 2000 composition as the Moscow concerto and 40 minutes long. The 2013 20-minute sonata isn't dedicated to Paris (clue 5), so must be a homage to Berlin, leaving the 55-minute étude written in 2004 dedicated to Paris.

2000, concerto, 40 mins, Moscow.
2004, étude, 55 mins, Paris.
2008, symphony, 38 mins, London.
2013, sonata, 20 mins, Berlin.
2018, cantata, 30 mins, Prague.

Lost and Found, p. 226

Ticket number 62 was for an item which took 12 minutes to find (clue 3) and number 29 was assigned to the umbrella (clue 4), so the gilet, which took ten minutes to find (clue 5) but wasn't number 38 or 51 (clue 5), must have been number 23. The hat belonged to Mrs. Wallace (clue 3), so Miss Kendal's item, which Jamie tried to assign number 51 but which wasn't the waterproof jacket (clue 1), must have been the overcoat. The hat wasn't number 62 (clue 3), so must have been assigned number 38, leaving number 62 given to the waterproof jacket. Mr. Selby's item took six minutes to find (clue 2), so Miss Kendal's overcoat, number 51, which didn't take 15 minutes to locate (clue 1), must have taken just three minutes. We now know either the diner or the time taken to find four items, so Mr. Selby's item, located after six minutes must have been the umbrella, numbered 29, leaving Jamie taking 15 minutes to find Mrs. Wallace's hat. Finally, from clue 5, the gilet didn't belong to Mr. Pickering, so he must have had the waterproof jacket, leaving Miss Joyce as the owner of the gilet.

Miss Kendal, No.51, overcoat, 3 minutes.
Miss Joyce, No.23, gilet, 10 minutes.
Mr. Pickering, No.62, jacket, 12 minutes.
Mr. Selby, No.29, umbrella, 6 minutes.
Mrs. Wallace, No.38, hat, 15 minutes.

A Good Mix, p. 228

Cousin Lou is sitting at table 5 (clue 6), so table 3, which isn't Grandad's (clue 2), Uncle Frank's (clue 1) or the one where Auntie Eileen and Ryan are sitting (clue 4), must be where Grandma and Uncle Henry are sitting, and, from clue 1, Uncle Frank must be at table 4. Janet is at table 6 (clue 3), so Auntie Eileen and Ryan must be at table 7 and Grandad must be at table 6. Now, from clue 2, Auntie Brenda and Linda must be at table 5. The groom's Uncle Tommy is not at table 4 or with the bride's Grandad at table 6 (clue 2), so he must be with Auntie Eileen on table 7. From clue 3, Janet is not sitting with the groom's Uncle Henry or Uncle Bob, so it must be Cousin Charles. So Uncle Bob must be at table 4 with Uncle Frank. The friend at their table is not Harriet (clue 5), so it must be Mark, which leaves Harriet at table 3 with Grandma and Uncle Henry.

Table 3, Grandma, Uncle Henry, Harriet.
Table 4, Uncle Frank, Uncle Bob, Mark.
Table 5, Cousin Lou, Auntie Brenda, Linda.
Table 6, Grandad, Cousin Charles, Janet.
Table 7, Auntie Eileen, Uncle Tommy, Ryan.

Arts Knight, p. 230

Sir Timid wrote the short story (clue 4) and the novelette features Eleanor (clue 2), so Sir Poltroon's work featuring Cassandra, which wasn't a ballad or an epic poem, must have been the play. Sir Sorely wrote about Sir Audace (clue 2), the ballad features Sir Noblesse (clue 1) and Liliane was rescued by Sir Paladin (clue 7), so Sir Poltroon's play, which didn't feature Sir Purefoy (clue 3), must have had Cassandra being rescued by Sir Valiant. We now know the author or brave knight in three types of work, so Sir Sorely's story of Sir Audace, which wasn't the novelette, must have been the epic poem, leaving Eleanor in the novelette being rescued by Sir Purefoy and Sir Paladin rescuing Liliane in Sir Timid's short story. The ballad *Sir Noblesse Oblige* doesn't feature Melisande (clue 1), so must feature Gwendoline, leaving Melisande being rescued by Sir Audace in Sir Sorely's poem. Finally, Gwendoline's rescue by Sir Noblesse wasn't written by Sir Coward, so Sir Spyneless must have written that ballad, leaving Sir Coward writing the novelette in which Eleanor is saved by Sir Purefoy.

Sir Coward de Custarde, novelette, Sir Purefoy, Eleanor.

Sir Poltroon à Ghaste, play, Sir Valiant, Cassandra.
Sir Sorely à Frayde, epic poem, Sir Audace, Melisande.
Sir Spyneless de Feete, ballad, Sir Noblesse, Gwendoline.
Sir Timid de Shayke, short story, Sir Paladin, Liliane.

Running Wild, p. 232

The trip to Mount Lunku, where 3 specimens were seen, was earlier than the Thursday trip in search of the spider-lizard (clue 1). However, 2 specimens were seen on Wednesday (clue 6) and the Monday trip was not to a mountain (clue 2), so the trip to Mount Lunku must have been on Tuesday. We know the creature being sought on Tuesday wasn't the spider-lizard, nor was it the copper monkey, which lives on the Sporo Plain (clue 5), or the whistling hog, 9 specimens of which were found (clue 6). The rainbow parrot wasn't sought on a mountain (clue 2), so Tuesday's trip to Mount Lunku must have been to find the ding-bat. The 9 whistling hogs weren't seen on Monday, so must have been seen on Friday. So it must have been in the Gwangi Valley that 2 specimens were seen on Wednesday (clue 4). By elimination, they must have been rainbow parrots and it must have been Monday when the team went to the Sporo Plain to find the copper monkey. From clue 3, the trip to Mount Borri must have been on Thursday and the one to the D'Kuna Forest on Friday, when the 9 whistling hogs were seen. There were fewer copper monkeys than there were creatures found on Mount Borri (clue 2), so Monday's trip must have found 6 copper monkeys and Thursday's must have found 8 spider-lizards on Mount Borri.

Monday, Sporo Plain, copper monkey, 6.
Tuesday, Mount Lunku, ding-bat, 3.

Wednesday, Gwangi Valley, rainbow parrot, 2.
Thursday, Mount Borri, spider-lizard, 8.
Friday, D'Kuna Forest, whistling hogs, 9.

Ssnake Charmers, p. 234

The female snake in position 10 (clue 4) isn't Ssue, Ssonia, or Ssuky (clue 1), or Ssal (clue 3), so must be Ssara. So, from clue 3, Ssal must be snake 5 and Sstan must be snake 9. So the female snake in position 1 (clue 4), who isn't Ssue or Ssonia (clue 1), must be Ssuky. Sstan's neighbor in position 8 is female (clue 3), but can't be Ssonia (clue 1) and must be Ssue. So Sseb, right of Ssal but not next to Ssue (clue 3), must be snake 6. Both of Ssue's neighbors are male (clue 1), so Ssonia must be snake 2, 3, or 4. So Ssaul, in an odd-numbered spot but not next to Ssonia (clue 1) can't be in position 3 and must be in position 7. Ssid is right of Ssonia but not two places right of Ssuky (clue 1), so he can't be in positions 2 or 3, so he must be spot 4. Finally, from clue 1, Ssonia must be snake 2 and Ssam snake 3.

1 Ssuky; 2 Ssonia; 3 Ssam; 4 Ssid; 5 Ssal; 6 Sseb; 7 Ssaul; 8 Ssue; 9 Sstan; 10 Ssara.

Flower Power, p. 235

Violet, a guitarist of some sort, is number 4 (clue 2). Number 2 is not Lily, who must have an odd number (clue 1), and, since Rose's position is numbered half that of the flute player (clue 1), she can't be number 2. Girl 2 can't be Daisy or Iris (clue 2), so must be Poppy. Violet hopes to play a guitar of some sort (clue 1), so Lily the wannabe trumpeter and her neighbor, the hopeful flautist, must be in positions 5 and 6, with, from clue 1, Rose in position 3. Girl 1 isn't Daisy (clue 2), so she must be the flautist-to-be in position 6, leaving Iris as girl 1. Rose isn't the bass guitarist or keyboardist (clue 1) and, with Violet learning a guitar, she can't be the drummer (clue 2), so must be the wannabe lead guitarist, leaving Violet intending to play bass guitar, Iris as the drummer, and Poppy as the keyboard player.

1, Iris, drums.
2, Poppy, keyboards.
3, Rose, lead guitar.
4, Violet, bass guitar.
5, Lily, trumpet.
6, Daisy, flute.

What the Flock?, p. 236

Esau Craggs' flock was 80 strong (clue 4) and Jacob Ramm's flock comprised more than 100 sheep (clue 1), so the flock of 70 sheep, which was not looked after by Isaiah Hills (clue 3) or Phil Penn (clue 4), must have been Job Herdin's flock on Badleigh Meadow (clue 1). His sheepdog was not Bob (clue 3), Dan (clue 1), Jem, who looked after the flock of 110 sheep (clue 5), or Ben, who worked on Tripton Meadow (clue 2), so it must have been Pip. The flock of 50 sheep did not graze on Tripton Meadow, Staggerdon Meadow, Badleigh Meadow, where the flock of 70 was, or Alldown Meadow, where the 105 grazed (clue 6), so it must have been Rosen Meadow. Jem helped shepherd the 110 sheep, so Ben on Tripton Meadow must have helped Esau Craggs with the flock of 80, leaving the 110 sheep on Staggerdon Meadow. Their shepherd was not Jacob Ramm (clue 1), so he must have looked after the flock of 105 on Alldown Meadow. Isaiah Hills was not the shepherd on Staggerdon Meadow (clue 3), so he must have looked after the 50 sheep on Rosen Meadow and, as his sheepdog was not Bob, it must have been Dan. By elimination, the Staggerdon Meadow shepherd must have been Phil Penn and Jacob Ramm must have looked after the flock of 105 with the help of his sheepdog Bob.

Esau Craggs, Tripton Meadow, 80 sheep, Ben.
Isaiah Hills, Rosen Meadow, 50 sheep, Dan.
Jacob Ramm, Alldown Meadow, 105 sheep, Bob.
Job Herdin, Badleigh Meadow, 70 sheep, Pip.
Phil Penn, Staggerdon Meadow, 110 sheep, Jem.

Bio Logical, p. 238

Blackburn, author of *Chosen*, wasn't an army officer or a navy officer (clue 1). The heart surgeon's book is *So Little Time* (clue 3) and the movie director's surname is Lancing (clue 5), so Blackburn must be the sports manager, Paul Blackburn (clue 5). Now, from clue 4, Gordon must be Gordon Tonbridge, and, from clue 3, the heart surgeon is Nigel. So Anthony, who isn't the army officer or the navy officer (clue 1), must be the movie director, Anthony Lancing. We've now matched occupations to three first names, so Gordon, who isn't the navy officer (clue 4), must be the army officer, leaving Tom as the navy officer. His surname isn't Warwick (clue 2), so he must be Tom Farnham, leaving Warwick as Nigel Warwick the heart surgeon. From clue 2, Tom Farnham's book isn't *Four Seasons*, and clue 6 rules out *Man Bites Dog*, so his book must be *Jack of Diamonds*. From clue 2, *Four Seasons*, which isn't by the army officer, must be by movie director Anthony Lancing, leaving Gordon Tonbridge, the army officer, as author of *Man Bites Dog*.

Anthony Lancing, movie director, *Four Seasons*.
Gordon Tonbridge, army officer, *Man Bites Dog*.
Nigel Warwick, heart surgeon, *So Little Time*.
Paul Blackburn, sports manager, *Chosen*.
Tom Farnham, navy officer, *Jack of Diamonds*.

Driven to Destruction, p. 240

Red Devil was car 5 (clue 2), so, from clue 4, the Ram must have been car 20 and *Hell on Wheels* must have been car 10. So the Ram wasn't Rex Carr's *Black Magic* (clue 3) or *Firestorm*, which was the VW (clue 5), so it must have been *Greased Lightning*, leaving Isadora Stallon's car 7 (clue 1) as the VW *Firestorm*, and Rex Carr's *Black Magic* must have carried the number 15. It was not based on a Jeep chassis (clue 3) or a Ford, which was Des Troy's car (clue 6), so it must have been the Dodge. Tilly Brakes wasn't driving car 5 or car 10 (clue 2), so must have been in car 20, the Ram *Greased Lightning*, leaving the Jeep as Justin Bitts' car. This was not car 5 (clue 5), so must have been car 10 *Hell on Wheels*, leaving Des Troy's Ford as car 5, *Red Devil*.

Car 5, Ford, Des Troy, *Red Devil*.
Car 7, VW, Isadora Stallon, *Firestorm*.
Car 10, Jeep, Justin Bitts, *Hell on Wheels*.
Car 15, Dodge, Rex Carr, *Black Magic*.
Car 20, Ram, Tilly Brakes, *Greased Lightning*.

Secret Identities, p. 242

Terry Wiles is going to Minneapolis (clue 3) and Gary Hearn is a vampire (clue 6), so the industrial spy going to Pittsburgh, who is also male (clue 2), must be Sean Tallis. Babs Curry isn't going to Atlanta (clue 5), nor, since she's a dentist (clue 5), to St. Louis, the TV critic's destination (clue 4), so she must be going to Memphis. So she's not the alien (clue 1) or the hired killer, who's traveling as an attorney (clue 3), so she must be the jewel thief. Terry Wiles isn't the hired killer (clue 3), so must be the alien, leaving the hired killer traveling as an attorney as Jessica Kay. From her stated occupation, her destination isn't St. Louis, so must be Atlanta and the TV critic going to St. Louis must be Gary Hearn, the vampire. Finally, Sean Tallis isn't the engineer (clue 6), so must be a pilot and the engineer must be Terry Wiles, going to Minneapolis, who is really an alien.

Babs Curry, dentist, Memphis, jewel thief.
Gary Hearn, TV critic, St. Louis, vampire.
Jessica Kay, attorney, Atlanta, hired killer.
Sean Tallis, pilot, Pittsburgh, industrial spy.
Terry Wiles, engineer, Minneapolis, alien.

Sylvia's Mother, p. 244

Sylvia parked at the gym on Monday (clue 1) and saved $7.60 on Wednesday (clue 5), so the day on which she saved $7.30 by parking at the hotel (clue 2), which wasn't Sunday (clue 1) or Thursday (clue 2), must have been Tuesday. Sylvia saved $6.80 by walking 600 yards (clue 4), walked 750 yards on Sunday (clue 1), and 500 yards from the shopping mall, so the hotel, parked at on Tuesday to save $7.30, which isn't 900 yards from the hospital must be 1,400 yards away. Sunday's saving was less than Monday's (clue 1), so, with what we have so far decided, it must have been less than $7.00. Sunday's walking distance rules out $6.80, so Sylvia must have saved $6.65 on Sunday. We now know the day or the money saved for three distances, so Wednesday's $7.60, which wasn't saved by walking only 500 yards, must have been saved with the 900-yard walk. It wasn't from the swimming pool (clue 5), so must have been from the bar, leaving the 600-yard walk saving $6.80 from the gym on Monday and the swimming pool as the place where Sylvia left her car on Sunday. By final elimination, she must have parked at the shopping mall on Thursday, walked 500 yards, and saved $7.00.

Sunday, Swimming pool, 750 yards, $6.65.
Monday, Gym, 600 yards, $6.80.
Tuesday, Hotel, 1,400 yards, $7.30.
Wednesday, Bar, 900 yards, $7.60.
Thursday, Shopping mall, 500 yards, $7.00.

Altared Arrangements, p. 246

Grace Hall wasn't supposed to get married at St. Mary's (clue 1), Parkside Church (clue 5), St. Paul's, which was where Carol Bell's wedding was booked (clue 2), or Hart Rd. Baptist (clue 3), so must have booked St. Francis RC. The wedding there wasn't canceled because the groom was arrested or because the bride was in hospital, which was why the St. Mary's wedding was called off (clue 1), because the bride ran away, which was what Ellen French did (clue 4), or because the groom fled (clue 5), so must have been canceled due to bats in the belfry. So Grace Hall should have married Tim Vance. Kay Lane's groom should have been Ben Crabtree (clue 3), and Ian Johnson must have been due to marry either Ellen French or Olive Price (clue 3), so Carol Bell, whose groom at St. Paul's wasn't due to be John Impey (clue 2), must have been going to marry Robin Shaw. So the wedding wasn't called off because the groom had fled (clue 5) and we know either the bride or the church to go with three other reasons, so Carol Bell's groom, Robin Shaw, must have been arrested. The wedding canceled because the groom had run away wasn't booked at Parkside Church (clue 5), so it must have been at Hart Rd. Baptist So the errant groom was Ian Johnson (clue 3), and the wedding at Parkside Church must have been called off because bride Ellen French fled, leaving the bride who should have married Ian Johnson at Hart Rd. Baptist as Olive Price. By elimination, Kay Lane and Ben Crabtree must have been due to marry at St. Mary's, but must have been prevented because she was in hospital, leaving Ellen French's groom, from whom she fled, as John Impey.

Carol Bell, Robin Shaw, St. Paul's, groom arrested.
Ellen French, John Impey, Parkside Church, bride ran away.
Grace Hall, Tim Vance, St. Francis RC, bats in belfry.
Kay Lane, Ben Crabtree, St. Mary's, bride in hospital.
Olive Price, Ian Johnson, Hart Road Baptist, groom fled.

Paranoica Pioneers, p. 248

The journalist who became 0002 couldn't have had a nine-letter first name (clue 7) and Desmond Childers was 0006, so, from clue 5, Charlotte Fleming must have been 0004. Also from clue 5, the historian must have been 0006, Desmond Childers. We know that the journalist wasn't Charlotte Fleming or Desmond Childers, and clue 7 tells us that he or she wasn't Rowena Maugham, Sebastian Le Queux or Frederick Gardner. Valerie Deighton was a civil servant (clue 1), and Monica Buchan can't have been 0002 (clue 6), so the journalist who had that number must have been Edmund Ambler. From clue 3, the psychologist must have become 0001. Now, from clue 1, Valerie Deighton, the civil servant, must have been 0003. We now know the names of 0002, 0003, and 0004. Since Desmond Childers, the historian, was 0006, from clue 6, Monica Buchan can't have been 0001, 0005, or 0008, so she must have been 0007, and the teacher must have been 0005. From clue 8, the politician must have been 0008 and the linguist must have been 0007, Monica Buchan. This leaves 0004, Charlotte Fleming, as the broadcaster. Sebastian Le Queux was neither 0001 nor 0008 (clue 4), so he must have been 0005, the teacher, and, from clue 4, Frederick Gardner must have been 0008, the politician. Finally, by elimination, 0001, the psychologist must have been Rowena Maugham.

0001: Rowena Maugham, psychologist.
0002: Edmund Ambler, journalist.
0003: Valerie Deighton, civil servant.
0004: Charlotte Fleming, broadcaster.
0005: Sebastian Le Queux, teacher.
0006: Desmond Childers, historian.

0007: Monica Buchan, linguist.
0008: Frederick Gardner, politician.

Skeery Spectres, p. 250

Mungo the Wicked's death in 1681 wasn't in the Master Bedroom (clue 4), while Lachlan the Diabolic's was in the Library (clue 5), and the 1535 death in the Gallery (clue 1). Clue 2 rules out 1681 for the death in the Blue Room, so Mungo the Wicked must have died in the Music Room. So, from clue 3, Duncan the Sinner, whose ghost is invisible but gives audible screams, must have died in 1469, and clue 5 rules out Hamish the Vile as the man who died in the Gallery in 1535 or the one who died in 1873. We know who died in 1469 and 1681, so Hamish the Vile must have died in 1744 and manifests himself as a skeletal figure (clue 6). Now, from clue 5, Lachlan the Diabolic's death in the Library must have been in 1873. So, from clue 2, Duncan the Sinner's death in 1469 must have been in the Blue Room, and Hamish the Vile must have died in the Master Bedroom and Angus the Bad must have died in the Gallery in 1535. Neither he nor Lachlan the Diabolic can be the invisible ghost which throws things (clue 2), so that must be Mungo the Wicked's ghost in the Music Room. Clue 7 also rules out Lachlan the Diabolic as the shadowy figure ghost, so he must appear as a headless figure, and it must be Angus the Bad who manifests as a shadowy figure.

Angus the Bad, shadowy figure, Gallery, 1535.
Duncan the Sinner, invisible: screams, Blue Room, 1469.
Hamish the Vile, skeletal figure, Master Bedroom, 1744.
Lachlan the Diabolic, headless figure, Library, 1873.
Mungo the Wicked, invisible: throws things, Music Room, 1681.

Spare Room, p. 252

The garage with the black door belongs to No.1 (clue 5) and the garage with a white door contains junk (clue 6), so the family living at No.2, who use their garage as a gym (clue 4) but whose garage door isn't navy or red (clue 4), must be the Franklins with their green garage door (clue 2). The garage containing junk doesn't belong to Nos.3 or 5, so must belong to the Saunders at No.4 (clue 3). Mr. Jones keeps his car in his garage (clue 1), so the family that has converted their garage into an office, which isn't the Reillys (clue 2), must be the Carlsons, leaving the Reilly family using their garage as a workshop. The family at No.5 isn't the Reillys (clue 2) or, since they must be the immediate neighbor of the Franklins at No.2 (clue 2), the Carlsons with their garage turned office, so the Joneses' car must live in the garage at No.5. The garage door here isn't navy blue (clue 1), so it must be red. Finally, No.1 isn't home to the Reillys' workshop garage (clue 5), so it must house the Carlsons' office behind its black garage door, leaving the Reillys at No.3 with the workshop behind the navy blue garage door.

No.1, Carlson, office, black.
No.2, Franklin, gym, green.
No.3, Reilly, workshop, navy blue.
No.4, Saunders, junk room, white.
No.5, Jones, car, red.

Progressive Disorders, p. 254

The spin-off GPI is the Genuine GPI (clue 2) and the Official band's rival version has been formed by the keyboardist (clue 3). Exodus' disgruntled singer, who does not claim his new incarnation to be the One and Only (clue 1) or Authentic (clue 4), must have formed the Real Exodus, occasioned by creative differences (clue 6). The Genuine GPI has not been formed by a bass or lead guitarist (clue 2), so must be led by the drummer.

This dispute was not over management issues (clue 5), Queen Scarlet's members are at odds over royalties (clue 3), and the bass guitarist has walked out over musical direction (clue 2), so the GPI split was caused by personality clashes. Queen Scarlet's royalties dispute was not caused by their keyboardist (clue 3), or the bass player wanting a different musical direction (clue 2), so they must have a breakaway incarnation led by the lead guitarist, leaving management issues forcing one band's keyboardist to form an Official faction. Maybe hasn't split thanks to their bass player (clue 5), so they must now have an Official Maybe version led by their former keyboard player, unhappy with the management, and the band whose bassist disputes their musical direction must be Gush. They do not have a spin-off Authentic version (clue 4), so the renegade bassist must claim his version to be the One and Only Gush, leaving Queen Scarlet's lead guitarist touring his new band under the name Authentic Queen Scarlet.

Exodus, singer, Real, creative differences.
GPI, drummer, Genuine, personality clashes.
Gush, bass guitarist, One and Only, musical direction.
Maybe, keyboardist, Official, management issues.
Queen Scarlet, lead guitarist, Authentic, royalty payments.

Misses Right, p. 256

Keydate.com introduced one of the men to Sandy (clue 4) and the QPid.com member went to the cinema (clue 5), so Donna's meeting at the theater, which was not arranged by Overture.com or Heart2Heart.com (clue 1), must have been set up by Solemates.com. Their member was not Mark (clue 2), Neil, who signed up with Heart2Heart (clue 1), Karl, who took his companion to

a concert (clue 3), or Joe, who met Laura (clue 6), so it must have been Ralph. Neil's Heart2Heart date wasn't Sandy, whose date was arranged through Keydate, nor was it Jill (clue 1), so Neil must have met Gina. So they didn't go out to dinner (clue 2) and must have visited a bar. Mark didn't take his companion to dinner (clue 2), so he must have organized the cinema trip and met her through QPid (clue 5), leaving the lady who was taken to dinner as Joe's date Laura, and so Joe must have been signed up to Overture. So Keydate must have introduced Karl to his concert partner, and Mark must have been introduced to Jill.

Joe, Overture.com, Laura Wryte, dinner.
Karl, Keydate.com, Sandy Write, concert.
Mark, QPid.com, Jill Ryatt, cinema.
Neil, Heart2Heart.com, Gina Wright, bar.
Ralph, Solemates.com, Donna Rite, theatre.

Equus October, p. 258

The Suburani were sponsoring the Corusci (clue 3) and the Via Recta chariot came to grief at the Temple of Neptune (clue 4), so the Pennipedes team, who lost their wheel at the Temple of the Castors but weren't sponsored by the men of the Via Sacra or Via Lata (clue 6), must have been sponsored by the Praetoriani. The Suburani's Corusci team weren't aided and abetted by Gormlus (clue 3) or Hopelus (clue 4). Branelus was helping with the Fulmina (clue 1) and Euselus was employed by the Via Sacra sponsors (clue 6), so the Suburani were enjoying the services of Cluelus. So the servant who failed to tighten the wheel for the Praetoriani/ Pennipedes team, who wasn't Gormlus (clue 3), must have been Hopelus. The crash at the Temple of Neptune, which befell the chariot sponsored by the men of the Via Recta (clue 4), wasn't the fault of Euselus or Cluelus, so must have been the fate of the Fulmina with Branelus, leaving the hope of the men of the Via Lata's ending at the Temple of Mars, with Gormlus denying all responsibility (clue 3). Cluelus' team didn't crash at the Circus Flaminius (clue 2), so this must have been where the Via Sacra chariot lost its harness and Cluelus' Suburani team must have reached the Trigarium. They weren't sponsoring the Veloces (clue 2) or the Scintillae (clue 5), so it must have been the Corusci. Finally, the Veloces weren't the victims at the Circus Flaminius (clue 2), so they must have been helped by Gormlus and crashed at the Temple of Mars, leaving the men of the Via Sacra and Euselus' coming to grief when their Scintillae team chariot lost its harness at the Circus Flaminius.

Branelus, Fulmina, Via Recta, Temple of Neptune.
Cluelus, Corusci, Suburani, Trigarium.
Euselus, Scintillae, Via Sacra, Circus Flaminius.
Gormlus, Veloces, Via Lata, Temple of Mars.
Hopelus, Pennipedes, Praetoriani, Temple of the Castors.

Getting Alarmed, p. 260

Angie bought jeans from PJ Fashions (clue 1) and the jacket cost $57.99 (clue 4), so the item costing $49.95 which was bought from MC Highstreet (clue 3), which wasn't the dress or sneakers (clue 3), must have been the shoes purchased in April (clue 6). The jacket wasn't bought from HF Store or KR Trends (clue 4), so must have been bought from JD Gear in August (clue 2). Nor was the dress bought from KR Trends (clue 4), so it must have been purchased at HF Store, leaving KR Trends as the shop where the sneakers were bought. Angie's new jeans weren't bought in May or July, so must have been the February purchase costing $54.50 (clue 5). The sneakers didn't cost $34.99 (clue 7), so must have cost $62.50, leaving

the dress as the $34.99 item. Finally, the May item wasn't the most expensive (clue 1), so must have been the $34.99 dress bought from HF Store, leaving the sneakers being bought from KR Trends for $62.50 in July.

HF Store, dress, $34.99, May.
JD Gear, jacket, $57.99, August.
KR Trends, sneakers, $62.50, July.
MC Highstreet, shoes, $49.95, April.
PJ Fashions, jeans, $54.50, February.

What a Picture, p. 262

Brooklyn was placed first (clue 5) and the rider in red and orange was third (clue 4), so, from clue 1, Sandpiper wasn't second or fourth and must have come in third, and Luke Grenfell, in black and blue, must have been riding the fourth-placed horse. We now know the horse or jockey for three places, so King's Ransom, ridden by Marvin Gale (clue 2), must have been second, leaving Luke's fourth-placed horse as Blue Streak. Marvin did not wear pink and white (clue 2), so he must have been in yellow and green, leaving pink and white as the colors worn by the winning jockey. This wasn't Jackie Moran (clue 3), so it must have been Conor O'Brien, leaving Jackie Moran's mount as the third-placed Sandpiper.

First, Brooklyn, Conor O'Brien, pink and white.
Second, King's Ransom, Marvin Gale, yellow and green.
Third, Sandpiper, Jackie Moran, red and orange.
Fourth, Blue Streak, Luke Grenfell, black and blue.

Sign In, p. 263

4	1	3	5	2	6
2	4	6	1	5	3
5	2	1	6	3	4
1	3	4	2	6	5
6	5	2	3	4	1
3	6	5	4	1	2

Sudoku, p. 263

3	8	4	7	9	6	5	1	2
2	6	5	8	1	4	3	7	9
7	9	1	5	2	3	4	8	6
6	4	2	9	8	1	7	5	3
9	5	3	4	6	7	1	2	8
8	1	7	2	3	5	9	6	4
1	3	9	6	7	8	2	4	5
5	2	6	1	4	9	8	3	7
4	7	8	3	5	2	6	9	1

Les Chevaliers, p. 264

Knight 1 rode Fureur, Maraudeur was Aubin's mount (clue 3), and knight 2 was not le Rouge mounted on Le Gris (clue 1), so knight 2, who did not ride Licorne (clue 7) or Flamme (clue 4), must have ridden Guerrier. So Aubin must have been knight 5 (clue 3). Knight 6 was le Borreau, who was not Thibaut (clue 6), and we know he wasn't Aubin. Levric was knight 3 (clue 4), Vesey was l'Estocade (clue 2) and he couldn't have been Hugues (clue 5), so he must have been Giraud. So le Rouge on Le Gris can't have been knight 2, 3,

5, or 6 (clue 1), so he must have been knight 4. So knight 1 can't have been le Sauvage (clue 1), and we know he wasn't le Borreau. Clue 5 rules out des Roches and de la Lance, so he must have been Vesey l'Estocade. We know de la Lance wasn't knight 4 or knight 6, so, from clue 5, he must have been knight 5, Aubin, and knight 2 must have been Hugues. Now knight 4, mounted on Le Gris, must have been Thibaut. Clue 4 now tells us that Flamme's rider must have been Giraud le Borreau, leaving Licorne as Levric's mount. Finally, from clue 4, knight 3, Levric, was not le Sauvage and must have been de Roches, leaving knight 2, Hugues, as le Sauvage.

1, Vesey l'Estocade, Fureur.
2, Hugues le Sauvage, Guerrier.
3, Levric des Roches, Licorne.
4, Thibaut Le Rouge, Le Gris.
5, Aubin de la Lance, Maraudeur.
6, Giraud le Borreau, Flamme.

Sitting Pretty, p. 266

Edith Howard was Angus Dunn's favorite model (clue 6), Claude Middleton's picture was painted in the 1890s (clue 1), and Montague Hope's *Constance* must have been painted later than 1884 (clue 3), so Morag Kennedy, who sat for the 1884 work but not for Alfred Jenkins (clue 2), must have posed for Herbert Ballard. Fanny March posed for *Bluebells* more than seven years before Montague Hope painted *Constance* (clue 3), so it wasn't in the 1890s when Claude Middleton's work was created, and we know either the sitter or work for three other artists so Alfred Jenkins must have painted Fanny March. He didn't do so in 1878 (clue 2), so *Bluebells* must date from 1886 and, from clue 3, Hope's *Constance* must have been painted in 1895 and Claude Middleton's picture must have been done in 1893. By elimination, Angus Dunn's painting must have been done in 1878. *Queen Guinevere* was painted earlier than 1886 (clue 2), but it was not by Herbert Ballard, so it must have been Angus Dunn. Middleton didn't paint *Eternal Hope* (clue 1), so that must have been Ballard's work, leaving Middleton as the painter of *Spring Dream*. The model for this was not Rosie Tranter (clue 5), so it must have been Lily Gough, leaving Miss Tranter as Montague Hope's model for his 1895 work *Constance*.

1878, Angus Dunn, *Queen Guinevere*, Edith Howard.

1884, Herbert Ballard, *Eternal Hope*, Morag Kennedy.

1886, Alfred Jenkins, *Bluebells*, Fanny March.

1893, Claude Middleton, *Spring Dream*, Lily Gough.

1895, Montague Hope, *Constance*, Rosie Tranter.

Carnival Crime, p. 268

Sunday night's incident did not involve Sgt. Collaham (clue 4), Sgt. Ningall (clue 1), or Sgt. Sorliss (clue 3), and Sgt. Lowe was called in on Thursday (clue 2), so the last night's arrest must have been performed by Sgt. Trunchan. It didn't take place at the Rifle Range (clue 3), or the Ghost Train, or Bumper Cars (clue 4), and Sgt. Ningall was in action at the Big Wheel (clue 1), so Sgt. Trunchan must have been the officer catching the diamond thieves red-handed in the Fortune Teller's tent. The officer called in to control the brawl on Saturday wasn't Sgt. Ningall (clue 1) or Sgt. Sorliss, who caught the pickpocket (clue 3), so must have been Sgt. Collaham, leaving Sgt. Sorliss' arrest on Wednesday or Friday. Sunday's incident was at the Fortune Teller's tent, so, from clue 3, the pickpocket must have been collared on Wednesday and, by elimination, the officer in action on Friday was Sgt. Ningall. Also from clue 3, the incident at the Rifle Range must have been Saturday's brawl attended by Sgt. Collaham. The drunk wasn't apprehended on the Ghost Train or the Bumper Cars (clue 4), so must have been Sgt. Ningall's collar at the Big Wheel, leaving Sgt. Lowe called to the case of assault. It wasn't on the Ghost Train (clue 2), so must have been at the Bumper Cars. Finally, Sgt. Sorliss must have caught the pickpocket on Wednesday as he operated in the dark of the Ghost Train.

Wed., Sgt. Sorliss, Ghost Train, pickpocket.

Thurs., Sgt. Lowe, Bumper Cars, assault.

Fri., Sgt. Ningall, Big Wheel, drunk.

Sat., Sgt. Collaham, Rifle Range, brawling.

Sun., Sgt. Trunchan, Fortune Teller, stolen gems.

Local Menu, p. 270

The witchety grub was eaten in Australia (clue 1), Alex tackled the octopus, and another man tried the eel (clue 2), so Carol, who visited Mauritius (clue 4) but who didn't eat snake (clue 4), must have been served the sea urchin and so made the trip in 2010 (clue 3). So, from clue 4, Greg must have made his trip in 2012. The 2018 visitor to Korea didn't eat snake or eel (clue 2), so must have been the octopus-devouring Alex. Kate didn't eat the witchety grub (clue 1) and a man ate the eel (clue 2), so she must have tucked into the snake. She didn't visit Japan (clue 3), so must have gone to China. She didn't travel there in 2014 (clue 3), so she must have traveled to China in 2016, leaving Phil traveling in 2014. From clue 2, he must have eaten the eel. So he didn't visit Australia (clue 1) and must have journeyed to Japan, leaving Greg dining on witchety grub in Australia in 2012.

2010, Carol, Mauritius, sea urchin.

2012, Greg, Australia, witchety grub.

2014, Phil, Japan, eel.

2016, Kate, China, snake.

2018, Alex, Korea, octopus.

Pod Casting, p. 272

Whale 3 excelled at deep diving (clue 4), so whale 6 isn't either Vic (clue 2) or Chic (clue 6). Nor is whale 6 Mick or Nic (clue 1), Flick (clue 2), Slick (clue 5), or Ahab (clue 6), and so must be Moby Rick. So, from clue 5, whale 7 must be going to Hawaii. He or she didn't excel in plankton identification or singing (clue 2), swimming (clue 5), or breaching (clue 6). The whale who was best at tail slapping is going to Mexico (clue 2) and, since Ahab can't be whale 8 (clue 3 and intro), whale 7 can't be the blowhole control expert (clue 6) and must have been the male whale who aced the krill recognition class (clue 3). He's not Mick (clue 1) or Slick (clue 5) and so must be Ahab and, from clue 6, whale 8 must be tops at blowhole control. Now, from clue 3, the whale going to California must be in the back row. Whale 2 is going to New Zealand (clue 4), so the whale heading for Colombia must be whale 1 and the California-bound whale must be deep-diving expert whale 3. From clue 3, whale 1 is female. She's not Nic (clue 1), Vic (clue 2), or Chic (clue 6) and so must be Flick and, from clue 2, whale 2 must have come top in plankton identification. Mick can't be whale 2 or, since whale 8 is female and he is numbered half that of a male whale (clues 3 and 1), whale 4, so he must be whale 3 and, from clue 1, whale 6, Rick, must be going to South Africa. So he isn't the star pupil at tail slapping or singing (clue 2) or breaching (clue 6) and must have got top marks in swimming. Slick's end of row spot isn't next to him (clue 5), so he must be whale 4 and so, Vic, numbered three higher than the best singer must be whale 8 with whale 5 possessing the best voice and, by elimination, Slick topping the scores at tail slapping and going to Mexico. Whale 5 isn't Chic (clue 6), so must be Nic, leaving Moby Chic as whale 2 with, from clue 6, whale 1, Flick, being the best breacher. Finally, Nic isn't going to Costa Rica (clue 1) and so must be holidaying in Alaska, leaving whale 8, Vic, going to Costa Rica to display her brilliant blowhole control.

1, Flick breaching, Colombia.
2 Chic, plankton identification, New Zealand.
3 Mick, deep diving, California.
4 Slick, tail slapping, Mexico.
5, Nic, singing, Alaska.
6, Rick, swimming, South Africa.
7, Ahab, krill recognition, Hawaii.
8, Vic, blowhole control, Costa Rica.

Lost in Translation, p. 274

Ellen helped to assemble the bunk beds (clue 3) and Jayne speaks Japanese (clue 5), so Tim's French-speaking girlfriend, who helped with the cocktail cabinet assembly (clue 2) must be Beverly. The kitchen cart flatpack was bought in March (clue 1), the instructions in Italian came with the item bought in April (clue 6), and the January assembly was assisted by Curtis (clue 4), so Beverly, who didn't help in May (clue 2), must have translated in February. The kitchen cart translator wasn't Lennie (clue 1), so it must have been Jayne who helped out with this in March. Curtis' January translation wasn't for the bedside cabinets (clue 4), so he must have translated the instructions for the wardrobe, leaving Lennie translating for the bedside cabinets. They were bought before the bunk beds (clue 4), so must have been the April item with the Italian instructions translated by Lennie, leaving Ellen translating the German bunk bed instructions in May.

January, Wardrobe, Spanish, Curtis.
February, Cocktail cabinet, French, Beverly.
March, Kitchen cart, Japanese, Jayne.
April, Bedside cabinets, Italian, Lennie.
May, Bunk beds, German, Ellen.

Robin the Rich, p. 276

Little John lives in Swagley Castle (clue 3) and Robin Hood is third in the list (clue 1), so Boodle House, which is the residence of the fifth richest of the five (clue 4) but isn't owned by Will Scarlet (clue 2) or Much the Miller's Son (clue 4), must be Friar Tuck's 1,000-acre estate (clue 5). The estate around Pillidge Castle is larger than Much's (clue 2), so it doesn't put its owner in second place, as he has 700 acres (clue 1), fifth, or first (clue 2). Pillidge Castle's owner is one position lower than Will Scarlet (clue 2), so, since Robin Hood is third (clue 2), he is not fourth and must be Robin himself, in third place, with Will Scarlet in second place with a 700-acre estate. Will's home is not the 900-acre Looton Manor (clue 6), so it must be Dunrobin Hall, leaving Looton Manor as Much's estate. The acreage of Little John's Swagley Castle estate is less than 1,000 (clue 3), so it must be 800, and the 1,100-acre estate must be Robin's Pillidge Castle. Much is not the wealthiest of the five (clue 6), so he must be in fourth position, leaving the richest of the former outlaws as Little John of Swagley Castle.

First, Little John, Swagley Castle, 800 acres.

Second, Will Scarlet, Dunrobin Hall, 700 acres.

Third, Robin Hood, Pillidge Castle, 1,100 acres.

Fourth, Much the Miller's Son, Looton Manor, 900 acres.

Fifth, Friar Tuck, Boodle House, 1,000 acres.

One Page, p. 278

Beth Oliver wrote *Museum Piece* (clue 5) and *Performance* won third prize (clue 2), so the fifth-placed story, written by Darren Quayle, which was not *Sunday Dinner* (clue 3) and can't have been *All About Alan* (clue 4), must have been *Last Resort*, which is 550 words long (clue 6). Ann Norton's story is longer than *Sunday Dinner* (clue 4), so wasn't the second prize winner, which was only 400 words (clue 1), nor did it win first prize (clue 4). Since it came just behind *All About Alan* (clue 4), it didn't take the fourth prize, as *Performance* was third, so Ann Norton must have written the third prize winner *Performance* and 400-word second prize winner must have been *All About Alan*. Cliff Parks' story was 500 words long (clue 1), so the 400-word *All About Alan* must be by Edna Roberts, leaving Cliff Parks' 500-word story as *Sunday Dinner*. Beth Oliver's *Museum Piece* is less than 550 words long (clue 5), so it must be 450 words long, and the 600-word story must be Ann Norton's *Performance*, which took third place. Cliff Parks' *Sunday Dinner* didn't win first prize (clue 1), so it must have come fourth, leaving the first-prize winner as Beth Oliver's *Museum Piece*.

First, Beth Oliver, *Museum Piece*, 450 words.

Second, Edna Roberts, *All About Alan*, 400 words.

Third, Ann Norton, *Performance*, 600 words.

Fourth, Cliff Parks, *Sunday Dinner*, 500 words.

Fifth, Darren Quayle, *Last Resort*, 550 words.

Saintly Lessons, p. 280

St. Peter's is where the Drama lesson is taking place (clue 4), so the name of the saint at the school where Mrs. Gaunt is observing the Music lesson, which must have five or six letters (clue 2), must be St. Martin's, Mr. Edge's school (clue 5). Mrs. Sterne is inspecting Mr. Mortense's school, dedicated to a saint with a name beginning with M (clue 1). It isn't St. Matthew's, which is being inspected by Mr. Stark (clue 4), so it must be St. Michael's. Mr. Cavill is not inspecting St. Bernadette's (clue 6), so it must be Mr.

Checkley, leaving Mr. Cavill as the inspector at St. Peter's. The lesson being inspected at St. Bernadette's is not Math (clue 6) or History (clue 3), so it must be English and the teacher must be Miss Trembull (clue 5). We know that the name of the saint to whom Mrs. Fretwell's school is dedicated must have seven letters (clue 2), so it must be St. Matthew's, leaving St. Peter's as Miss Pannick's school. Finally, St. Michael's is not where the History class is being observed (clue 3), so it must be the Math lesson, leaving St. Matthew's as the school where the inspector is observing the History lesson.

St. Bernadette's, Miss Trembull, Mr. Checkley, English.
St. Martin's, Mr. Edge, Mrs. Gaunt, Music.
St. Matthew's, Mrs. Fretwell, Mr. Stark, History.
St. Michael's, Mr. Mortense, Mrs. Sterne, Math.
St. Peter's, Miss Pannick, Mr. Cavill, Drama.

Hollywood Hats, p. 282

She Fell for Him was made in 1934 (clue 1). The top hat was worn in the 1935 movie (clue 4), which cannot have been *Coming Home* (clue 2) or *City Life* starring Clark Maybank (clue 6), while it was the derby which was worn in *What's Cooking?* (clue 5), so *Stepping Out* must have been shot in 1935. So, from clue 7, Victor O'Sullivan starred in *She Fell for Him* in 1934. We already know the star of *Stepping Out* was not Clark or Victor and clue 2 rules out Gene Parker for 1935 and clue 3 tells us Royston Wallace wore a Stetson, so the top hat in *Stepping Out* must have been worn by Jefferson Rodgers. Royston's headgear rules out his movie as *What's Cooking?*, so his western must have been *Coming Home* and Gene Parker must have starred in *What's Cooking?* Clark Maybank did not wear the fedora (clue 6), so his hat must have been the trilby, leaving the fedora

for Victor O'Sullivan. From clue 2, the trilby, which we now know was not worn in the 1934 or 1935 movies, must have been worn by Clark Maybank in 1933, *Coming Home* must have been made in 1932, and *What's Cooking?*, starring Gene Parker, in 1931.

1931, *What's Cooking?*, Gene Parker, derby.
1932, *Coming Home*, Royston Wallace, Stetson.
1933, *City Life*, Clark Maybank, trilby.
1934, *She Fell for Him*, Victor O'Sullivan, fedora.
1935, *Stepping Out*, Jefferson Rodgers, top hat.

Don and Dusted, p. 284

The trainee in Marketing was 30 (clue 3) and the 28-year-old was the personal trainer person (clue 6), so the former gardener, who became a trainee in the HR department, but was not 23 or 24 (clue 1), must have been 27-year-old Guy Keene (clue 6). The caterer wasn't Dwight Mann (clue 4) or Marcus Best (clue 5), and Elwyn Post had been a student (clue 2), so the caterer must have been Hope Smee. She didn't become a trainee in Sales (clue 4), Marketing (clue 3), or Logistics (clue 5), so it must have been Accounts. Dwight Mann was allocated to Sales (clue 4), so the trainee in Logistics, who wasn't Marcus Best (clue 5), must have been the student Elwyn Post, leaving the personal trainer as 28-year-old Dwight Mann, who worked in Sales, and the Marketing trainee as the cab driver, who was Marcus Best. Elwyn Post was not the 23-year-old trainee (clue 2), so he must have been 24, leaving the 23-year-old as Hope Smee. Finally, Guy Keene didn't win the full-time job (clue 6), nor was it caterer Hope Smee (clue 4), 28-year-old Dwight Mann (clue 6) or Marcus Best (clue 5), so it must have been student Elwyn Post who has now been offered a high-flying job.

Marcus Best, 30, cab driver,
Guy Keene, 27, gardener, HR.
Dwight Mann, 28, personal trainer,
Elwyn Post, 24, student, Logistics.
Hope Smee, 23, caterer, Accounts.

…; 2 bored; 3 surprised; 4 angry; 5 thoughtful; 6 sad; 7 puzzled; 8 scared; 9 happy.

Domino Search, p. 286

0	2	3	5	0	3	3	5
1	5	4	5	4	4	6	0
3	1	1	2	5	3	0	2
4	5	6	4	1	0	5	0
6	6	4	2	3	0	2	4
1	6	1	2	5	2	1	4
3	3	6	1	6	2	0	6

Let's Face It, p. 287

Ed's final expression wasn't angry or bored (clue 1), surprised or tired (clue 1), puzzled, sad, or scared (clue 2), or thoughtful (clue 3), so it must have been his happy face. He didn't start the sequence with an angry or bored face (clue 1), surprised (clue 1), puzzled, sad, or scared (clue 2), or thoughtful (clue 3), and so must he have acted tired. So his second face wasn't angry (clue 1), surprised (clue 1), puzzled, sad, or scared (clue 3), or thoughtful (clue 3) and so must have been bored. So, from clue 1, Ed must have portrayed angriness fourth. Now, from clue 2, the odd-numbered position for Ed's puzzled face can't be 5 and must be 7, with the sad face sixth and scared expression eighth. Finally, the thoughtful expression wasn't next after bored, so wasn't third and must have been fifth, leaving the surprised face third.

The MeCam, p. 288

Lindsey's MeCam's picture was posted on MeTube (clue 3), Caroline's MeCam snapped some birds, and Ruth's MeCam posted its pictures on a site beginning with M (clue 2), so the mugger, whose image was forwarded to the police but who was not photographed by Brenda (clue 1), must have been snapped by the MeCam of the unfortunate Clara. Brenda's MeCam did not photograph the dog or herself (clue 1), so must have captured the flowers. So, from clue 3, Caroline must have been heading for the café when her MeCam posted a picture of birds to SnapMe. Now from clue 2, Clara must have been on the way to the business meeting when her MeCam photographed the mugger. The dog walker's MeCam took a picture of the dog (clue 1), so Ruth's MeCam must have taken a picture of Ruth herself on the way to the gym (clue 2). Her selfie wasn't sent to MyFace (clue 1) and Lindsey's picture went to MeTube (clue 3), so Ruth's selfie must have gone to MeBook. Now, Lindsey's MeCam must have filmed her dog while she walked it, and Brenda must have been going to work when her MeCam sent a photo of flowers to MyFace.

Brenda, work, flowers, MyFace.
Caroline, café, birds, SnapMe.
Clara, business meeting, mugger, police.
Lindsey, dog walk, dog, MeTube.
Ruth, gym, herself, MeBook.

Annie Get Your Gun, p. 290

Annie Mapley was a stagecoach robber before taking up showbiz (clue 1) and the bounty hunter hunted for bounties in New

Mexico (clue 2), so Annie Laurely from Colorado, who wasn't a deputy sheriff or a rustler (clue 3), must have been the barmaid and bouncer who left the saloon to join Moose Matt's Wild West Show (clue 6). Annie Alderley joined Coyote Clem's show (clue 5), so stagecoach robber Annie Mapley, who didn't join up with Longhorn Luke (clue 1) or Grizzly Gus (clue 4), must have joined Bison Ben's Wild West Show when it visited her home state of Utah (clue 5). Grizzly Gus' crack shot wasn't Annie Limey (clue 4), so must have been Annie Eldery, leaving Annie Limey joining Longhorn Luke. So neither Annie Eldery nor Annie Limey was from Texas (clue 7), so that must have been Annie Alderly. She wasn't a sheriff or a bounty hunter (clue 7), so must have been the rustler. Finally, Longhorn Luke's sharpshooter, Annie Limey, wasn't from Arizona (clue 1), so she must have be the bounty hunter from New Mexico, leaving Annie Eldery giving up her job as a deputy sheriff in Arizona to join Grizzly Gus' Wild West Show.

Annie Alderly, Texas, rustler, Coyote Clem.

Annie Eldery, Arizona, deputy sheriff, Grizzly Gus.

Annie Laurely, Colorado, saloon worker, Moose Matt.

Annie Limey, New Mexico, bounty hunter, Longhorn Luke.

Annie Mapley, Utah, stagecoach robber, Bison Ben.

Civil Service, p. 292

Cedric Dunn came from Preston (clue 4) and George Holt joined the Texas Light Cavalry (clue 1), so the man from Aberdeen who joined the Louisiana Tigers, who wasn't Alf Browder (clue 2) or Isaac Jones (clue 5), must have been Edgar Fitch, whose rank was private (clue 5). The man who joined the 17th Georgia Infantry became a corporal (clue 6), so the one who joined the 2nd Mississippi

become a lieutenant or a [clu]e 3) must have been the sergeant, [wa]s born in Ipswich (clue 6). We now [kno]w either the name or the unit to go with three home towns, so George Holt, who joined the Texas Light Cavalry but who wasn't from Edinburgh (clue 1), must have come from Bedford. He wasn't the lieutenant (clue 1), so must have been the major. The lieutenant wasn't from Edinburgh (clue 1), so he must have been Cedric Dunn from Preston and he must have served in the 1st Tennessee Artillery, leaving the man from Edinburgh as a corporal in the 17th Georgia Infantry. He wasn't Isaac Jones (clue 5), so he must have been Alf Browder and Isaac Jones must have been the man from Ipswich who joined the 2nd Mississippi Rifles and rose to the rank of sergeant.

Alf Browder, Edinburgh, 17th Georgia Infantry, corporal.

Cedric Dunn, Preston, 1st Tennessee Artillery, lieutenant.

Edgar Fitch, Aberdeen, Louisiana Tigers, private.

George Holt, Bedford, Texas Light Cavalry, major.

Isaac Jones, Ipswich, 2nd Mississippi Rifles, sergeant

Getting the Bird, p. 294

Daisy has 5 young (clue 2) and the goose is named Iris (clue 3), so the duck who has 3 chicks (clue 1), but who isn't named Ivy or Lily (clue 1), must be Rose, who is looked after by Harvey (clue 4). Lily doesn't have 4 chicks (clue 1) and Iris the goose has a larger brood than the swan (clue 3), so the 4 chicks must belong to Ivy. Dominique is the turkey's keeper (clue 2), so Beth, who doesn't look after the goose or ostrich (clue 3), must be the swan's keeper. Ernie looks after the mother with 6 chicks (clue 5), so Roxy, who doesn't attend to the mother with

4 or 7 young (clue 6), must look after Daisy and her 5 chicks. We now know the name of the mother or the name of the keeper for four types of bird, so Roxy must look after Daisy the ostrich and 5 ostrich chicks. Beth's mother swan can't have 7 chicks (clue 3), so she must be Ivy the swan with 4 chicks, leaving Lily as the mother turkey. By elimination, she must have 7 chicks, leaving Iris as the mother goose with 6 chicks tended to by Ernie.

Duck, 3 chicks, Rose, Harvey.
Goose, 6 chicks, Iris, Ernie.
Ostrich, 5 chicks, Daisy, Roxy.
Swan, 4 chicks, Ivy, Beth.
Turkey, 7 chicks, Lily, Dominique.

Killer Sudoku, p. 296

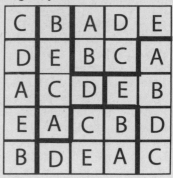

7	2	1	3	9	5	6	4	8
3	5	8	7	4	6	9	1	2
4	6	9	2	8	1	5	7	3
2	4	3	6	1	7	8	5	9
8	9	6	5	3	4	1	2	7
5	1	7	9	2	8	4	3	6
6	3	4	8	5	2	7	9	1
1	8	2	4	7	9	3	6	5
9	7	5	1	6	3	2	8	4

Logi-5, p. 297

C	B	A	D	E
D	E	B	C	A
A	C	D	E	B
E	A	C	B	D
B	D	E	A	C

Sign In, p. 296

5	3	2	4	6	1
1	4	3	2	5	6
6	2	4	5	1	3
4	5	1	6	3	2
3	6	5	1	2	4
2	1	6	3	4	5

Sudoku, p. 297

6	7	1	5	3	2	8	9	4
2	9	5	4	7	8	1	3	6
4	3	8	9	1	6	2	7	5
3	5	2	1	4	7	9	6	8
7	6	4	8	5	9	3	2	1
1	8	9	6	2	3	5	4	7
9	4	6	3	8	1	7	5	2
8	2	3	7	6	5	4	1	9
5	1	7	2	9	4	6	8	3

Domino Search, p. 299

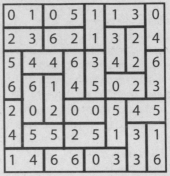

Not So Fast Food, p. 298

The tortoise at the front of the line isn't Shelbourne (clue 1), Shelley, Shelford or Hershel (clue 2), or Sheldon (clue 3), and so must be Michelle. So, from clue 1, Shelbourne must be second in line and the tortoise waiting in third place must be having lettuce leaves. The tortoise in sixth place won't be eating dandelions or red chard (clue 2) or spinach or watercress (clue 3) and so must be having kale salad. Now, Sheldon can't be in third place (clue 3) and, to make space immediately ahead of him for spinach and watercress (clue 3), he must be in sixth place with the spinach eater in fifth place and the watercress salad chosen by the tortoise in fourth place. So, from clue 2, Shelbourne in second place must have chosen red chard salad, Shelley must be the lettuce lover in third place and Shelford must be in fourth spot, leaving Michelle at the head of the line choosing dandelions and the spinach-eater in fifth spot being Hershel.

1st, Michelle, dandelion; 2nd, Shelbourne, red chard; 3rd, Shelley, lettuce; 4th, Shelford, water cress; 5th, Hershel, spinach; 6th, Sheldon, kale.

Lift Off, p. 300

The male passenger for the basement parking garage is not Sushila or Ena (intro), Zbigniew (clue 2), or Ali (clue 3), so must be Rennie. Ena, on the floor above Ali and below the movie theater (clue 3), cannot be on the first floor, since Ali cannot presently be on the ground floor, nor can she be in the basement or on the third floor, and Sushila is on the second floor, so she must be on the ground floor, Ali must be in the basement, and the movie theater must be on the first floor. Now, from clue 2, Zbigniew must be on the first floor, and the cafe must be on the third floor where, by elimination, Rennie must be waiting for a ride to the basement. Sushila now cannot be waiting for the elevator to transport her to the bathrooms on a higher floor (clue 1), so they must be on the second floor and must be Ena's destination. By elimination, Sushila must be waiting for the elevator to take her to the first-floor movie theater, and the news stand must be on the ground floor.

Third floor, cafe, Rennie, basement.
Second floor, bathrooms, Sushila, first floor.
First floor, movie theater, Zbigniew, third floor.
Ground floor, news stand, Ena, second floor.
Basement, parking garage, Ali, ground floor.

Audition, p. 301

Alexis read the artist third (clue 1), so, from clue 4, Alexis couldn't have read the role of author first or second and must have read that role last. Alexis' first role wasn't the auctioneer (clue 1), so must have been the architect, leaving the auctioneer second. The actor who read the artist's part last wasn't Angel (clue 2) or Ashley (clue 3), so must have been Ariel. Ariel didn't read the role of author second (clue 3), and we know Alexis took the role of auctioneer second, so Ariel's second role must have been the architect, which, from clue 2, must have been Angel's third role, leaving Ashley taking that role last. We know Alexis played the author last, so Ariel's first part and Angel's last (clue 2), which we know can't be the artist or the architect, must have been the auctioneer, leaving Ashley playing the auctioneer third and Ariel's third role as the author. Now, from clue 1, Alexis must have been next left to Ariel who, from clue 3, was next left to Ashley. Since Angel read the role of auctioneer last, she can't have been in seat D (clue 4), so that seat must have been Ashley's, with Alexis in seat B and Ariel in seat C, leaving Angel in seat A. Finally, from clue 1, Angel must have read the role of the author second and so began with the artist, leaving Ashley reading the author first and the artist second.

A, Angel, artist, author, architect, auctioneer.
B, Alexis, architect, auctioneer, artist, author.
C, Ariel, auctioneer, architect, author, artist.
D, Ashley, author, artist, auctioneer, architect.

Use By, p. 302

The pizza was 6 days past its use-by date (clue 2) and Mr. Jennings spotted something which was 8 days too old (clue 3), so Ms. Timms' carton of cream (clue 1), which was more than 4 days out of date (clue 1), must have been 5 days beyond its use-by date and she was given a $2 credit coupon (clue 3). Mr. Jennings wasn't looking for orange juice or veggie burgers (clue 3), so must have been after the salmon. A fresh carton of orange juice was offered to one customer at half price (clue 5), so Mr. Short, who was offered a fresh version of the product he wanted free of charge but which wasn't pizza (clue 2), must have wanted the veggie burgers. The orange juice wasn't 2 days past its date, so must have been 4 days, leaving the Mr. Short's veggie burgers' use-by date as 2 days ago. Ms. Hayward didn't shop for orange juice (clue 5), so she must have found the pizza, leaving Ms. Matthews buying the orange juice. Finally, Mr. Jennings didn't receive the $3 credit coupon (clue 3), so he must have received a free product (a box of candies) and Mrs. Hayward must have been given the $3 credit coupon.

Ms. Hayward, pizza, 6 days, $3 credit coupon.
Mr. Jennings, salmon, 8 days, free product.
Ms. Matthews, orange juice, 4 days, reduced price.
Mr. Short, veggie burgers, 2 days, replacement free.
Ms. Timms, cream, 5 days, $2 credit coupon.

Blooming Failures, p. 304

From clue 1, Martin and Paula's plant must have survived for either 10 or 12 days. The plant belonging to Georgie and Mike lasted for 12 (clue 5), so it must have taken Keith 10 days to see off Martin and Paula's specimen, with the plant which survived for 5 days belonging to the couple who had gone to Rio. They weren't Sadie and Tim (clue 1) and Deirdre and James went to Madeira (clue 3), so they must have been Brian and Jackie. Georgie and Mike hadn't gone to Cape Town (clue 5) or, from the length of time their plant hung on to life, Florida (clue 2), so they must have gone to Phuket. Their plant wasn't the clematis (clue 2) or the spider plant, which only lasted 6 days (clue 4), the herb garden, which was owned by the travelers to Cape Town (clue 5), or the aspidistra, which was Sadie and Tim's (clue 1), so Georgie and Mike's plant was the peace lily. Brian and Jackie's 5-day survivor while they were in Rio wasn't the herb garden (clue 5), so it must have been the clematis. Martin and Paula's plant lasted too long to be the spider plant (clue 1), so they must have owned the herb garden that withered while they were in Cape Town, leaving the spider plant belonging to Deirdre and James lasting only 6 days of their Madeira cruise and Sadie and Tim's aspidistra lasting for 8 days whilst they visited Florida.

Brian and Jackie, Rio, clematis, 5 days.
Deirdre and James, Madeira, spider plant, 6 days.
Georgie and Mike, Phuket, peace lily, 12 days.
Martin and Paula, Cape Town, herb garden, 10 days.
Sadie and Tim, Florida, aspidistra, 8 days.

Household Gods, p. 306

Leila's cat is called Hecate (clue 2) and Heather lives at No.24 (clue 3), so Mnemosyne at No.51, who does not belong to Abel or Max (clue 3), must belong to Lindsey. Apollo is a glowing shade of ginger (clue 1), so Abel's gray cat, who isn't Athena (clue 4), must be Phoebe. They don't live at either No.22 or No.49 (clue 4), so Phoebe and Abel must share 33 Olympus Street. Max doesn't live at No.22 (clue 4), so must own No.49, leaving Leila and Hecate at No.22. From clue 2, Heather's cat must be white and, by elimination, it must be Athena, leaving ginger Apollo living with Max at No.49. Finally, from clue 4, Leila's cat Hecate must be tabby and Mnemosyne at No.51 must be black.

No.22, Leila, Hecate, tabby.
No.24, Heather, Athena, white.
No.33, Abel, Phoebe, gray.
No.49, Max, Apollo, ginger.
No.51, Lindsey, Mnemosyne, black.

Phylum Feast, p. 308

Dish 8, opposite the chicken on plate 4 (clue 2), does not contain plain yogurt or scallops (clue 1), tuna (clue 2), pork or snails (clue 3), or mushrooms (clue 4), so must contain prawns. So, from clue 3, dish 7 must be steamed, dish 1 must be pork, and dish 5 must contain snails that have been boiled (clue 2). Now, from (clue 1), the plain yogurt cannot be in dishes 2, 4, or 8 and must be in dish 6, with the stewed food in dish 2 and the scallops in dish 3. Now, from clue 4, the mushrooms must be stewed and in dish 2, the chicken on plate 5 must have been baked and the pork on plate 1 must have been roast. By elimination, the steamed dish on plate 7 must be steamed tuna. Finally, the scallops were not fried (clue 1), so must have been broiled, leaving dish 8 as fried prawns.

Dish 1, roast pork.
Dish 2, stewed mushrooms.
Dish 3, broiled scallops.
Dish 4, baked chicken.
Dish 5, boiled snails.
Dish 6, plain yogurt.
Dish 7, steamed tuna.
Dish 8, fried prawns.

Logi-5, p. 309

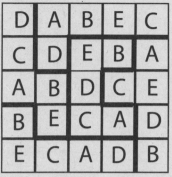

D	A	B	E	C
C	D	E	B	A
A	B	D	C	E
B	E	C	A	D
E	C	A	D	B

Battleships, p. 310

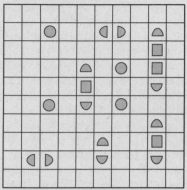

Killer Sudoku, p. 309

8	4	9	7	5	3	2	1	6
6	5	7	2	1	8	4	3	9
2	1	3	6	4	9	7	8	5
9	8	1	3	7	5	6	4	2
7	3	4	9	6	2	8	5	1
5	6	2	1	8	4	3	9	7
3	9	8	5	2	6	1	7	4
1	2	5	4	3	7	9	6	8
4	7	6	8	9	1	5	2	3

Pulling Strings, p. 311

The wine is attached to a string numbered three times that leading to the scarf (clue 2) so it must be numbered 3, 6, or 9 and be in the right-hand column, and the pen must be numbered 2, 5, or 8 and be in the center column. So the perfume, empty string, candies vertical combination (clue 3) must be in the left-hand column, with the perfume attached to string 1 and the candies tied to string 7. There is an unattached string in each row (clue 1) so the wine, directly right of the pen (clue 2) cannot be attached to strings 3 or 9 and must be tied to string 6, with the pen at 5, the scarf at 2 and the empty string at 3. We have now filled two rows, so the coffee, left of an unattached string (clue 3) must be at 8, with the string at 9 leading to nothing.

1, perfume; 2, scarf; 3, empty.
4, empty; 5, pen; 6, wine.
7, candies; 8, coffee; 9, empty.

Unboxing Days, p. 312

Polly is a parrot (clue 2), so Jolly, which was opened on the 31st and so isn't the fairy (clue 4), baby (clue 3), or cow (clue 2), must be the squishy blob which Hugh greeted with, "Ha ha ha!" (clue 1). So on the 30th, Hugh did not unpack the fairy (clue 4), parrot, or cow (clue 2), so must have unboxed the baby. So, from clue 3, Hugh must have said, "I love it" on the 29th and opened Dolly on the 28th. Now, from clue 2, Hugh must have unpacked Polly the parrot on the 29th and said, "I love it," the baby must be called Molly and the cow must be Dolly unwrapped on the 28th. By elimination, Lolly must be a fairy and was opened on the 27th to High's cries of, "Wow wow wow" (clue 1). Finally, from clue 4, Dolly the cow must have been described as "Super cute" on the 28th, leaving Molly the baby described as "Adorable" on the 30th.

27th, Lolly the fairy, "Wow wow wow!"
28th, Dolly the cow, "Super cute!"
29th, Polly the parrot, "I love it!"
30th, Molly the baby, "Adorable!"
31st, Jolly the squishy blob, "Ha ha ha!"

InnFluencers, p. 313

BeerGoggles' unique selling point is bottle caps (clue 1), so BarBarian's field, which isn't parties in breweries or wine tasting (clue 1), must be cocktails. So its owner, based at the Nightcrawler bar, is not Billie, who owns the Horse and Bucket, Jilly, whose site is PubLicity, or Lily (clue 2), and must be Millie. From clue 1, the owner of the Top Hat cannot be Jilly and must be Lily, leaving Jilly organizing the parties in breweries. By elimination, her bar must be the Green Monkey. Now, BeerGoggles, specializing in bottle caps, must be Billie's site, leaving Lily running the InnOvations website and knocking back wine by the bottle at the Top Hat.

Billie, BeerGoggles, bottle caps, Horse and Bucket.
Jilly, PubLicity, parties in breweries, Green Monkey.
Lily, InnOvations, wine tasting, Top Hat.
Milly, BarBarian, cocktails, Nightcrawler.

Battleships, p. 314

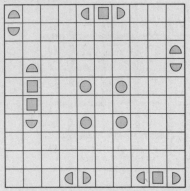

Domino Search, p. 315

4	6	5	6	4	0	1	1
1	5	5	5	4	6	2	0
3	1	2	0	5	1	2	3
2	1	4	6	6	0	0	4
0	3	5	3	4	1	6	1
2	5	2	2	4	3	3	5
3	6	0	3	0	2	6	2

Festival Bands, p. 316

The world music and jazz festivals and the one commemorated by a black band were all in the first half of the year and in that order (clue 3). The opera festival was in August (clue 2), so the black band, obtained 2 months before the pop festival (clue 4), cannot have been acquired in June and must have been obtained in May, with the world music festival in March and the jazz festival in April. From clue 4, the pop festival must have been in July and the folk festival in September commemorated by the white band (clue 4). Now, from clue 1, the rock festival must have been the May event associated with the black wristband, the reggae festival must have been in June, and the July pop festival must have featured a purple wristband, leaving the blues festival with the blue band (clue 2) in October. Now the only months available for the successive pink and yellow bands (clue 4) are March and April, respectively. The opera festival was not accessed by a red wristband (clue 2), so that must be the memento of June's reggae festival and the opera festival must have been commemorated by a band of gold.

March, world music, pink; April, jazz, yellow; May, rock, black; June, reggae, red; July, pop, purple; August, opera, gold; September, folk, white; October, blues, blue.

Sudoku, p. 317

7	3	1	4	8	9	6	2	5
2	9	5	3	6	1	8	7	4
4	6	8	5	7	2	3	1	9
3	5	9	8	1	4	7	6	2
1	2	6	9	3	7	5	4	8
8	7	4	6	2	5	9	3	1
5	1	7	2	9	3	4	8	6
6	4	3	1	5	8	2	9	7
9	8	2	7	4	6	1	5	3

Logi-5, p. 317

A	B	C	D	E
B	C	D	E	A
D	A	E	C	B
E	D	B	A	C
C	E	A	B	D

Domino Search, p. 318

3	1	4	1	3	6	1	3
5	1	4	0	4	2	2	5
6	6	5	5	1	1	2	5
6	3	4	6	0	6	0	3
0	6	4	5	0	2	3	0
1	0	3	3	0	5	4	1
2	4	2	5	2	6	4	2

Play these other fun puzzle books by USA TODAY

USA TODAY Sudoku

USA TODAY Everyday Sudoku

USA TODAY Crossword

USA TODAY Logic

USA TODAY Word Roundup and Word Search

USA TODAY Jumbo Puzzle Book

USA TODAY Jumbo Puzzle Book 2

USA TODAY Don't Quote Me®

USA TODAY Picture Puzzles Across America

USA TODAY Word Finding Frenzy

USA TODAY Sudoku 2

USA TODAY Crossword 2

USA TODAY Logic 2

USA TODAY Sudoku 3

USA TODAY Up & Down Words Infinity

USA TODAY Crossword 3

USA TODAY Sudoku Super Challenge

USA TODAY Sudoku Super Challenge 2

USA TODAY Sudoku Super Challenge 3

USA TODAY Crossword Super Challenge

USA TODAY Crossword Super Challenge 2

USA TODAY Crossword Super Challenge 3

USA TODAY Jumbo Puzzle Book Super Challenge

USA TODAY Jumbo Puzzle Book Super Challenge 2

USA TODAY Jumbo Puzzle Book Super Challenge 3

USA TODAY Logic Super Challenge

USA TODAY Logic Super Challenge 2

USA TODAY Logic Super Challenge 3

USA TODAY Sunshine Sudoku

USA TODAY Teatime Crosswords

USA TODAY Jazzy Jumbo Puzzle Book